SCIENCE.
BAD.

JONATHAN HICKMAN
WRITER

NICK PITARRA
ARTIST

MICHAEL GARLAND
COLORS

RUS WOOTON
LETTERS

IMAGE COMICS, INC.
Robert Kirkman – Chief Operating Officer
Erik Larsen – Chief Financial Officer
Todd McFarlane – President
Marc Silvestri – Chief Executive Officer
Jim Valentino – Vice-President

Eric Stephenson – Publisher
Corey Murphy – Director of Sales
Jeff Boison – Director of Publishing Planning & Book Trade Sales
Jeremy Sullivan – Director of Digital Sales
Kat Salazar – Director of PR & Marketing
Emily Miller – Director of Operations
Branwyn Bigglestone – Senior Accounts Manager
Sarah Mello – Accounts Manager
Drew Gill – Art Director
Jonathan Chan – Production Manager
Meredith Wallace – Print Manager
Briah Skelly – Publicity Assistant
Sasha Head – Sales & Marketing Production Designer
Randy Okamura – Digital Production Designer
David Brothers – Branding Manager
Ally Power – Content Manager
Addison Duke – Production Artist
Vincent Kukua – Production Artist
Tricia Ramos – Production Artist
Jeff Stang – Direct Market Sales Representative
Emilio Bautista – Digital Sales Associate
Leanna Caunter – Accounting Assistant
Chloe Ramos-Peterson – Administrative Assistant
IMAGECOMICS.COM

THE MANHATTAN PROJECTS, VOLUME 6
First Printing / April 2016 / ISBN: 978-1-63215-628-0

MP

THE MANHATTAN PROJECTS

6

TIME FOR
JUSTICE

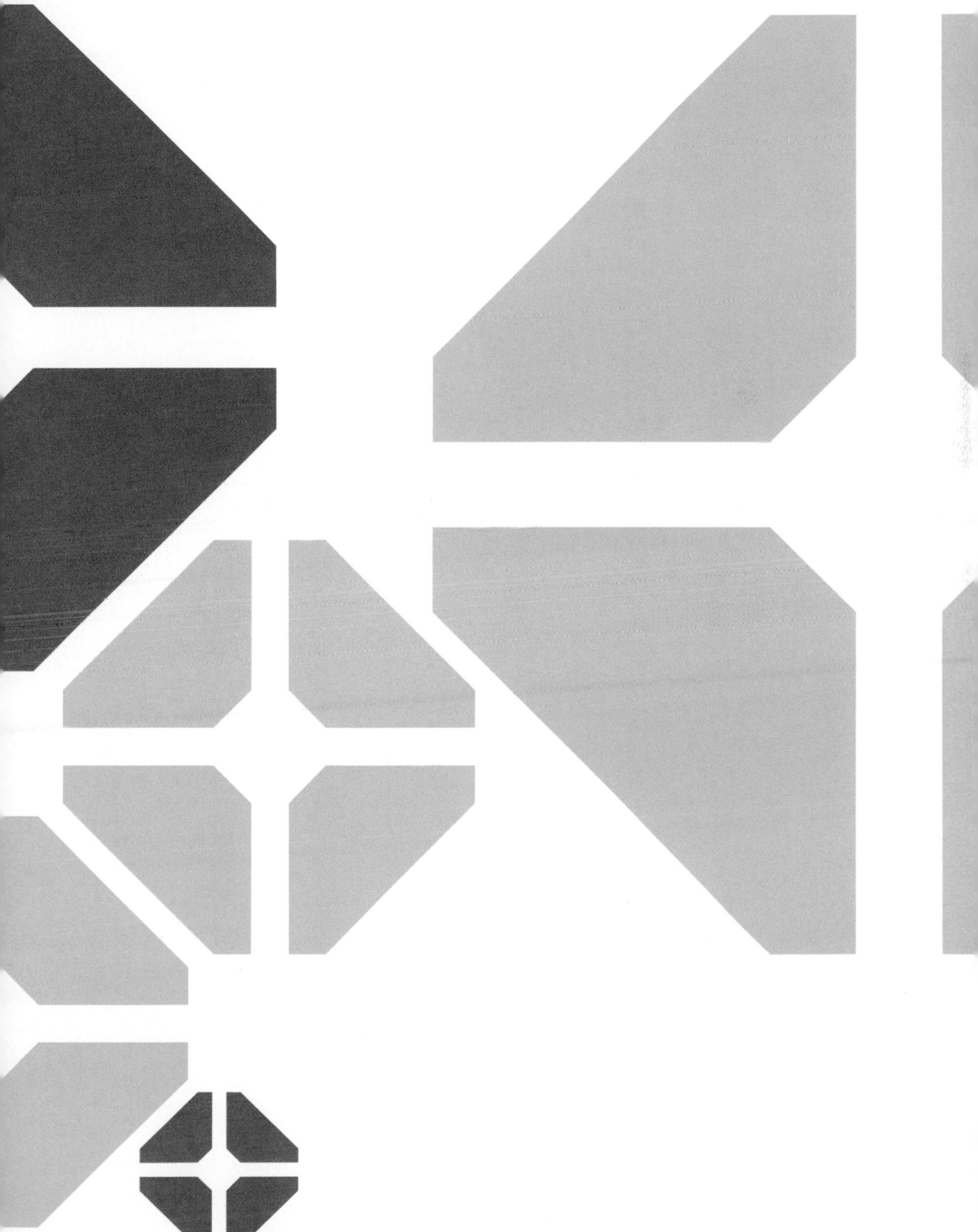

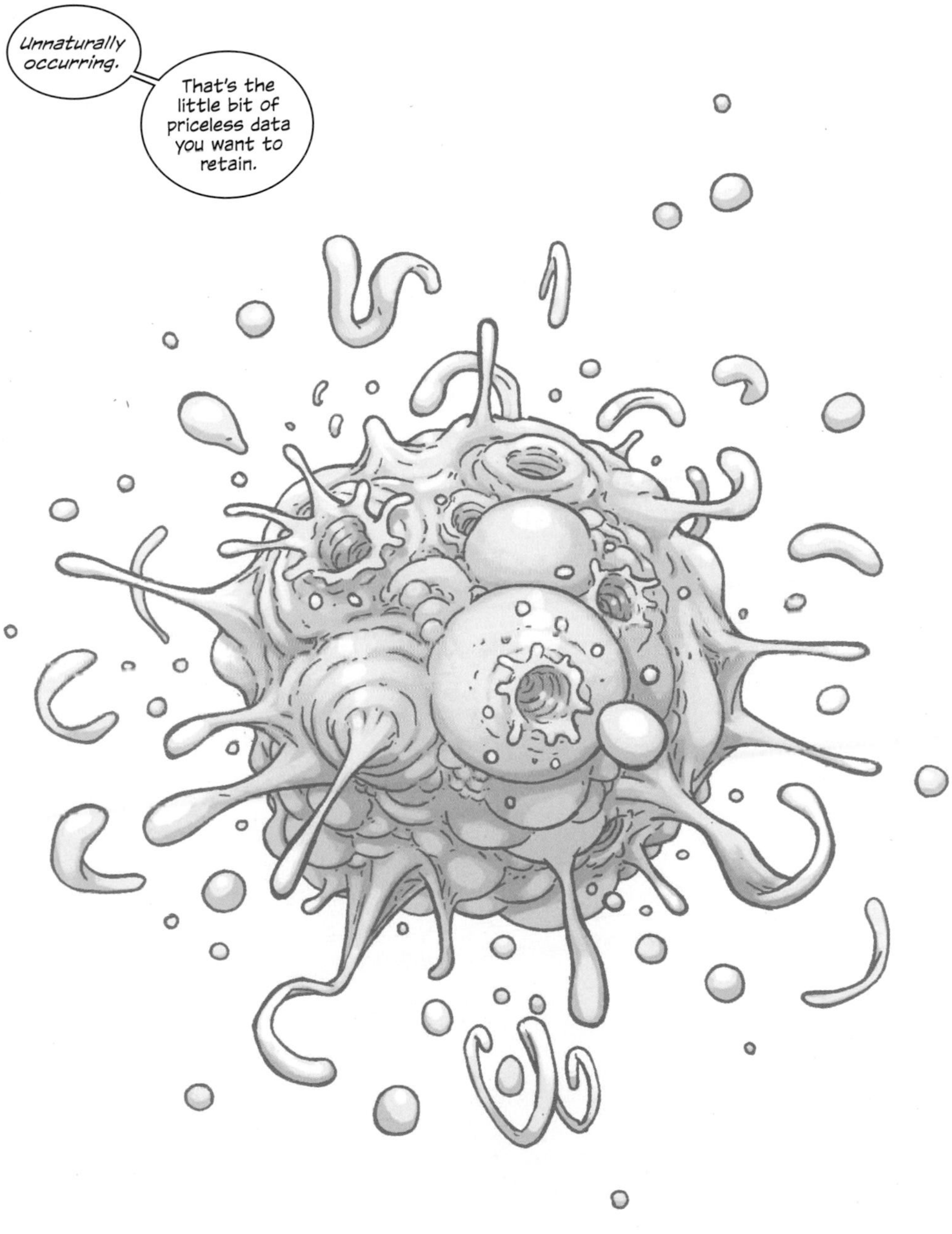
Unnaturally occurring.
That's the little bit of priceless data you want to retain.

A spore must be manufactured...
And we have done so. *Again.*
Readings say it's stable, and I've engaged the container sequence.
Yes...
Done! But *not* done!
The nesting material has been secured...
But it seems that your projections were too optimistic, Primor.
You said there would be a yield of twelve units, but after mining only three, we exhausted most of this planet's supply.
This fourth unit is only a partial...

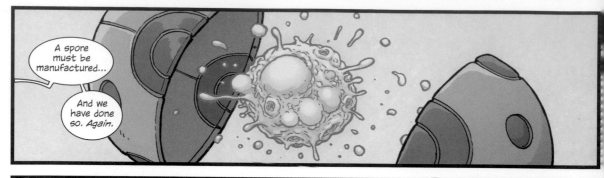

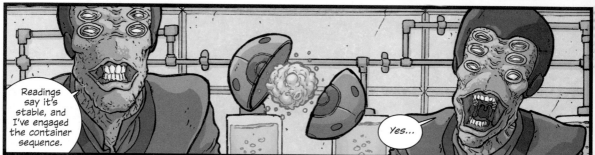

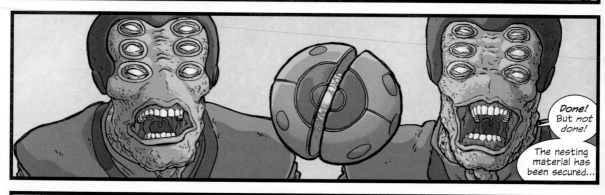

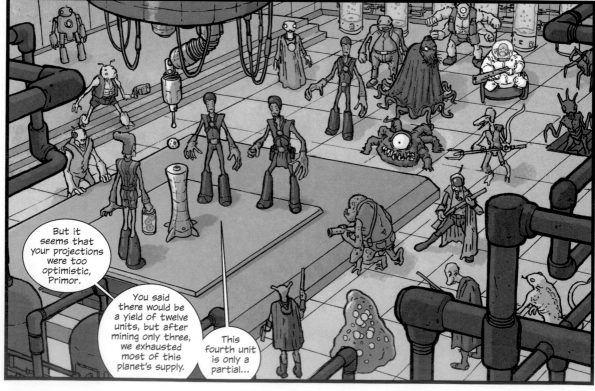

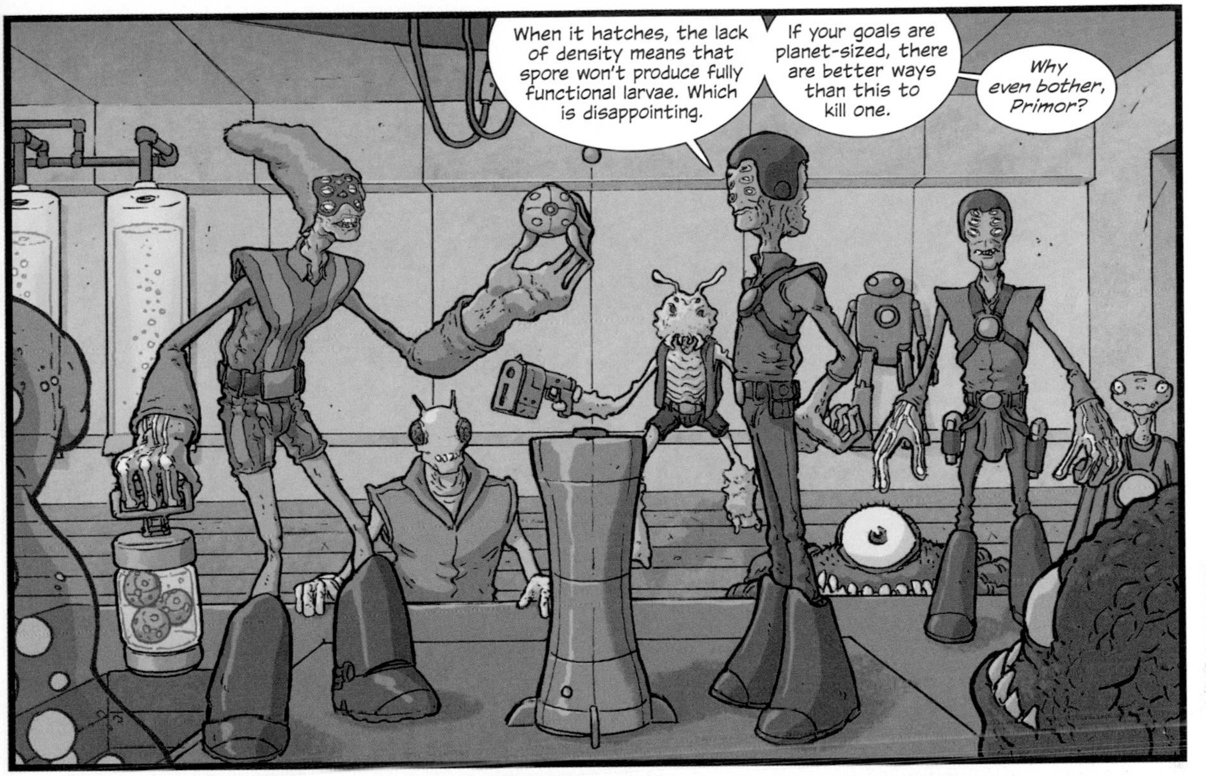
When it hatches, the lack of density means that spore won't produce fully functional larvae. Which is disappointing.
If your goals are planet-sized, there are better ways than this to kill one.
Why even bother, Primor?

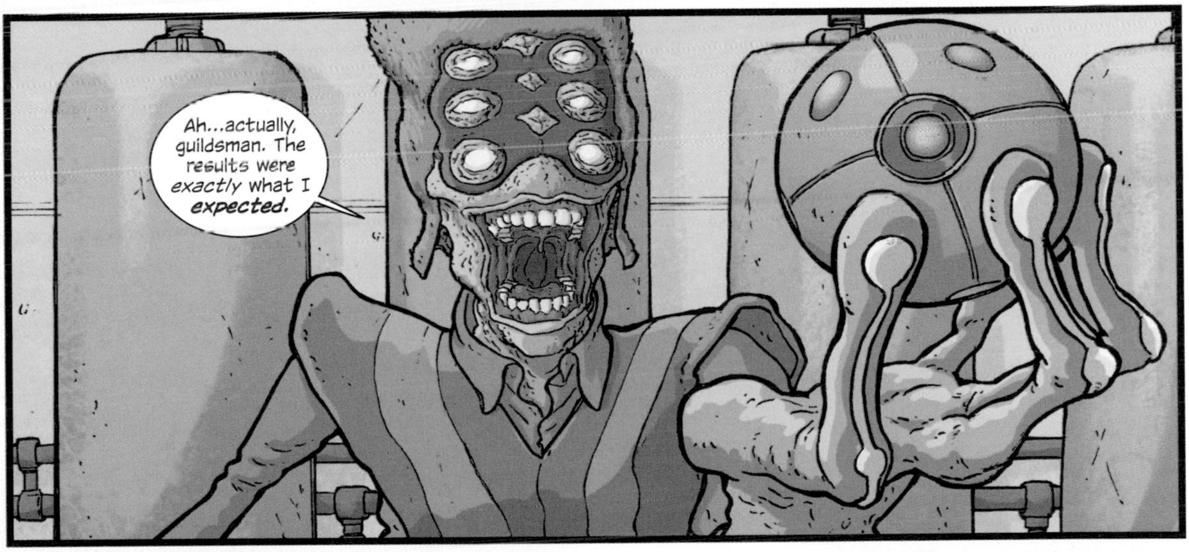
Ah...actually, guildsman. The results were *exactly* what I ***expected.***

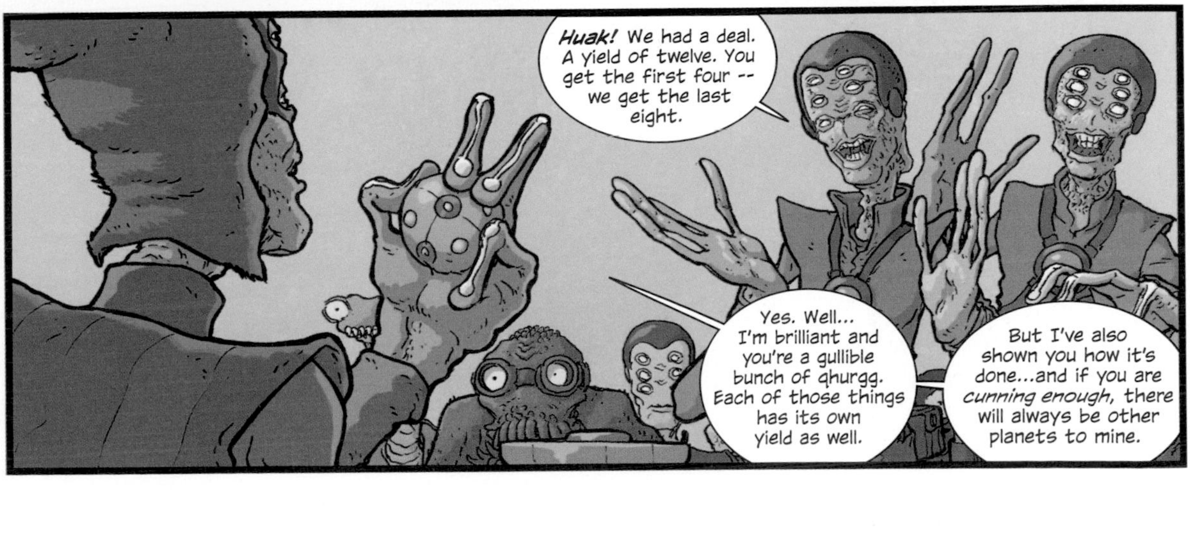
Huak! We had a deal. A yield of twelve. You get the first four -- we get the last eight.
Yes. Well... I'm brilliant and you're a gullible bunch of qhurgg. Each of those things has its own yield as well.
But I've also shown you how it's done...and if you are *cunning enough*, there will always be other planets to mine.

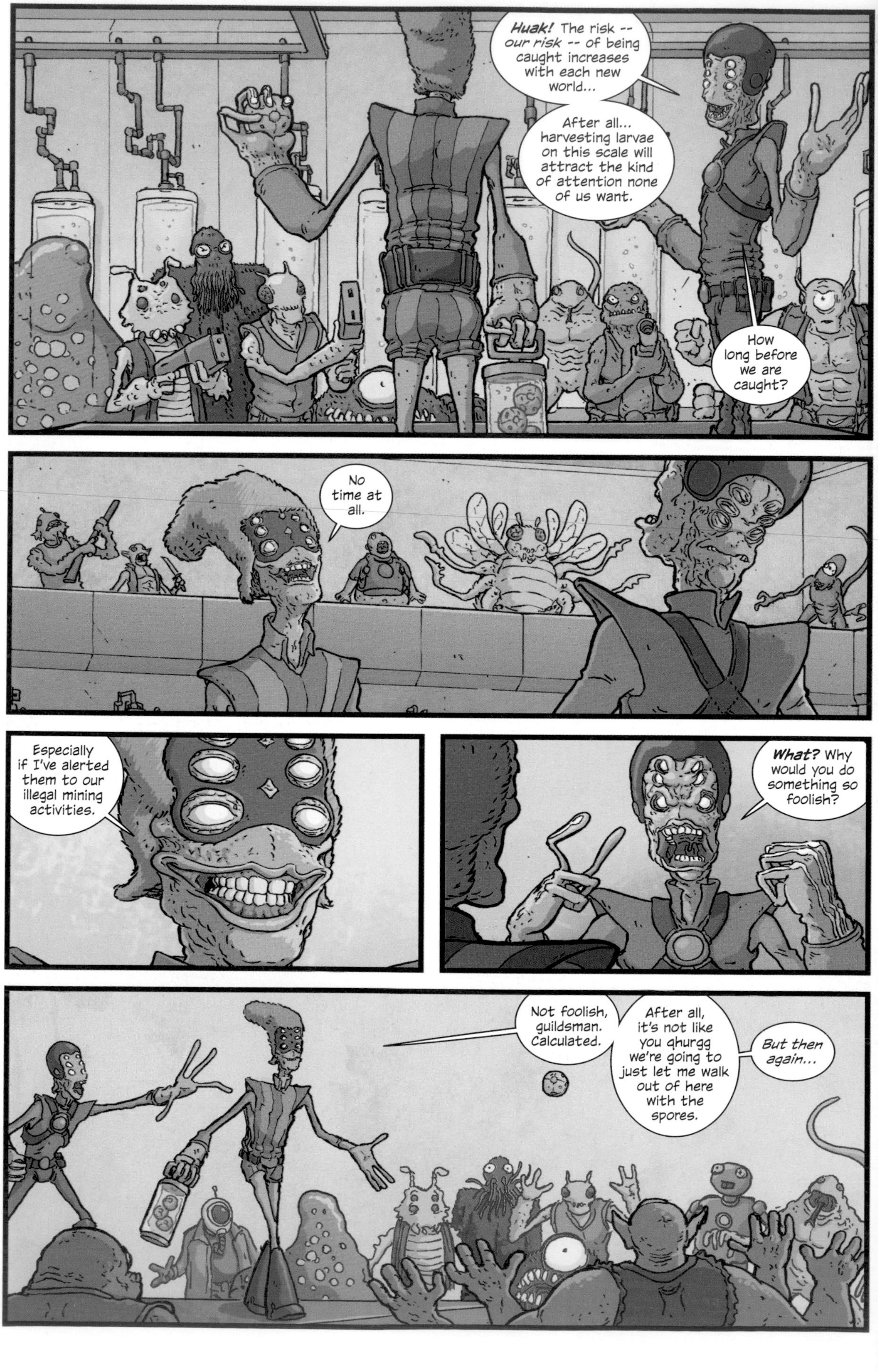
Huak! The risk -- *our risk* -- of being caught increases with each new world...
After all... harvesting larvae on this scale will attract the kind of attention none of us want.
How long before we are caught?
No time at all.
Especially if I've alerted them to our illegal mining activities.
What? Why would you do something so foolish?
Not foolish, guildsman. Calculated.
After all, it's not like you qhurgg we're going to just let me walk out of here with the spores.
But then again...

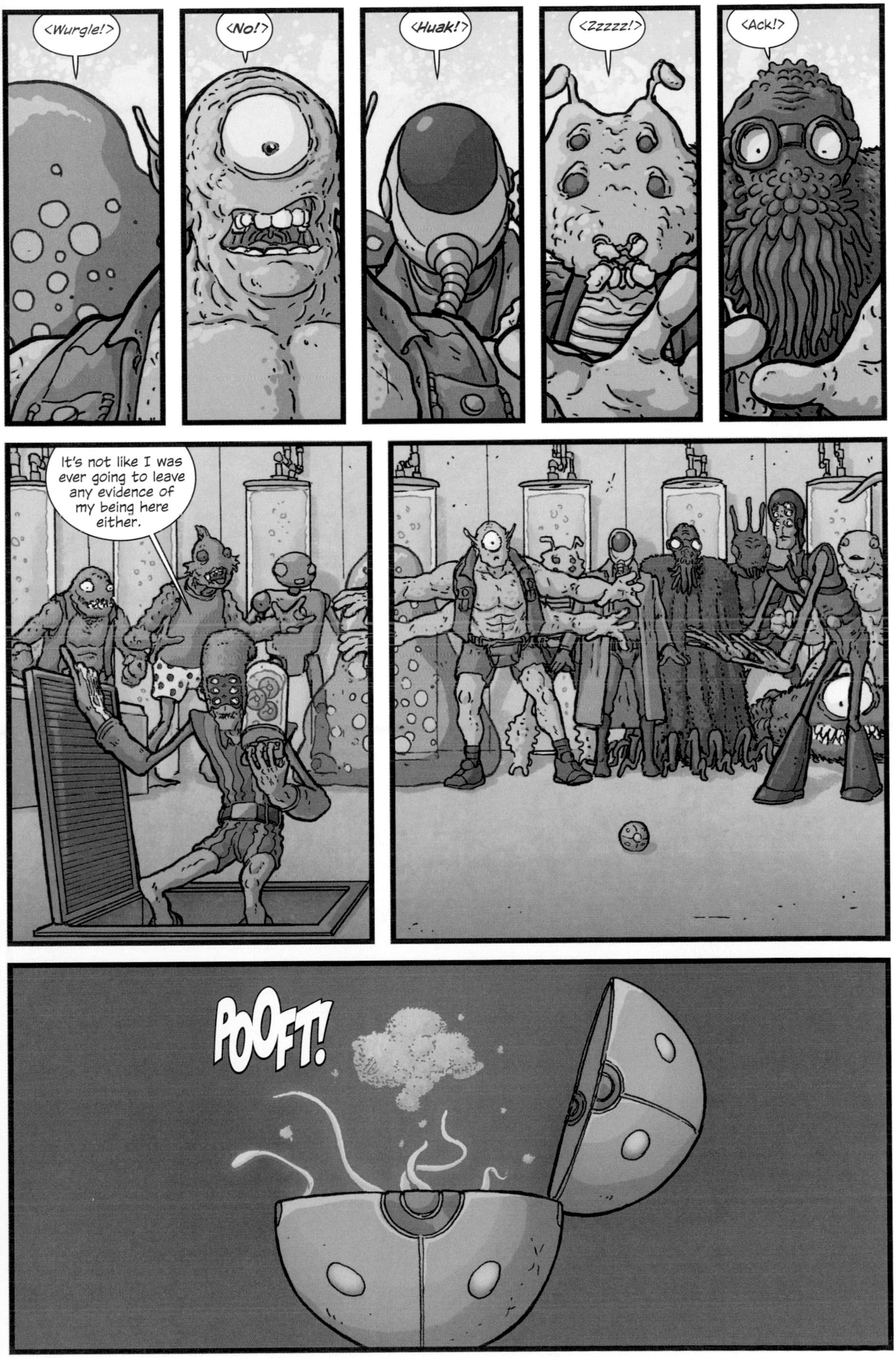
<Wurgle!>
<No!>
<Huak!>
<Zzzzz!>
<Ack!>
It's not like I was ever going to leave any evidence of my being here either.
POOFT!

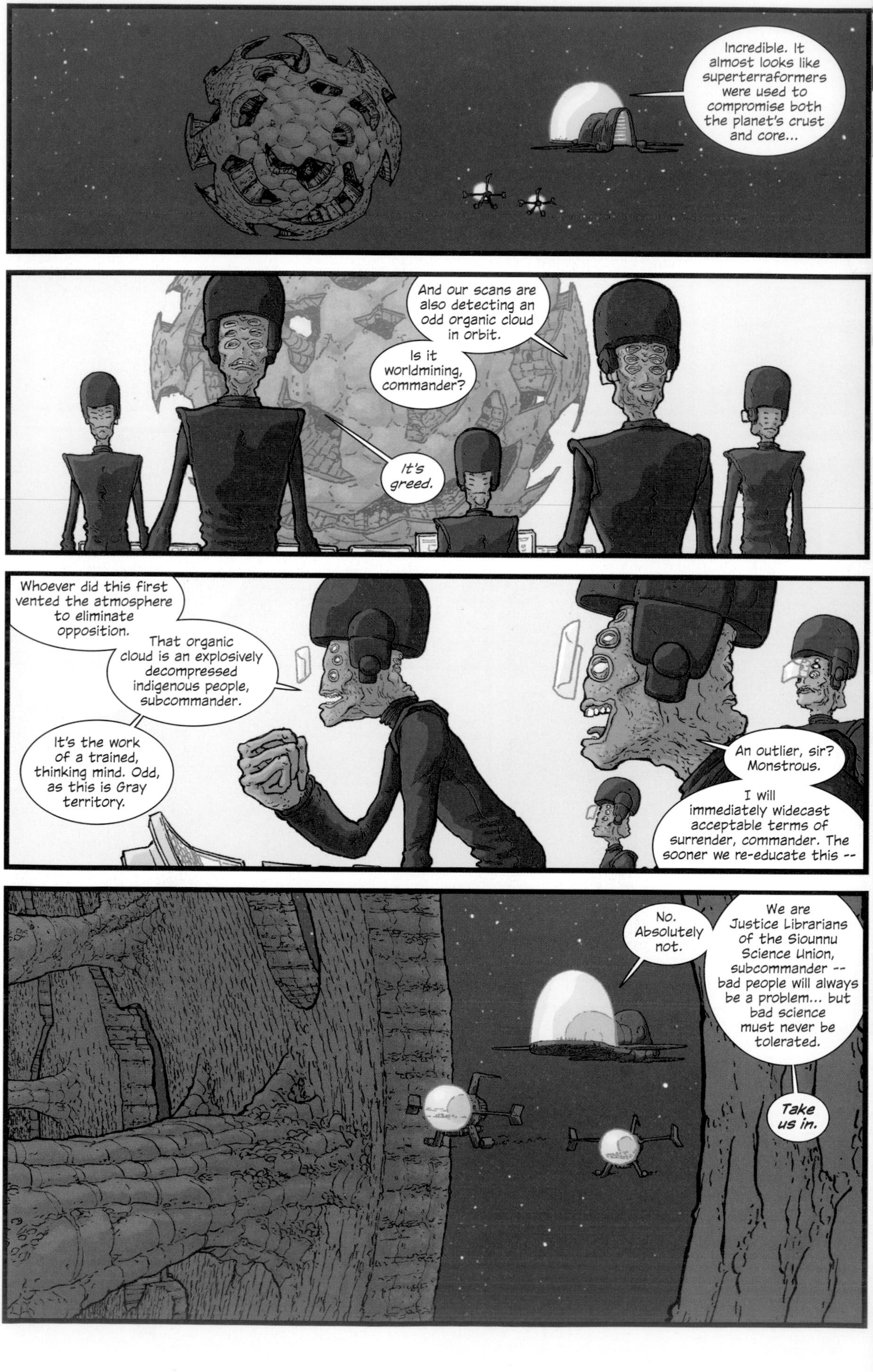
Incredible. It almost looks like superterraformers were used to compromise both the planet's crust and core...
And our scans are also detecting an odd organic cloud in orbit.
Is it worldmining, commander?
It's greed.
Whoever did this first vented the atmosphere to eliminate opposition.
That organic cloud is an explosively decompressed indigenous people, subcommander.
It's the work of a trained, thinking mind. Odd, as this is Gray territory.
An outlier, sir? Monstrous.
I will immediately widecast acceptable terms of surrender, commander. The sooner we re-educate this --
No. Absolutely not.
We are Justice Librarians of the Siounnu Science Union, subcommander -- bad people will always be a problem... but bad science must never be tolerated.
Take us in.

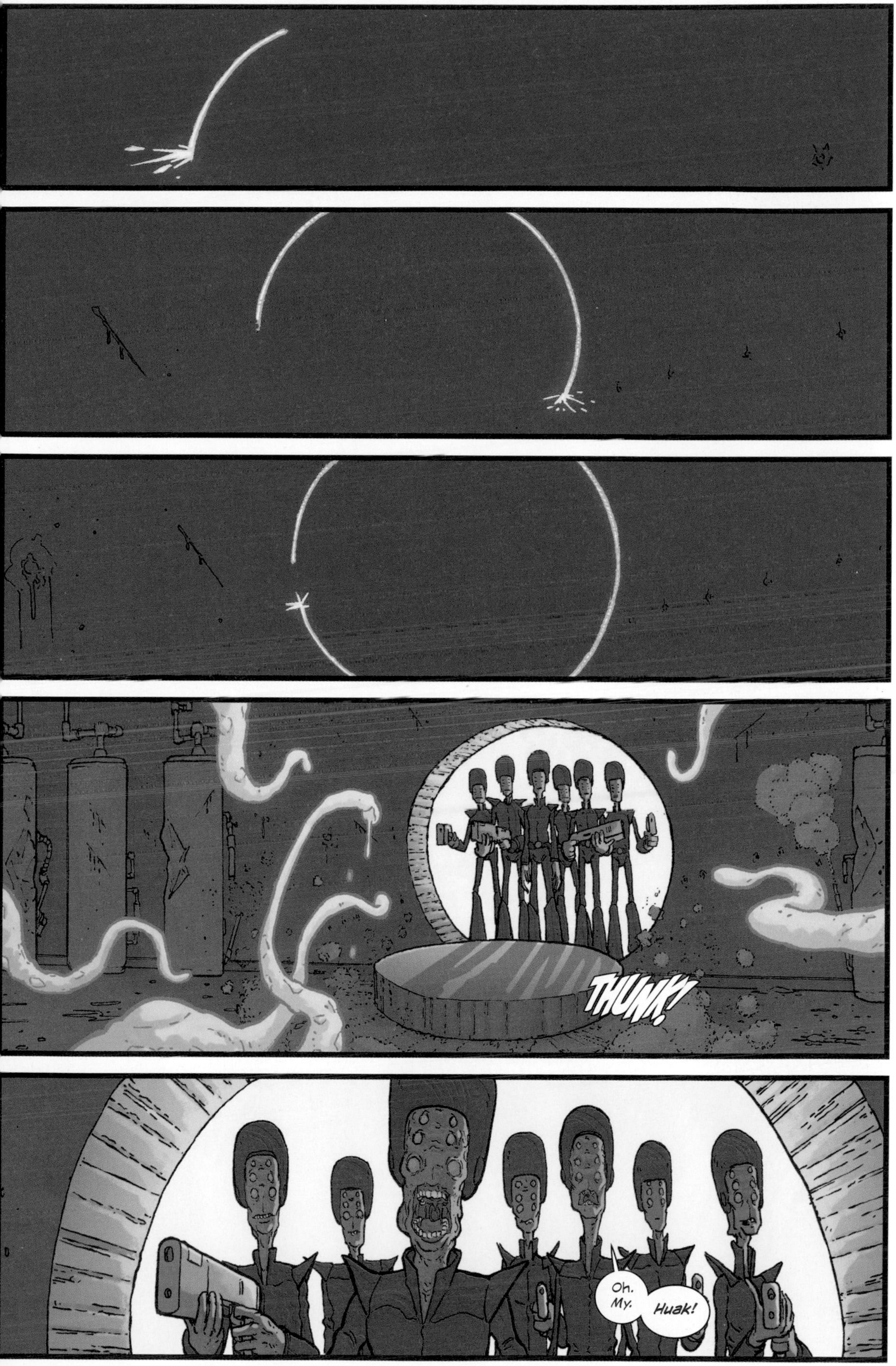
THUNK!
Oh. My.
Huak!

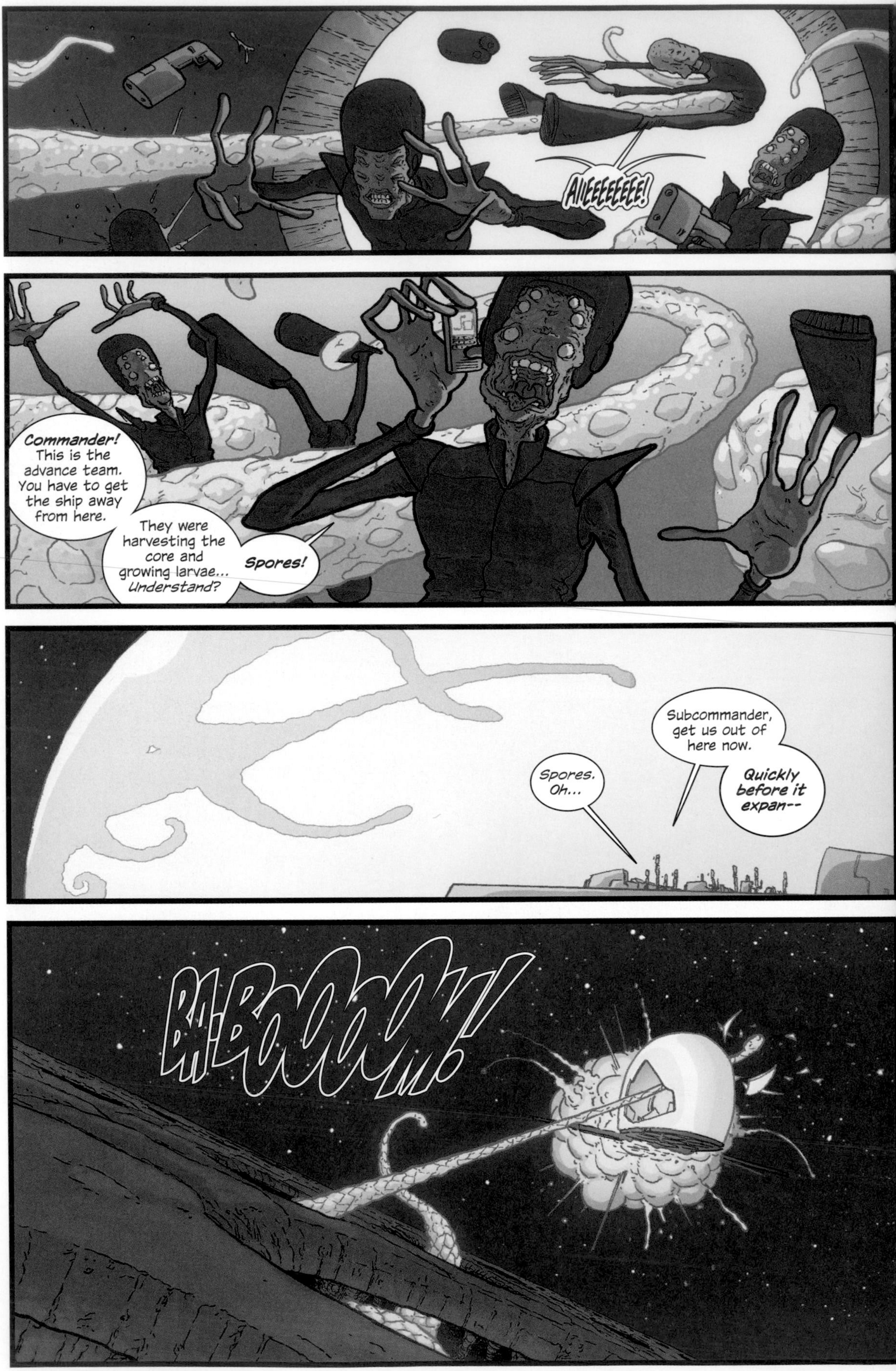
AIEEEEEEEE!
Commander! This is the advance team. You have to get the ship away from here.
They were harvesting the core and growing larvae... Understand?
Spores!
Spores. Oh...
Subcommander, get us out of here now.
Quickly before it expan--
BA-BOOOOOM!

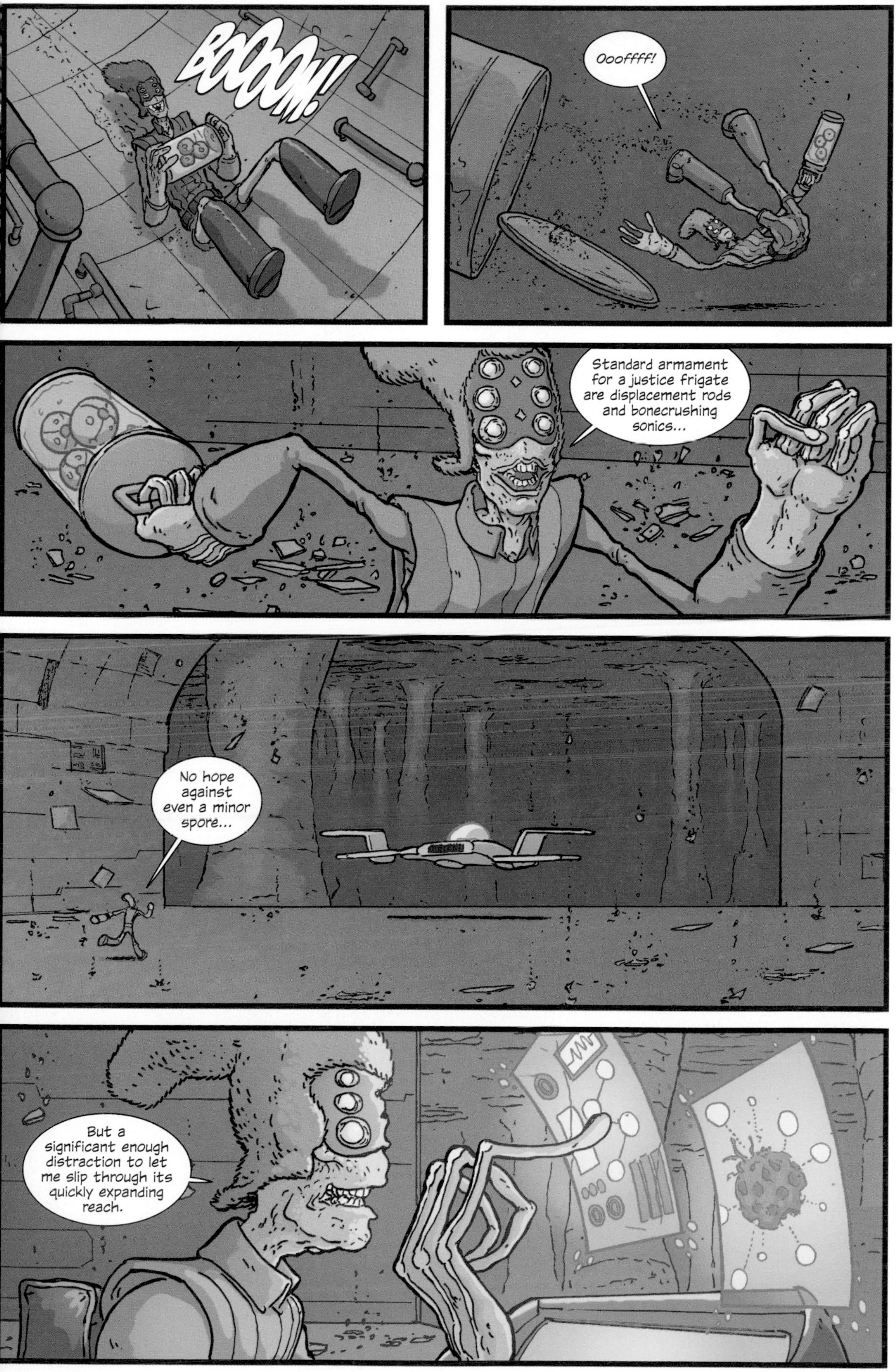
BOOOOM!!
Oooffff!
Standard armament for a justice frigate are displacement rods and bonecrushing sonics...
No hope against even a minor spore...
But a significant enough distraction to let me slip through its quickly expanding reach.

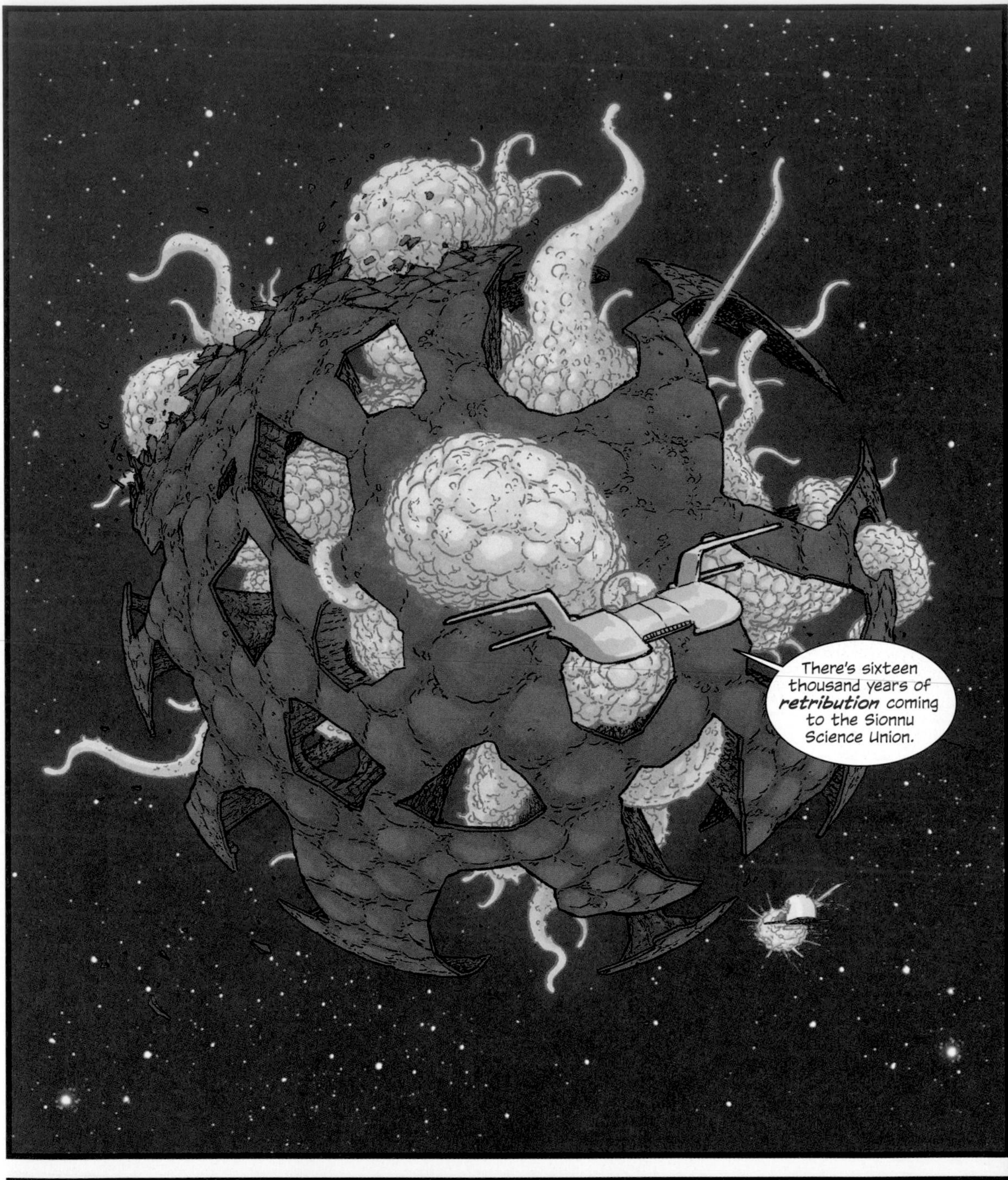
There's sixteen thousand years of ***retribution*** coming to the Sionnu Science Union.

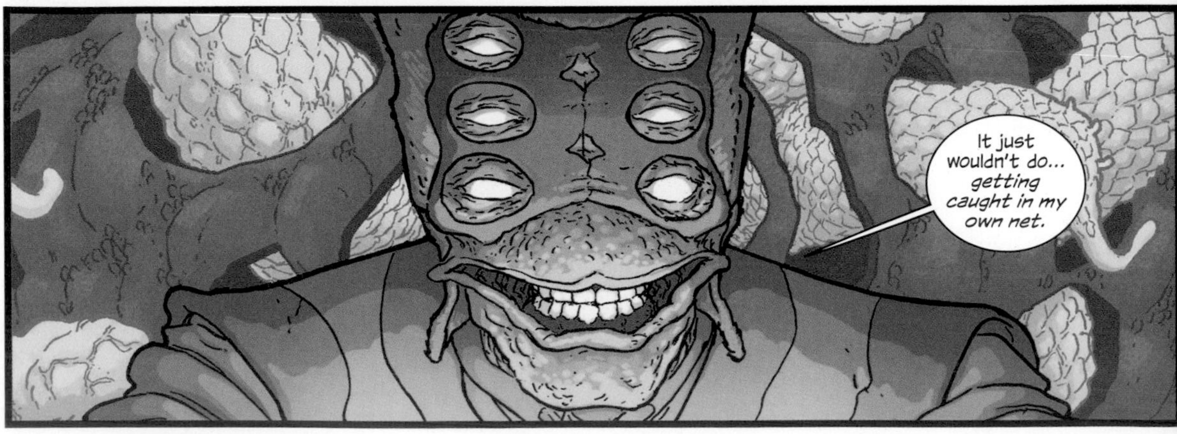
It just wouldn't do... *getting caught in my own net.*

"LOVE WILL CARRY YOU HALFWAY AROUND THE UNIVERSE IF YOU LET IT. YOU'LL GET LOST OUT THERE IN THE HEAVENS, AND NEVER COME HOME AGAIN."

CLAVIS AUREA
THE RECORDED FEYNMAN | **VOL. 4**

26

THE SUN BEYOND THE STARS

They don't bother to tell you. *I don't know why,* but they just don't.

Of course, there was a sign when you entered the building, but it's not like it was in standard basic or anything. *Hrmptuoola. Oolaparump.*

Sitting here now, I ask myself...what was the thinking behind this kind of marketing confusion: Making their most holy of unholies look like the most appealing of commercial establishments?

I wasn't asking for a lot of help, but some help would have been good. *I dunno,* maybe someone standing outside yelling...

ATTENTION: You are now entering a Huzali zone -- any behavior not in line with our pseudo-religious dogma is punishable by constant whining until the station security forces show up and throw you in the slammer.

I mean, *really.* How was I supposed to know what looked like a fairly standard eatery was actually a sacred reproduction center. And that those things I thought were tasty bite-sized morsels were actually the next generation of the Huzali people.

Didn't help they were so damn tasty.

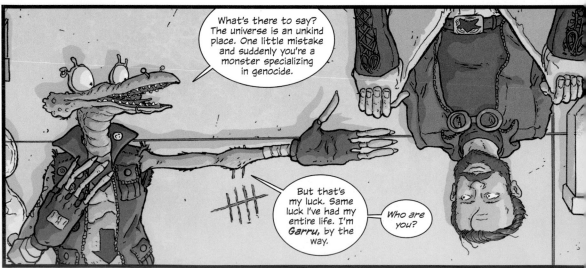

What's there to say? The universe is an unkind place. One little mistake and suddenly you're a monster specializing in genocide.

But that's my luck. Same luck I've had my entire life. I'm *Garru,* by the way.

Who are you?

Don't Drink
My name is Yuri Gagarin.
I'm a cosmonaut. I was also the first one of my people to journey into spa--
Amazing. Just fascinating.
You got anything to eat?
I'm surprised little babies aren't more filling.
You'd think, wouldn't you? But actually, no. Not filling at all.
S'okay, don't worry about it... we'll be out of here in the next couple of hours anyway.
Drink
How do you know that?
Feez, Cosmo...
Nearest star's in ascendence. It's the harmonic festival -- all local government offices are closed for the holidays...
Skeleton crew except for the standard security forces and the midnight court to abjudicate the work of said security.
I'm going to court? There's going to be a trial?
You got it.

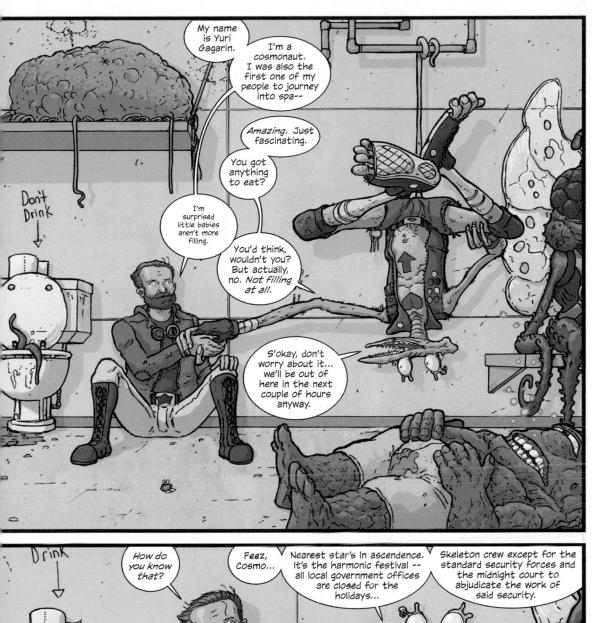

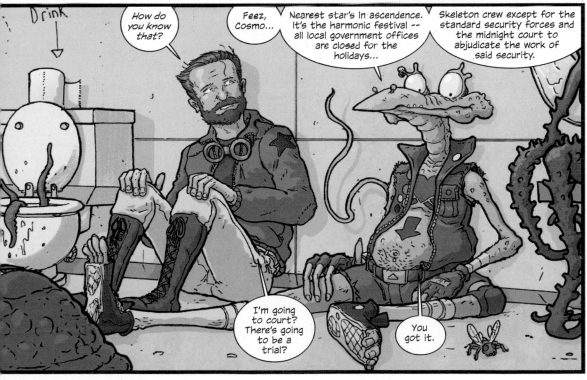

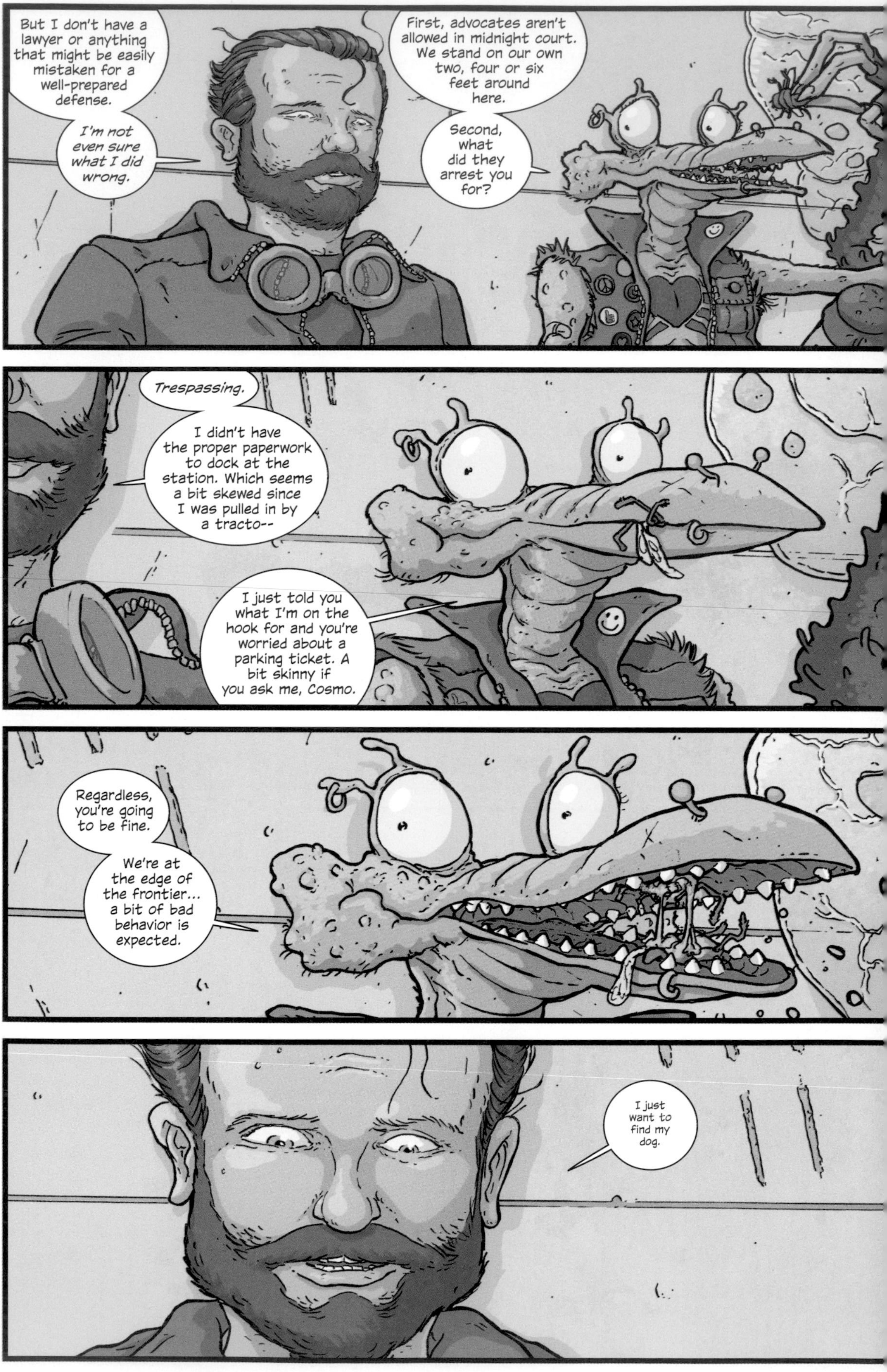
But I don't have a lawyer or anything that might be easily mistaken for a well-prepared defense.
I'm not even sure what I did wrong.
First, advocates aren't allowed in midnight court. We stand on our own two, four or six feet around here.
Second, what did they arrest you for?
Trespassing.
I didn't have the proper paperwork to dock at the station. Which seems a bit skewed since I was pulled in by a tracto--
I just told you what I'm on the hook for and you're worried about a parking ticket. A bit skinny if you ask me, Cosmo.
Regardless, you're going to be fine.
We're at the edge of the frontier... a bit of bad behavior is expected.
I just want to find my dog.

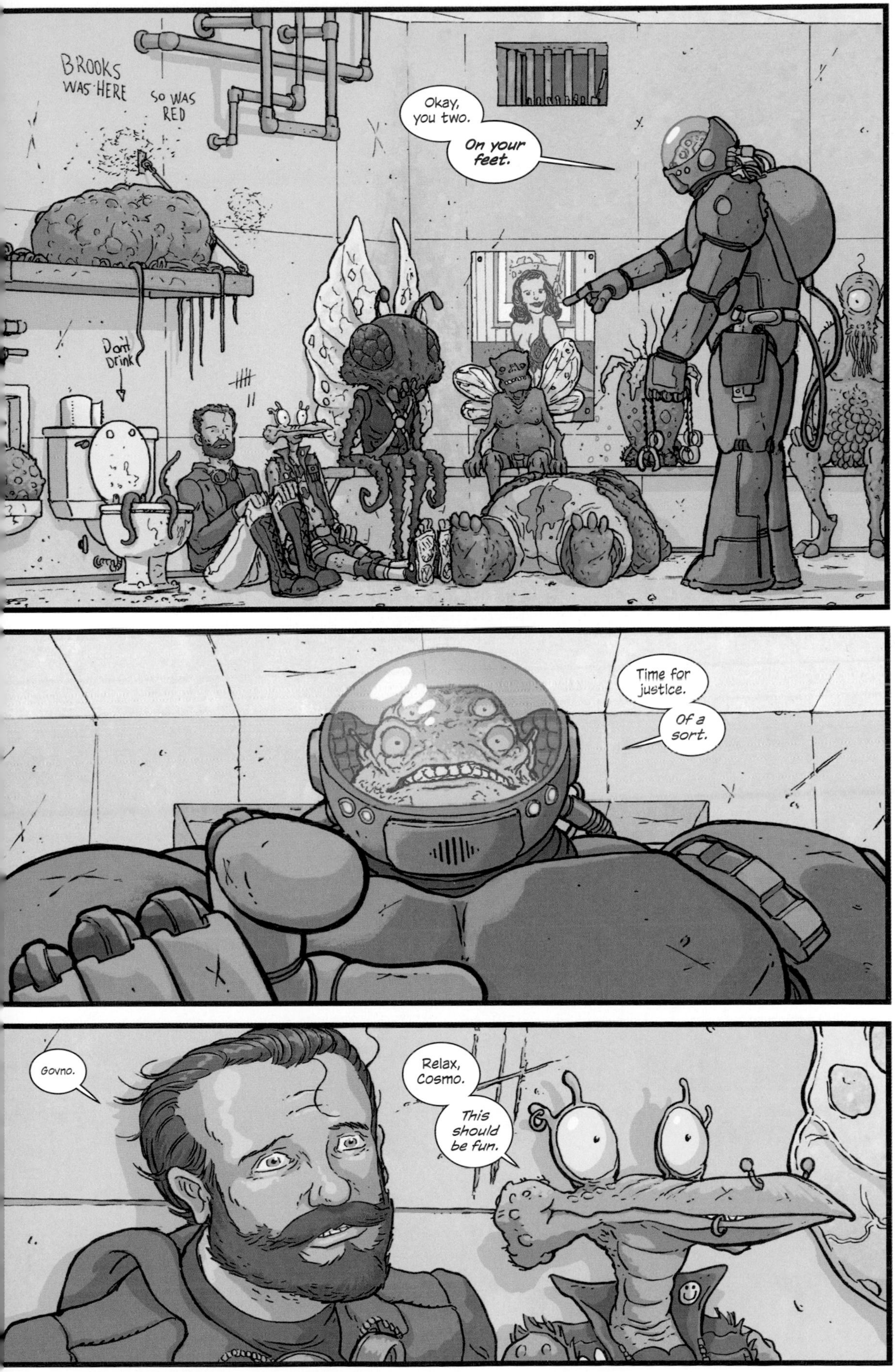

BROOKS WAS HERE
SO WAS RED
Don't Drink
Okay, you two.
On your feet.
Time for justice.
Of a sort.
Govno.
Relax, Cosmo.
This should be fun.

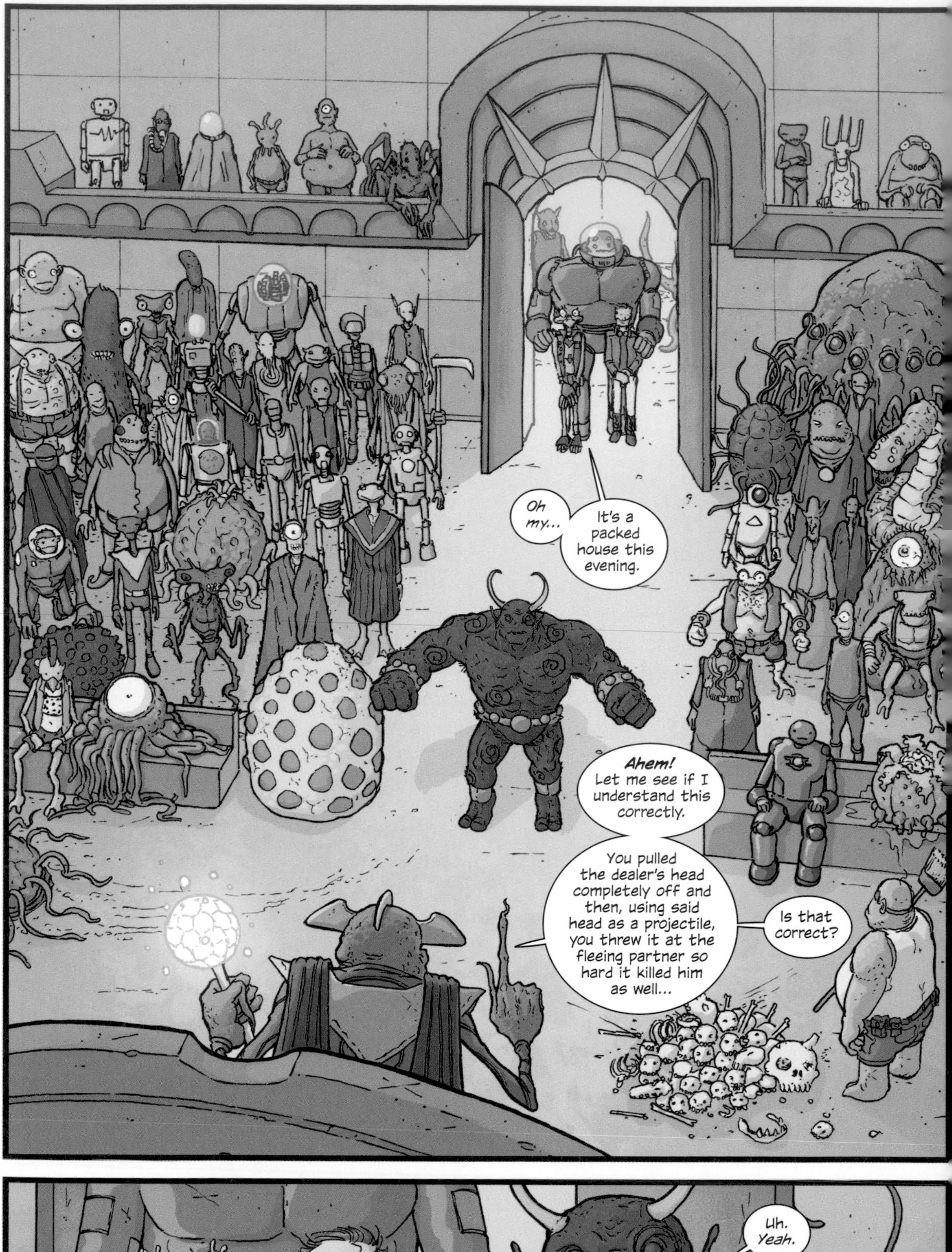
Oh my...
It's a packed house this evening.
Ahem! Let me see if I understand this correctly.
You pulled the dealer's head completely off and then, using said head as a projectile, you threw it at the fleeing partner so hard it killed him as well...
Is that correct?

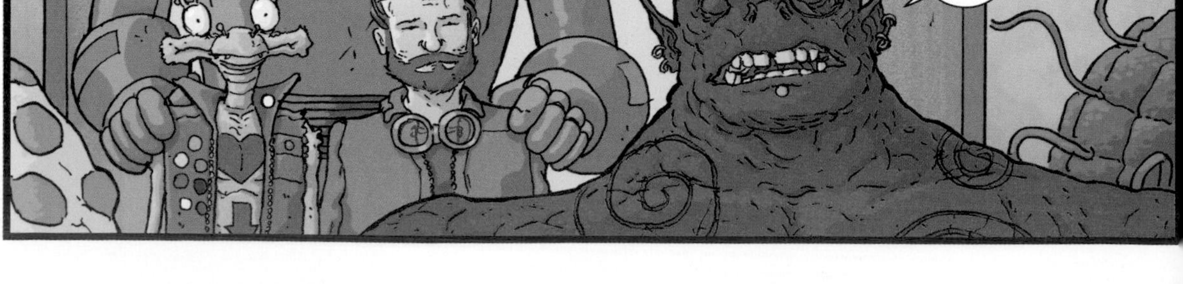
Uh. Yeah.

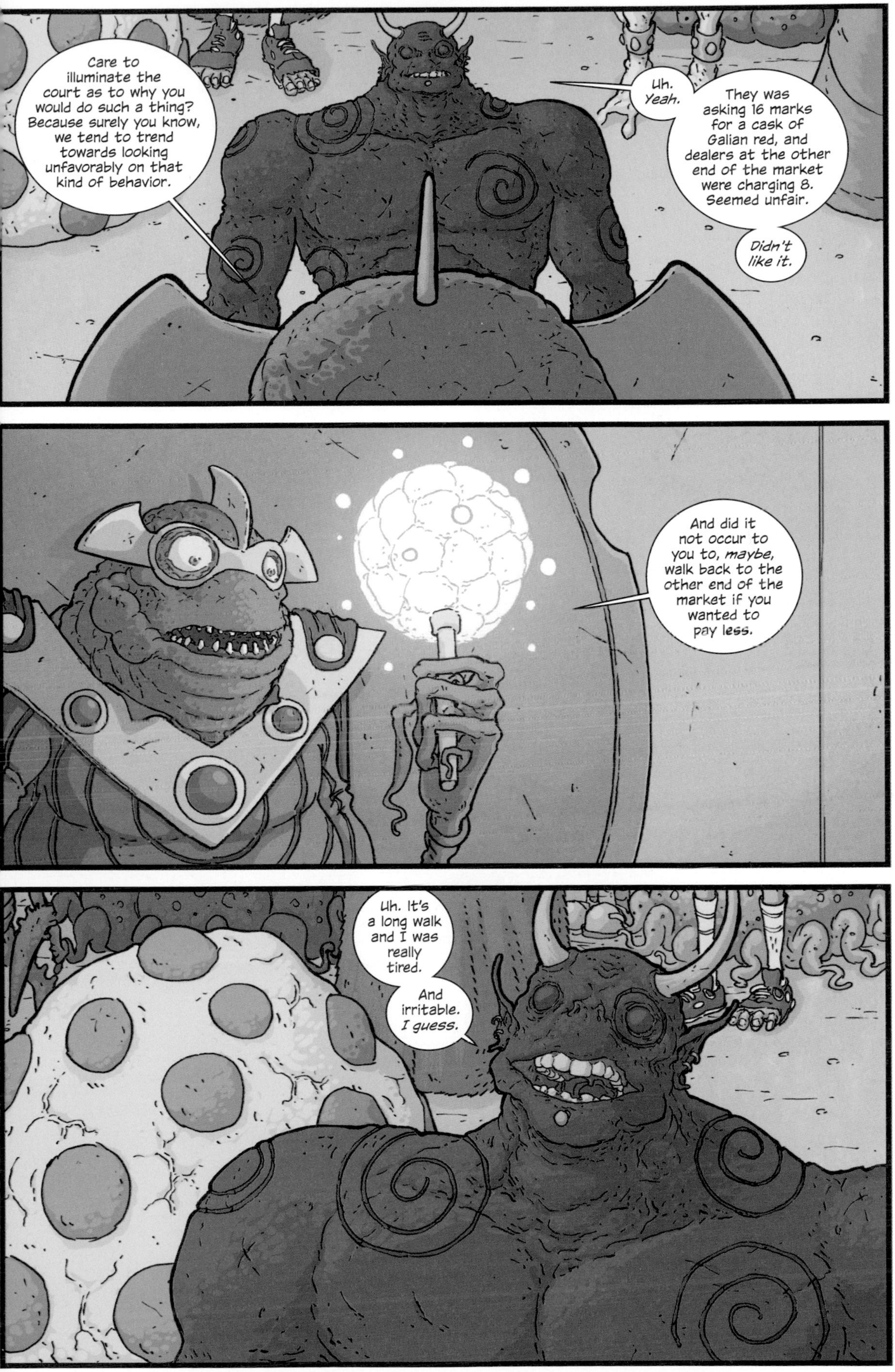
Care to illuminate the court as to why you would do such a thing? Because surely you know, we tend to trend towards looking unfavorably on that kind of behavior.
Uh. *Yeah.*
They was asking 16 marks for a cask of Galian red, and dealers at the other end of the market were charging 8. Seemed unfair.
Didn't like it.
And did it not occur to you to, *maybe*, walk back to the other end of the market if you wanted to pay less.
Uh. It's a long walk and I was really tired.
And irritable. *I guess.*

Well. Seems like you certainly held to your own remarkable brand of internal logic.

Fringe as it is...*I love it.* You're free to go. Sally forth and behead no more.

Uh.

Okay.

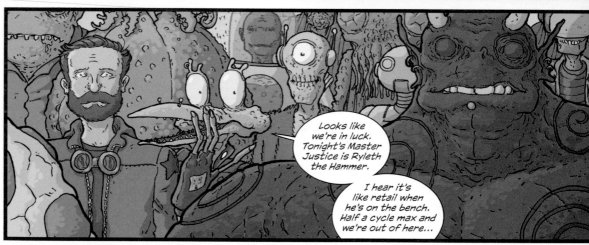

Looks like we're in luck. Tonight's Master Justice is Ryleth the Hammer.

I hear it's like retail when he's on the bench. Half a cycle max and we're out of here...

I'll show you around.

You're gonna love this place.

Next case!

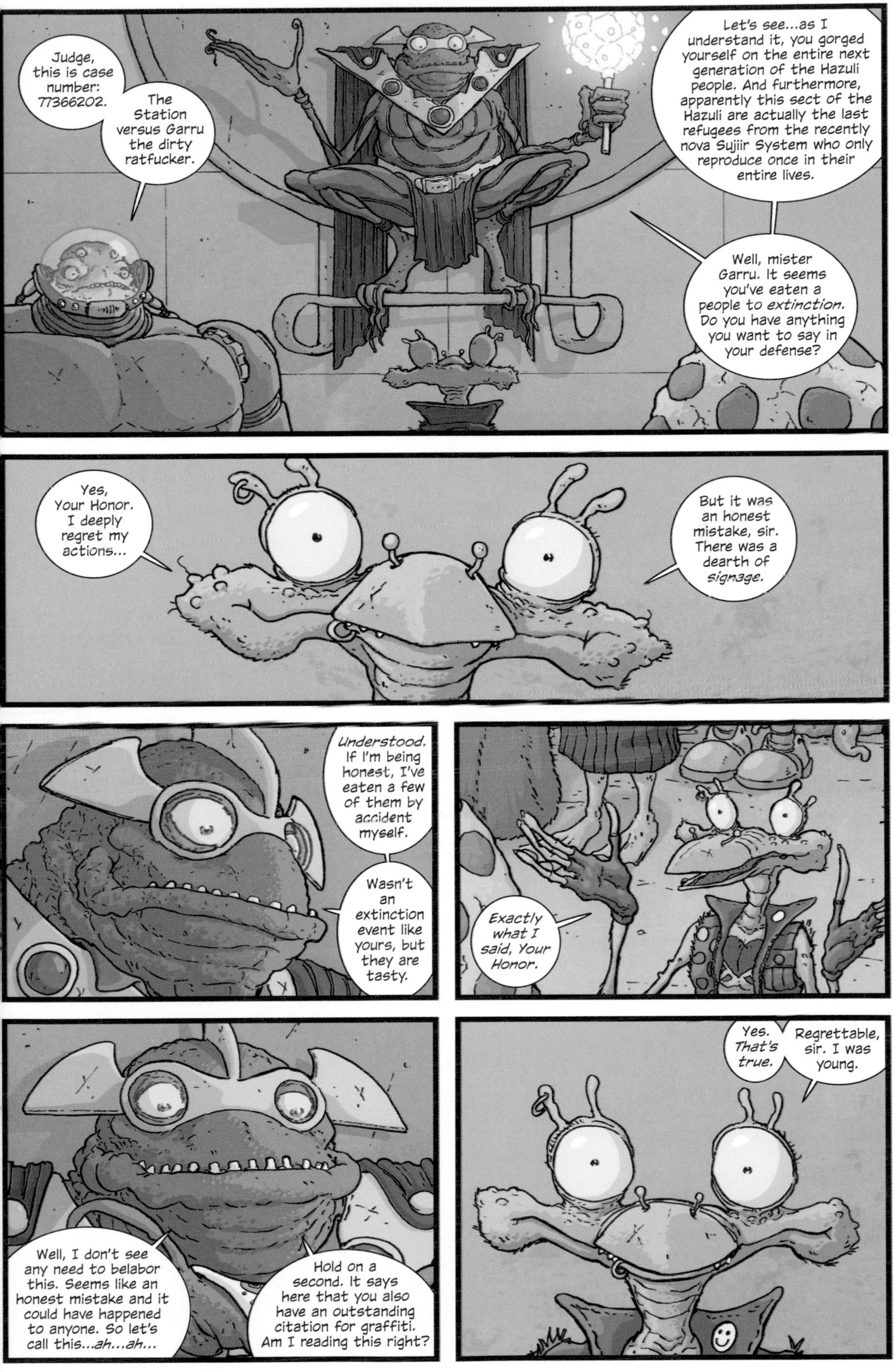
Judge, this is case number: 77366202.
The Station versus Garru the dirty ratfucker.
Let's see...as I understand it, you gorged yourself on the entire next generation of the Hazuli people. And furthermore, apparently this sect of the Hazuli are actually the last refugees from the recently nova Sujiir System who only reproduce once in their entire lives.
Well, mister Garru. It seems you've eaten a people to *extinction.* Do you have anything you want to say in your defense?
Yes, Your Honor. I deeply regret my actions...
But it was an honest mistake, sir. There was a dearth of *signage.*
Understood. If I'm being honest, I've eaten a few of them by accident myself.
Wasn't an extinction event like yours, but they are tasty.
Exactly what I said, Your Honor.
Well, I don't see any need to belabor this. Seems like an honest mistake and it could have happened to anyone. So let's call this...*ah...ah...*
Hold on a second. It says here that you also have an outstanding citation for graffiti. Am I reading this right?
Yes. *That's true.*
Regrettable, sir. I was young.

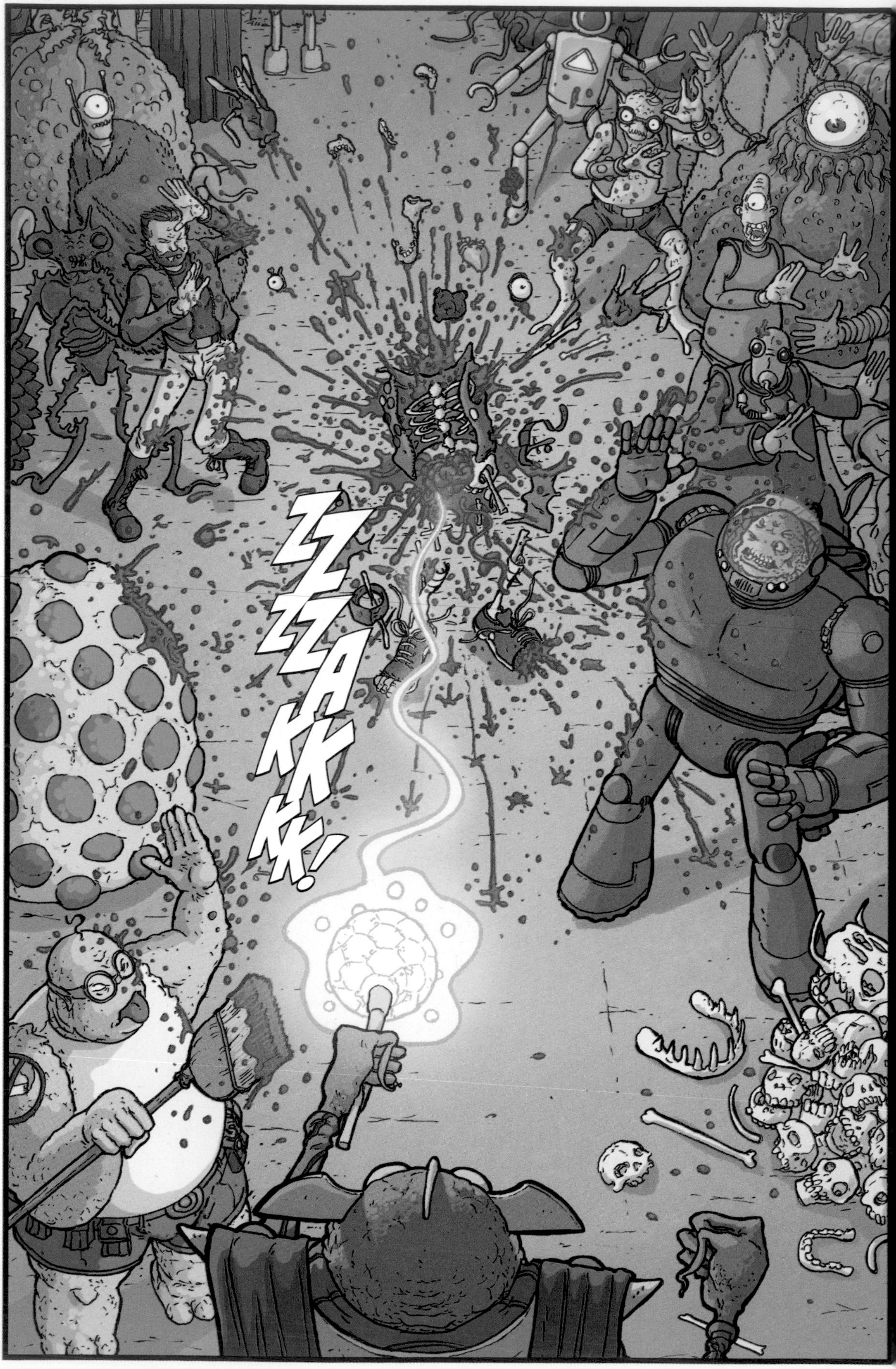
ZZZZAKKKK!

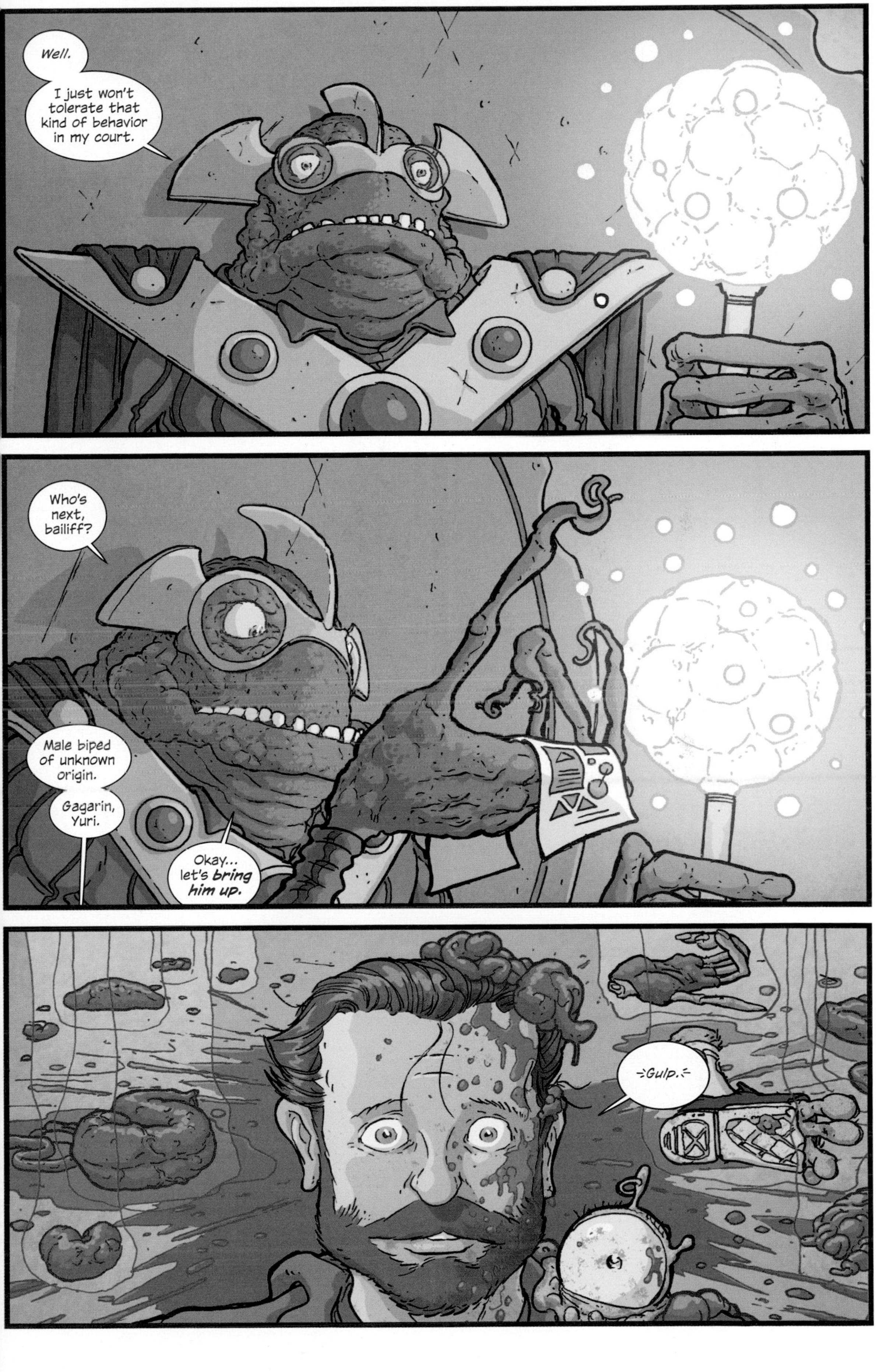
Well.
I just won't tolerate that kind of behavior in my court.
Who's next, bailiff?
Male biped of unknown origin.
Gagarin, Yuri.
Okay... let's *bring him up.*
Gulp.

Later.

Are you sure this is where you want to send me?

Absolutely. Trust me.

I saw the report on your 'spacecraft' that was towed in...

It might not look like much, but because this station is located in the neutral zone between galactic empires we get all kinds of *free spirits* and *fast ships.*

Which is exactly what you're looking for, even if you don't quite know it yet.

No. I mean, are you sure this is where you want to send me for trespassing...

I just got Garru's guts off my jacket, so his punishment is still fresh on my mind and mine seems, ah, a little light.

Oh, that...

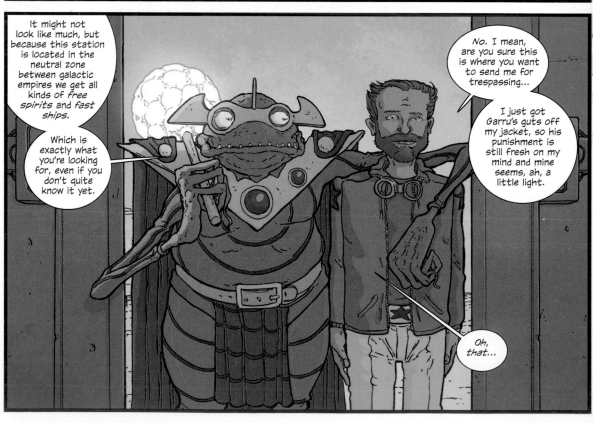

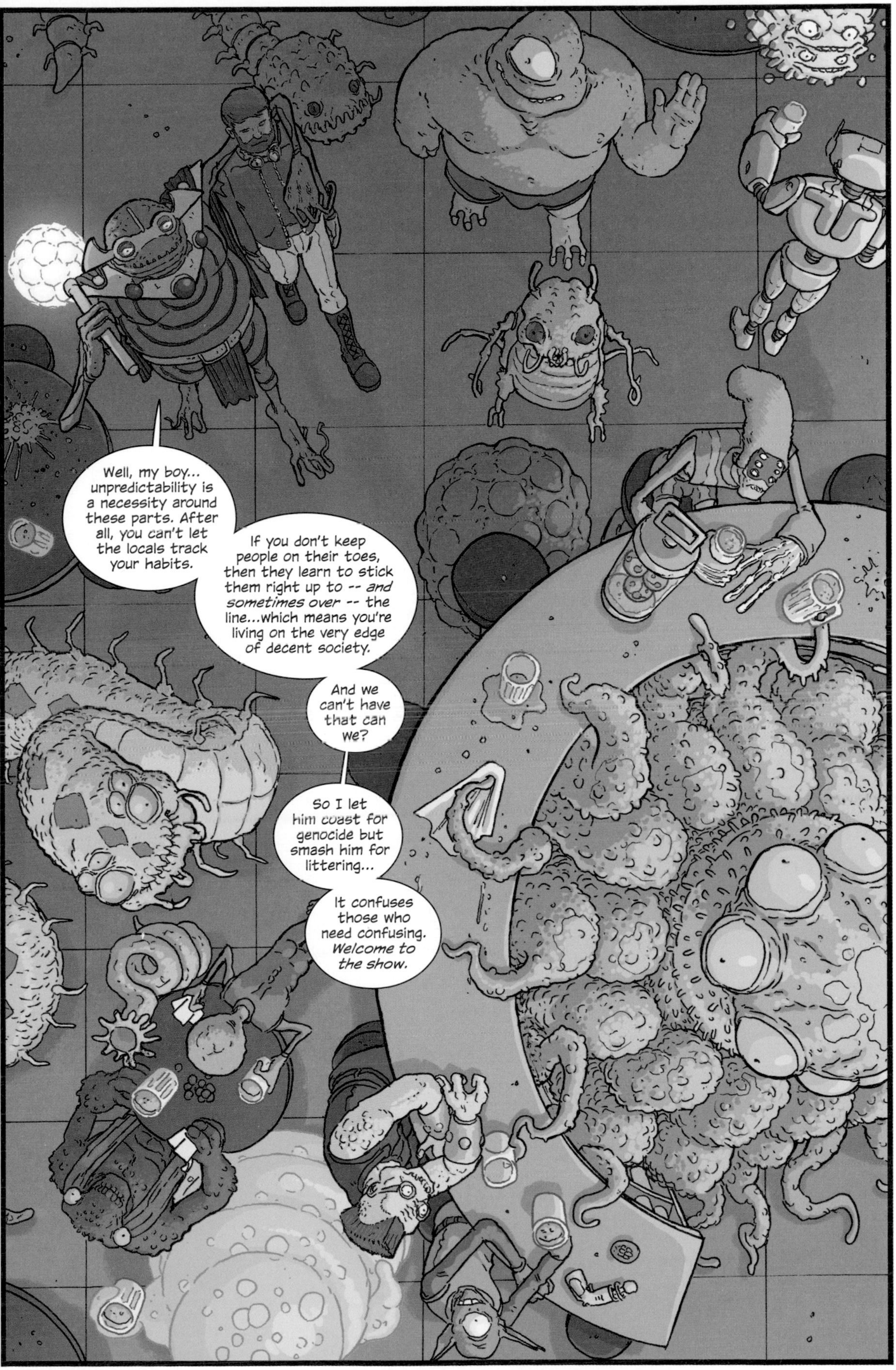
Well, my boy... unpredictability is a necessity around these parts. After all, you can't let the locals track your habits.
If you don't keep people on their toes, then they learn to stick them right up to -- *and sometimes over* -- the line...which means you're living on the very edge of decent society.
And we can't have that can we?
So I let him coast for genocide but smash him for littering...
It confuses those who need confusing. *Welcome to the show.*

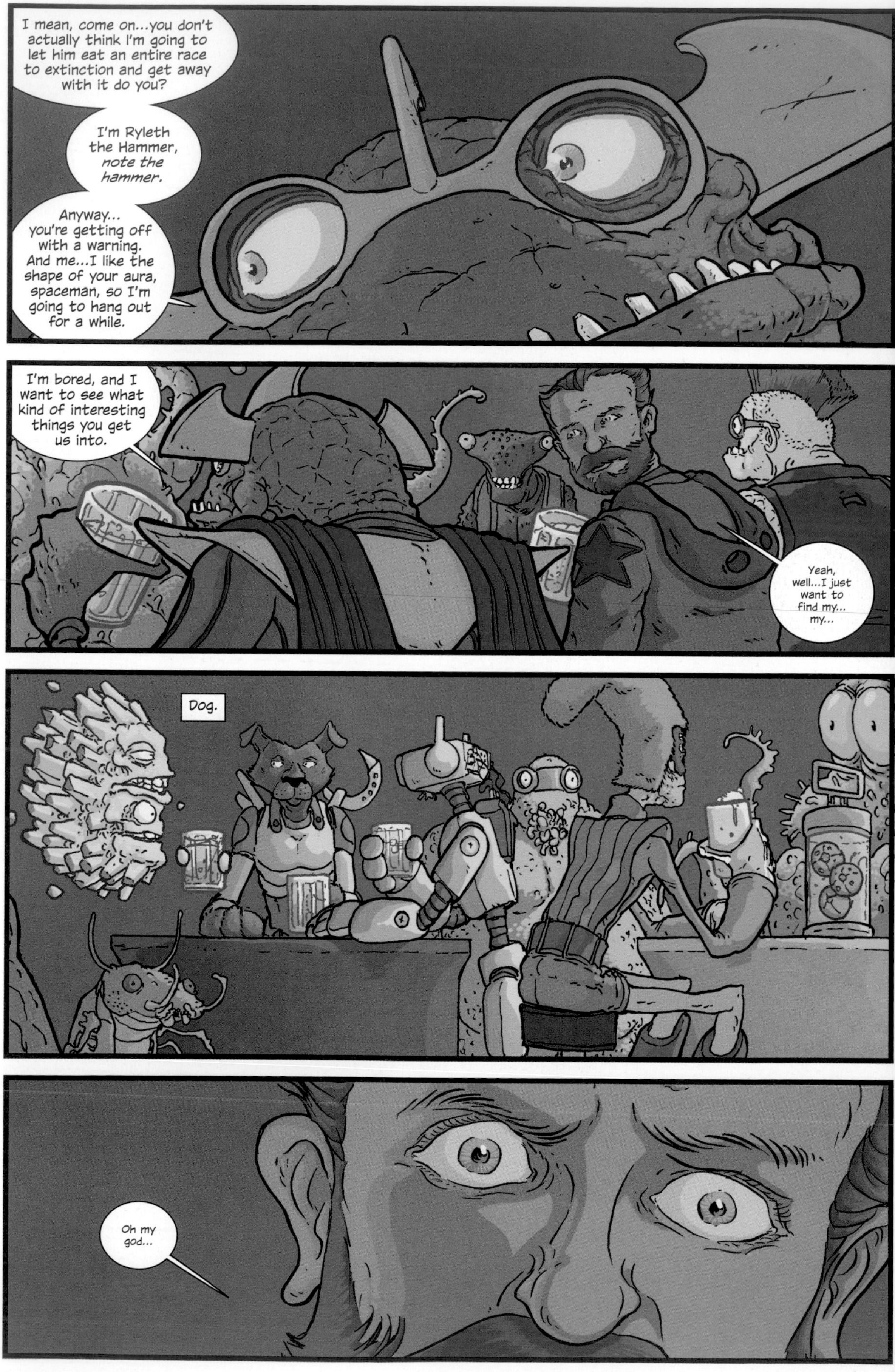
I mean, come on...you don't actually think I'm going to let him eat an entire race to extinction and get away with it do you?
I'm Ryleth the Hammer, *note the hammer.*
Anyway... you're getting off with a warning. And me...I like the shape of your aura, spaceman, so I'm going to hang out for a while.
I'm bored, and I want to see what kind of interesting things you get us into.
Yeah, well...I just want to find my... my...
Dog.
Oh my god...

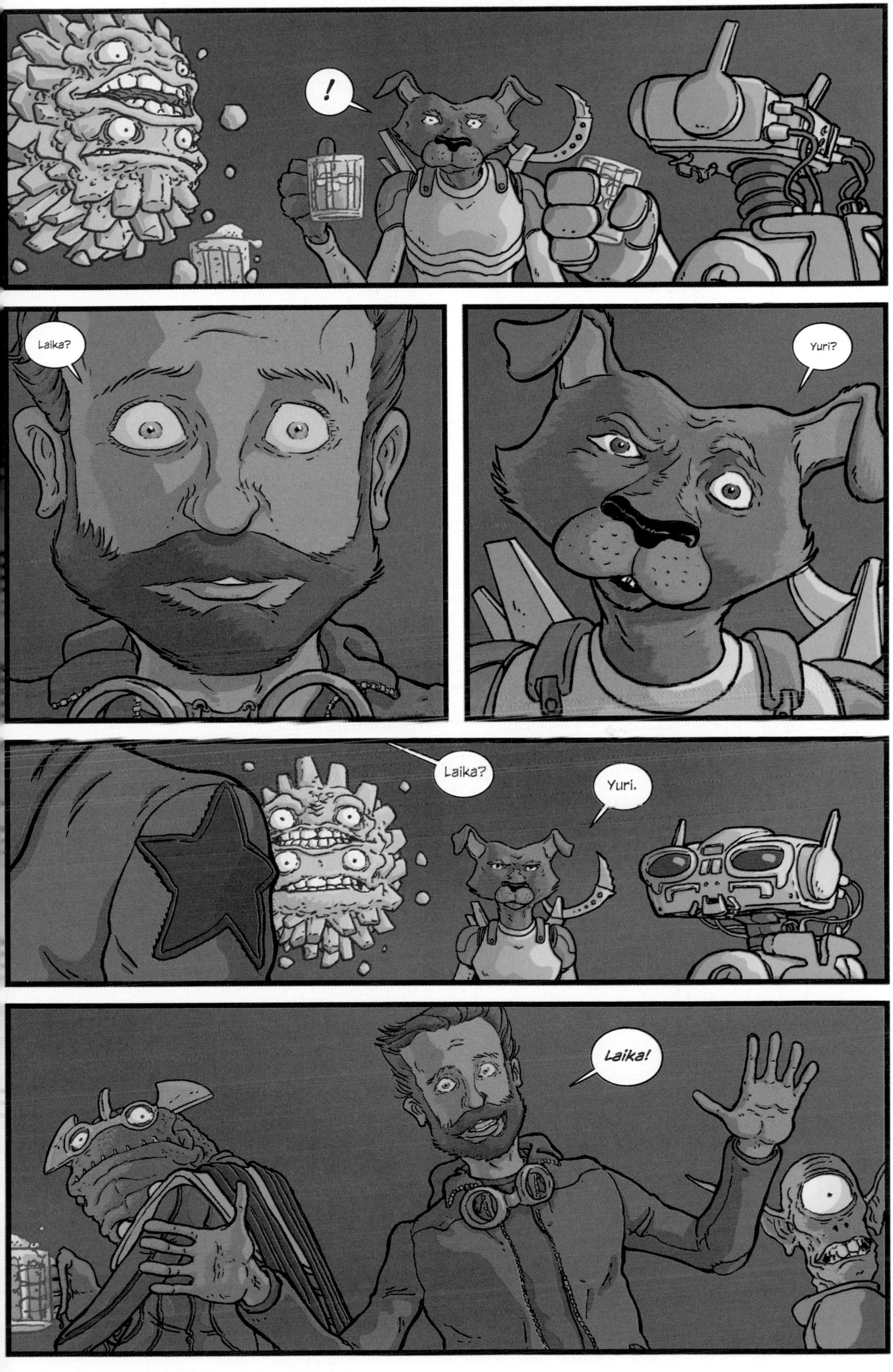
!
Laika?
Yuri?
Laika?
Yuri.
Laika!

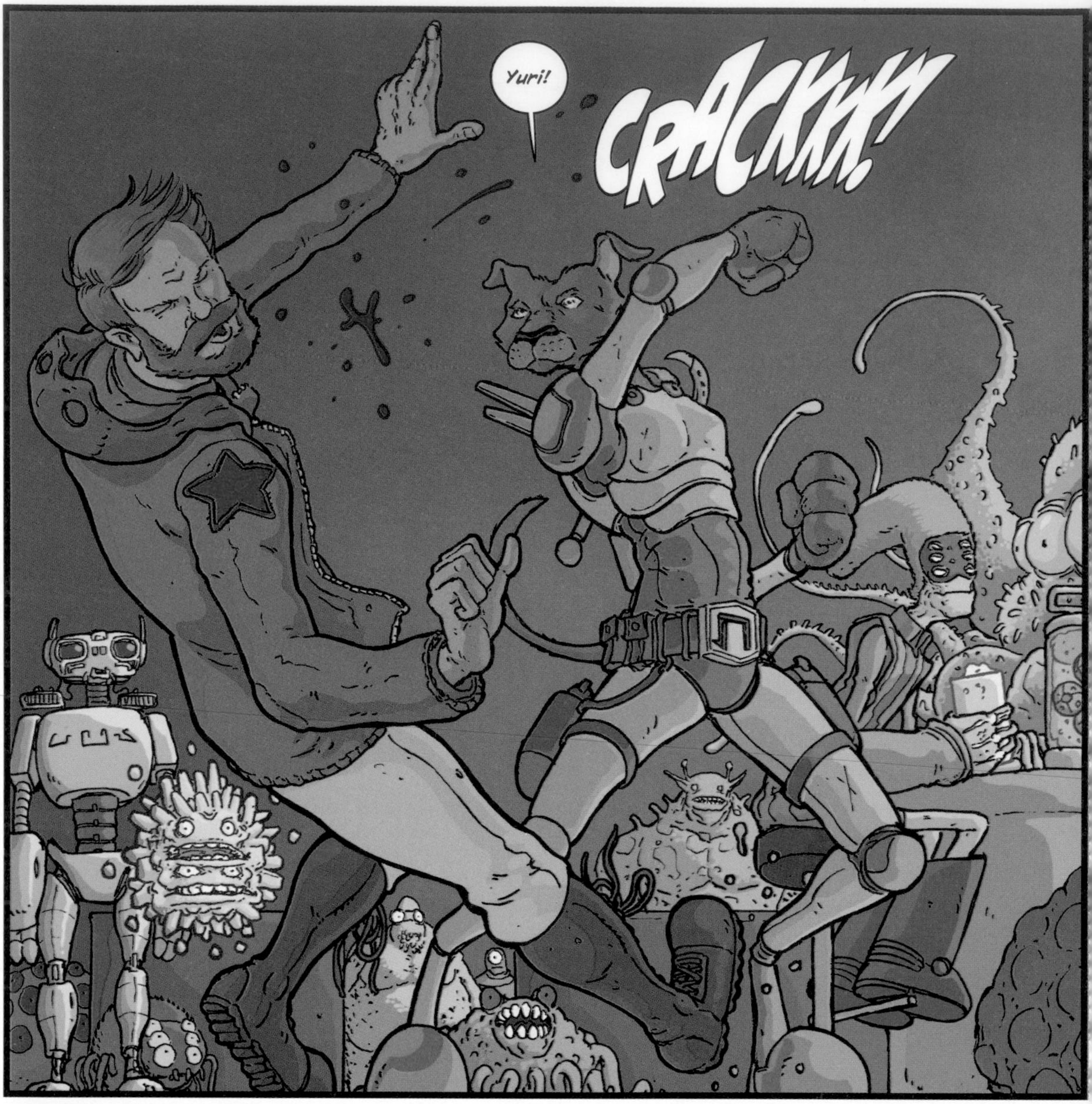
Yuri!
CRACKKK!

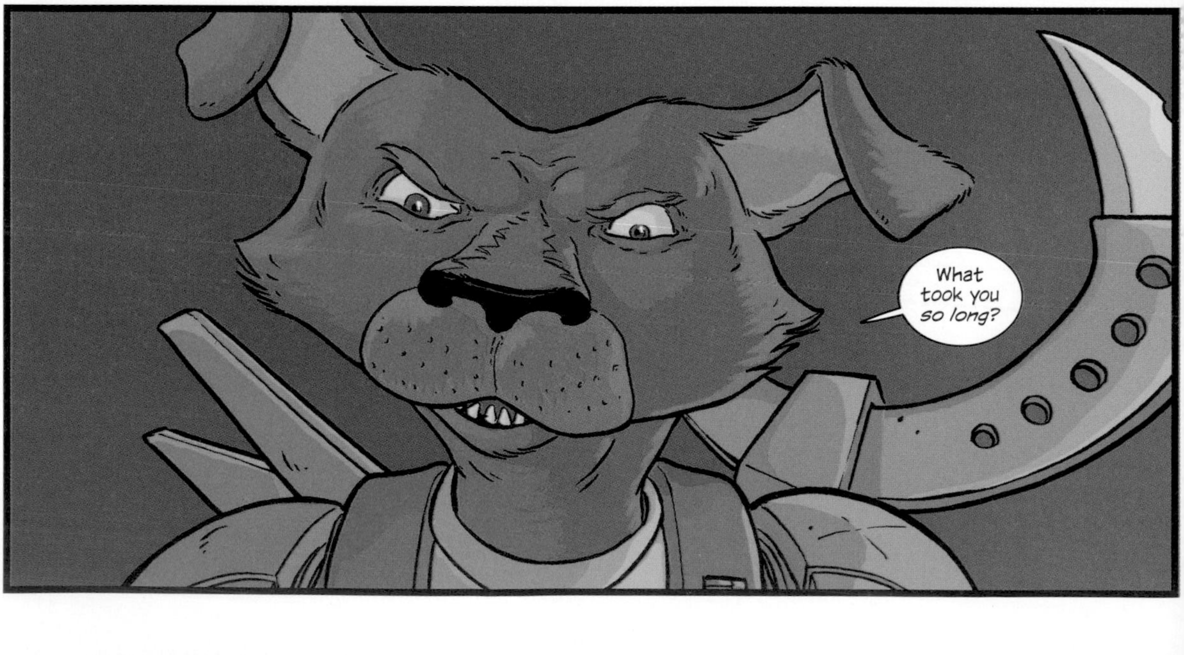
What took you so long?

FEED ME
UNDERSTANDIN

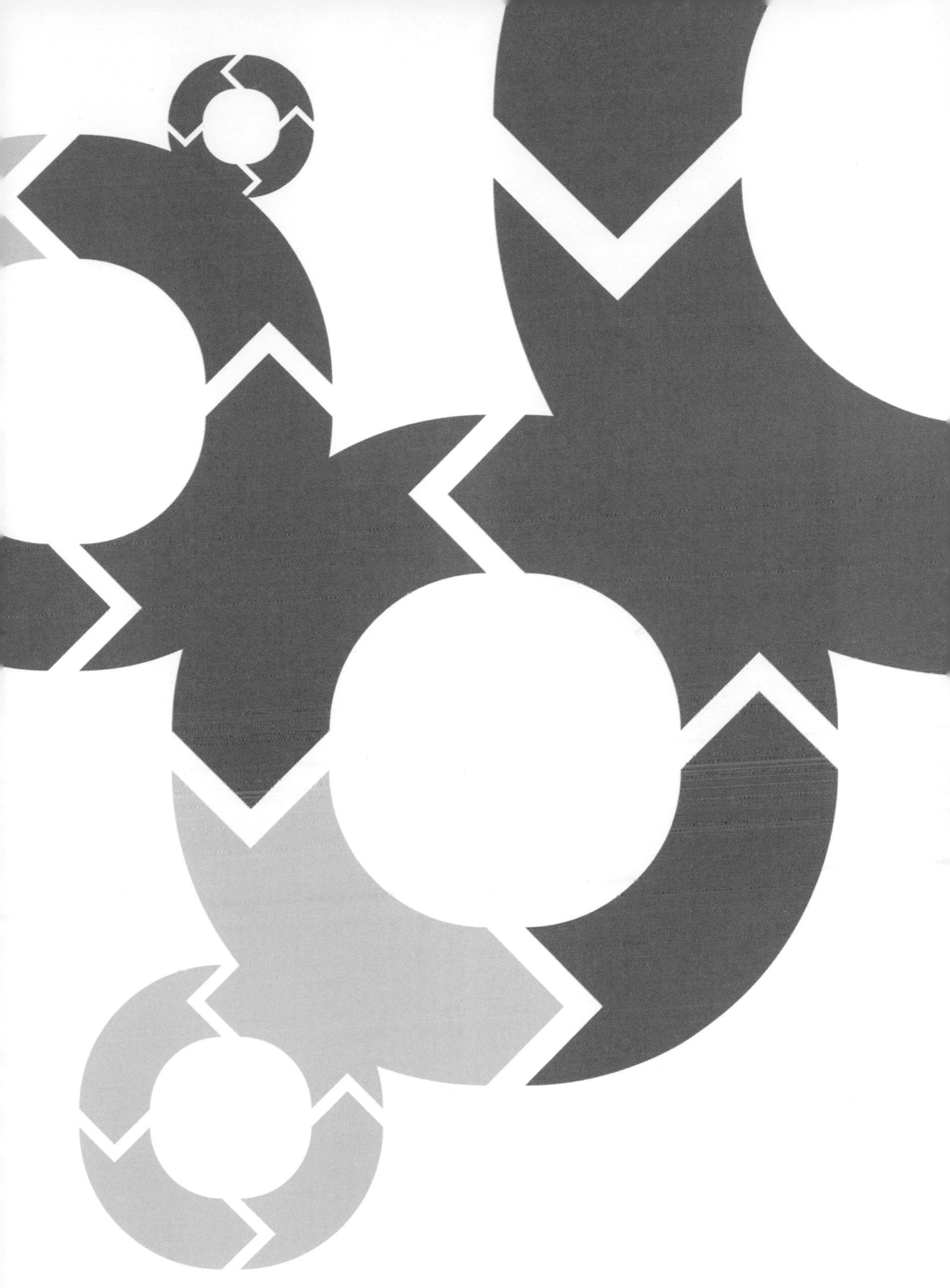

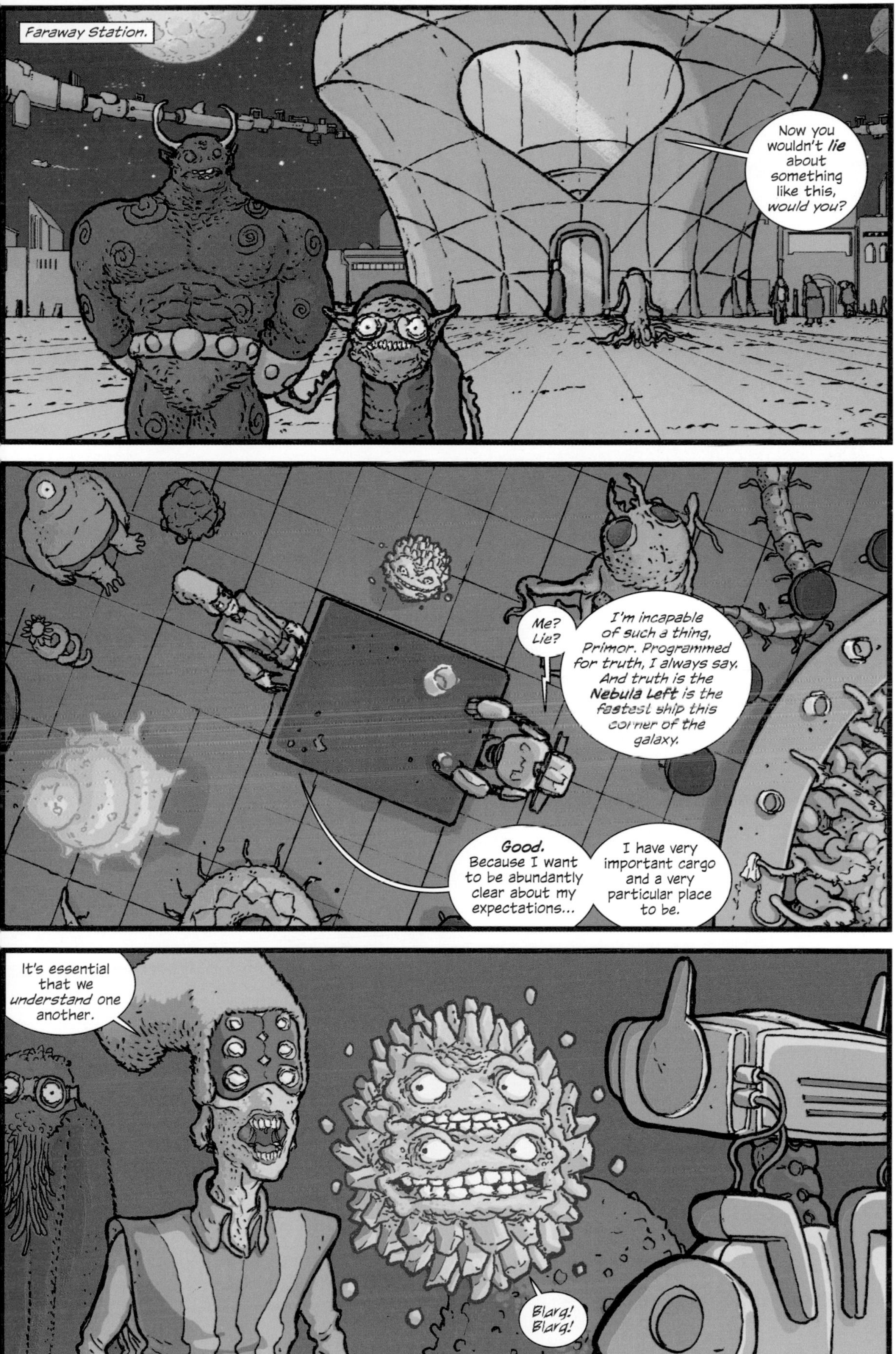
Faraway Station.
Now you wouldn't *lie* about something like this, *would you?*
Me? Lie?
I'm incapable of such a thing, Primor. Programmed for truth, I always say. And truth is the **Nebula Left** is the fastest ship this corner of the galaxy.
Good. Because I want to be abundantly clear about my expectations...
I have very important cargo and a very particular place to be.
It's essential that we *understand* one another.
Blarg! Blarg!

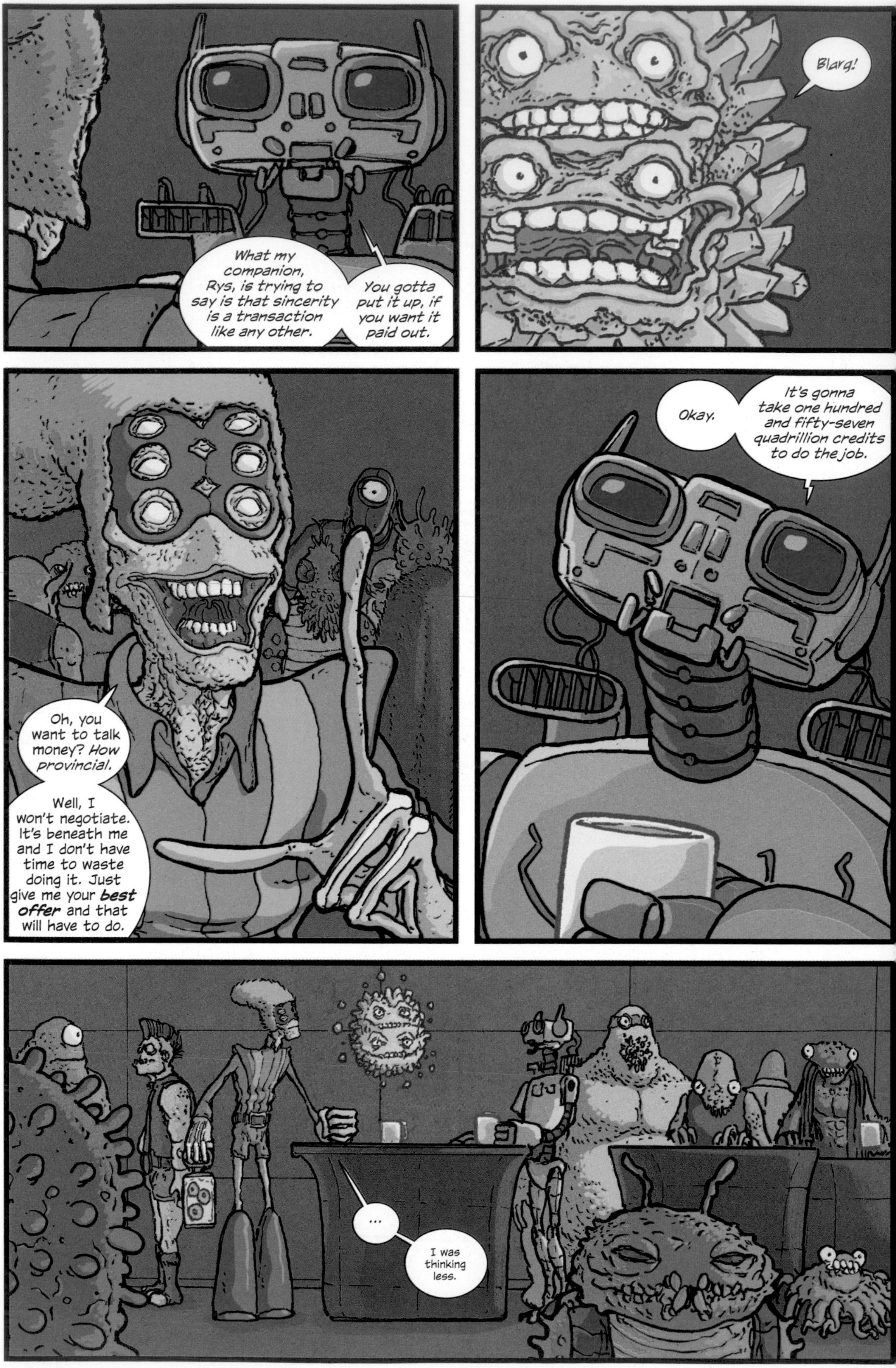
What my companion, Rys, is trying to say is that sincerity is a transaction like any other.
You gotta put it up, if you want it paid out.
Blarg!
Oh, you want to talk money? How provincial.
Well, I won't negotiate. It's beneath me and I don't have time to waste doing it. Just give me your best offer and that will have to do.
Okay.
It's gonna take one hundred and fifty-seven quadrillion credits to do the job.
...
I was thinking less.

Later.

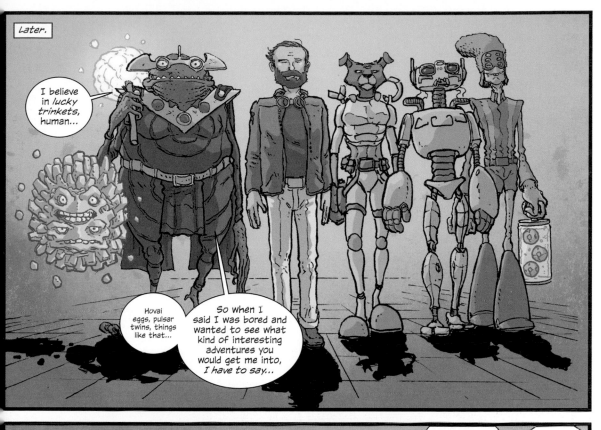

I believe in *lucky* trinkets, human...

Hovai eggs, pulsar twins, things like that...

So when I said I was bored and wanted to see what kind of interesting adventures you would get me into, I have to say...

I had grander plans in mind than this.

You seemed a bit too charmed for courier duty.

Luckier than being *second hand* help on a second rate ship.

Let's go back to the bar...

I think you can do better.

I think there are *more exciting* things out there for us.

I told you, all I wanted to do was find my dog...

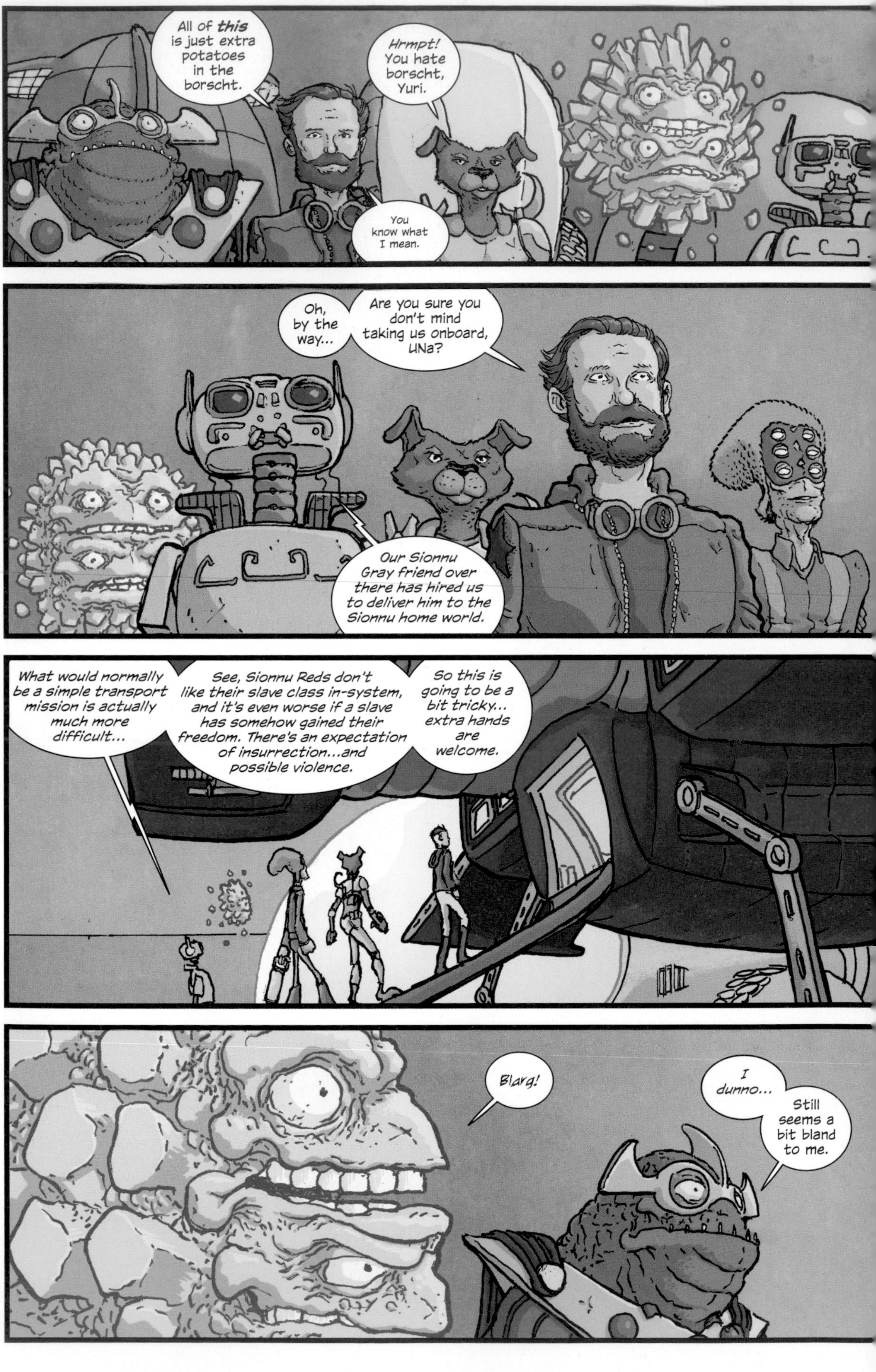
All of *this* is just extra potatoes in the borscht.
Hrmpt! You hate borscht, Yuri.
You know what I mean.
Oh, by the way...
Are you sure you don't mind taking us onboard, UNa?
Our Sionnu Gray friend over there has hired us to deliver him to the Sionnu home world.
What would normally be a simple transport mission is actually much more difficult...
See, Sionnu Reds don't like their slave class in-system, and it's even worse if a slave has somehow gained their freedom. There's an expectation of insurrection...and possible violence.
So this is going to be a bit tricky... extra hands are welcome.
Blarg!
I dunno...
Still seems a bit bland to me.

Well, I don't care what the judge says, Laika... *this is some ship.*

How did you--

We stole it.

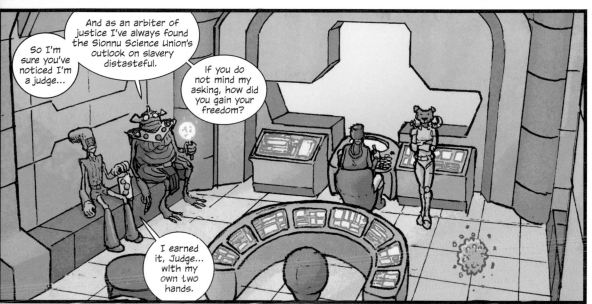

So I'm sure you've noticed I'm a judge...

And as an arbiter of justice I've always found the Sionnu Science Union's outlook on slavery distasteful.

If you do not mind my asking, how did you gain your freedom?

I earned it, Judge... with my own two hands.

The idea that I was property...that my body -- and *more importantly* -- my mind belonged to someone else...

It was a concept I had to purge with blood.

So I murdered everyone that would call themselves my master.

And I am not done yet.

Well...

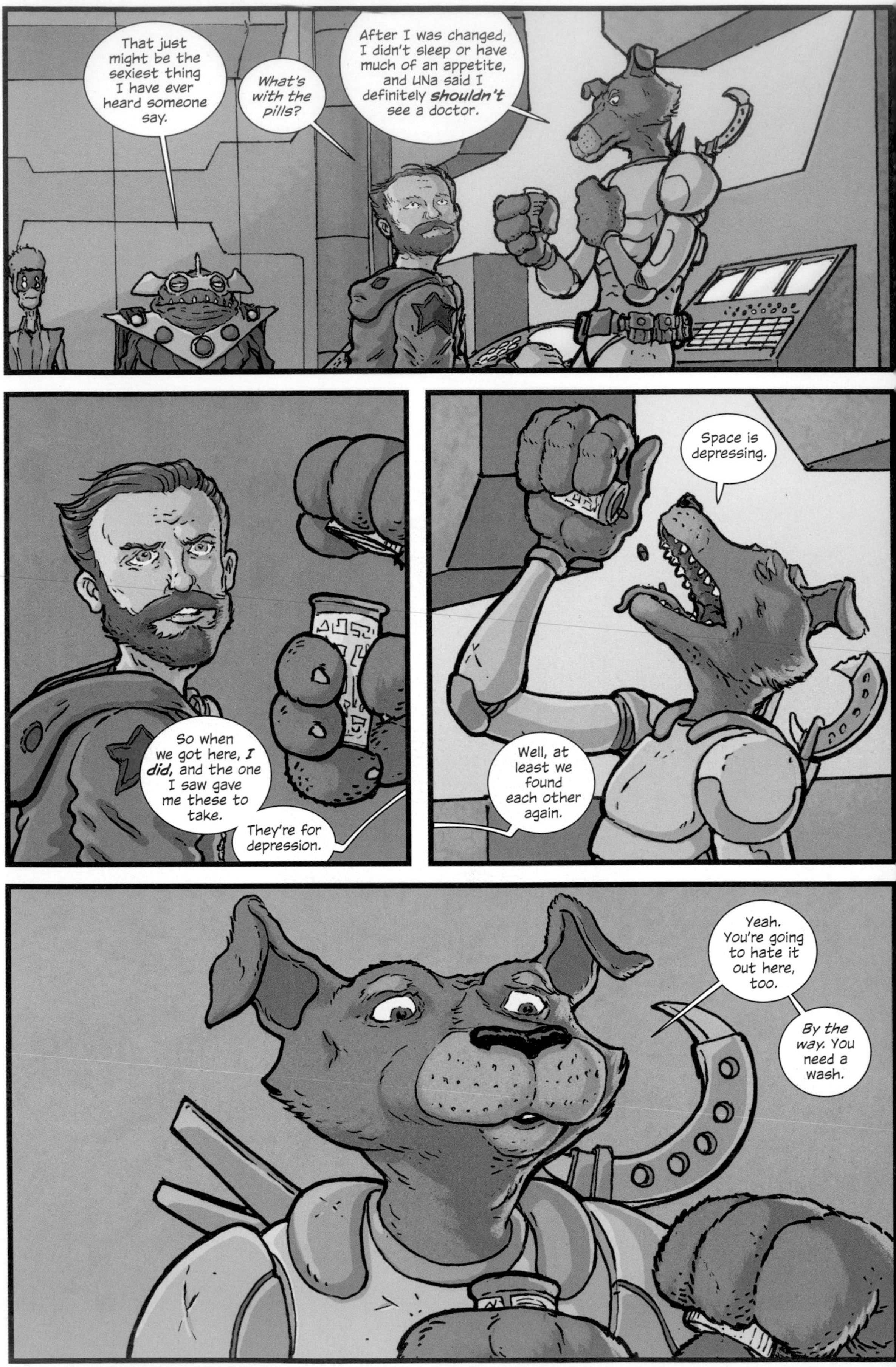
That just might be the sexiest thing I have ever heard someone say.
What's with the pills?
After I was changed, I didn't sleep or have much of an appetite, and UNa said I definitely ***shouldn't*** see a doctor.
So when we got here, ***I did,*** and the one I saw gave me these to take.
They're for depression.
Space is depressing.
Well, at least we found each other again.
Yeah. You're going to hate it out here, too.
By the way. You need a wash.

"LOVE WILL ALSO PUNCH YOU IN THE FACE..."

CLAVIS AUREA
THE RECORDED FEYNMAN │ **VOL. 4**

27

THE SUN BEYOND
THE STARS

"...BECAUSE YOU HAD IT COMING."

CLAVIS AUREA
THE RECORDED FEYNMAN | **VOL. 4**

The Sionnu Ternary System.

The Science Council Homeworld.

Great Sionox...

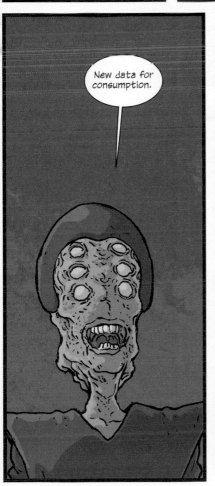

New data for consumption.

I will partake of knowledge, minister.

I will accept your new data.

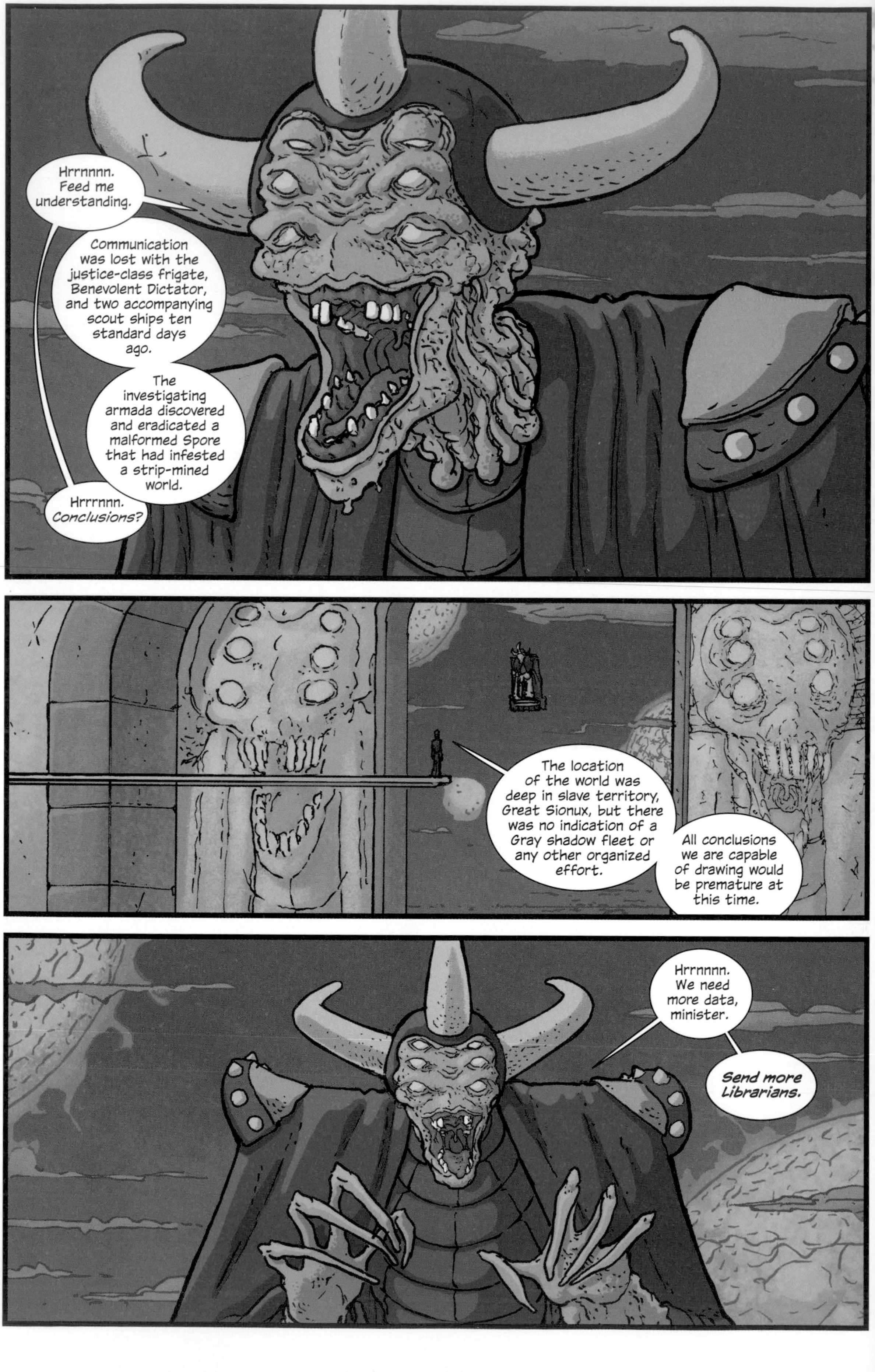

Hrrnnnn. Feed me understanding.
Communication was lost with the justice-class frigate, Benevolent Dictator, and two accompanying scout ships ten standard days ago.
The investigating armada discovered and eradicated a malformed Spore that had infested a strip-mined world.
Hrrnnnn. *Conclusions?*
The location of the world was deep in slave territory, Great Sionux, but there was no indication of a Gray shadow fleet or any other organized effort.
All conclusions we are capable of drawing would be premature at this time.
Hrrnnnn. We need more data, minister.
Send more Librarians.

Blarg!

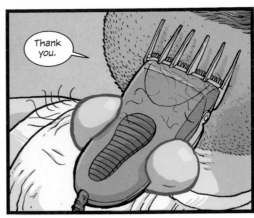

Thank you.

But I don't just smell better, I feel better.

Blarg!

I understand how that might be confusing, but I've seen some pretty momentous things at this point in my life.

Yeah.

All of them somehow exciting, terrifying, or for some reason or the other *baffling*. I'm talking about paradigm-shifting stuff. Shake you to your core kinds of events.

And what I've learned is that the only consistent thing that you cannot predict is how people will react during traumatic -- or **shocking** -- incidents.

You just never know what people are going to do.

But, yeah, I get it...

I wish she wouldn't have punched me either.

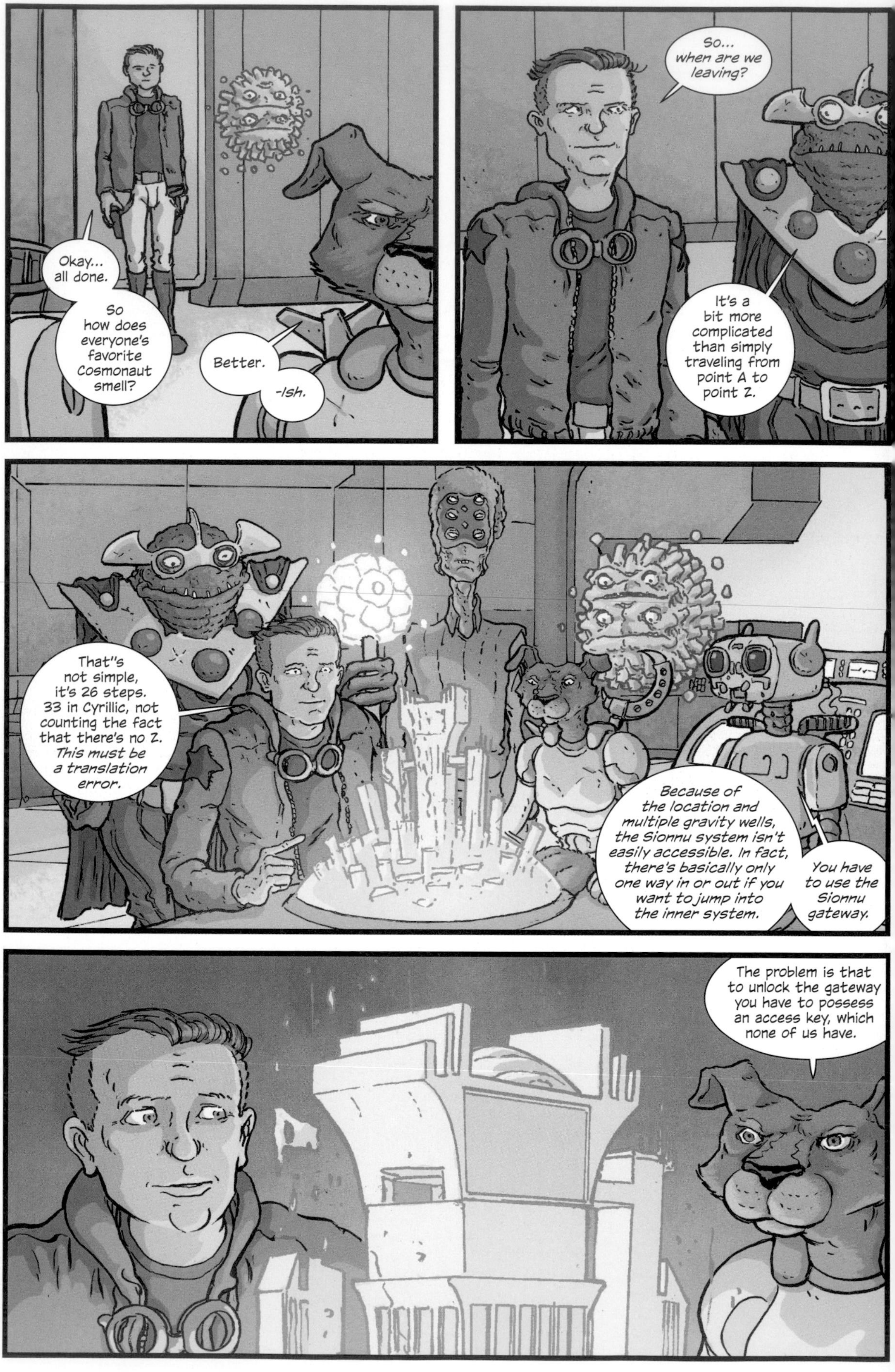

Okay... all done.
So how does everyone's favorite Cosmonaut smell?
Better.
-Ish.
So... when are we leaving?
It's a bit more complicated than simply traveling from point A to point Z.
That''s not simple, it's 26 steps. 33 in Cyrillic, not counting the fact that there's no Z. *This must be a translation error.*
Because of the location and multiple gravity wells, the Sionnu system isn't easily accessible. In fact, there's basically only one way in or out if you want to jump into the inner system.
You have to use the Sionnu gateway.
The problem is that to unlock the gateway you have to possess an access key, which none of us have.

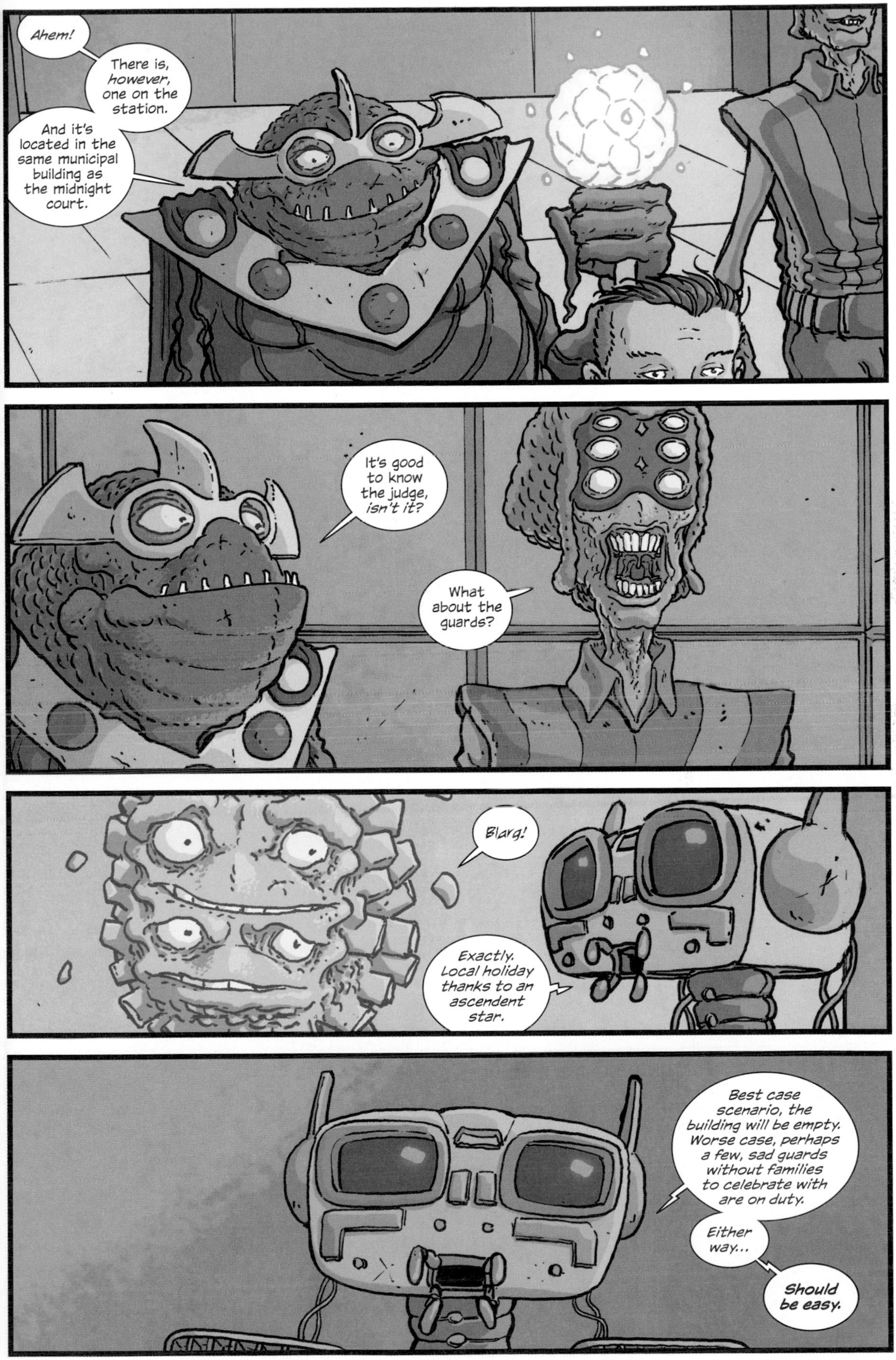
Ahem!
There is, *however*, one on the station.
And it's located in the same municipal building as the midnight court.
It's good to know the judge, *isn't it?*
What about the guards?
Blarg!
Exactly. Local holiday thanks to an ascendent star.
Best case scenario, the building will be empty. Worse case, perhaps a few, sad guards without families to celebrate with are on duty.
Either way...
Should be easy.

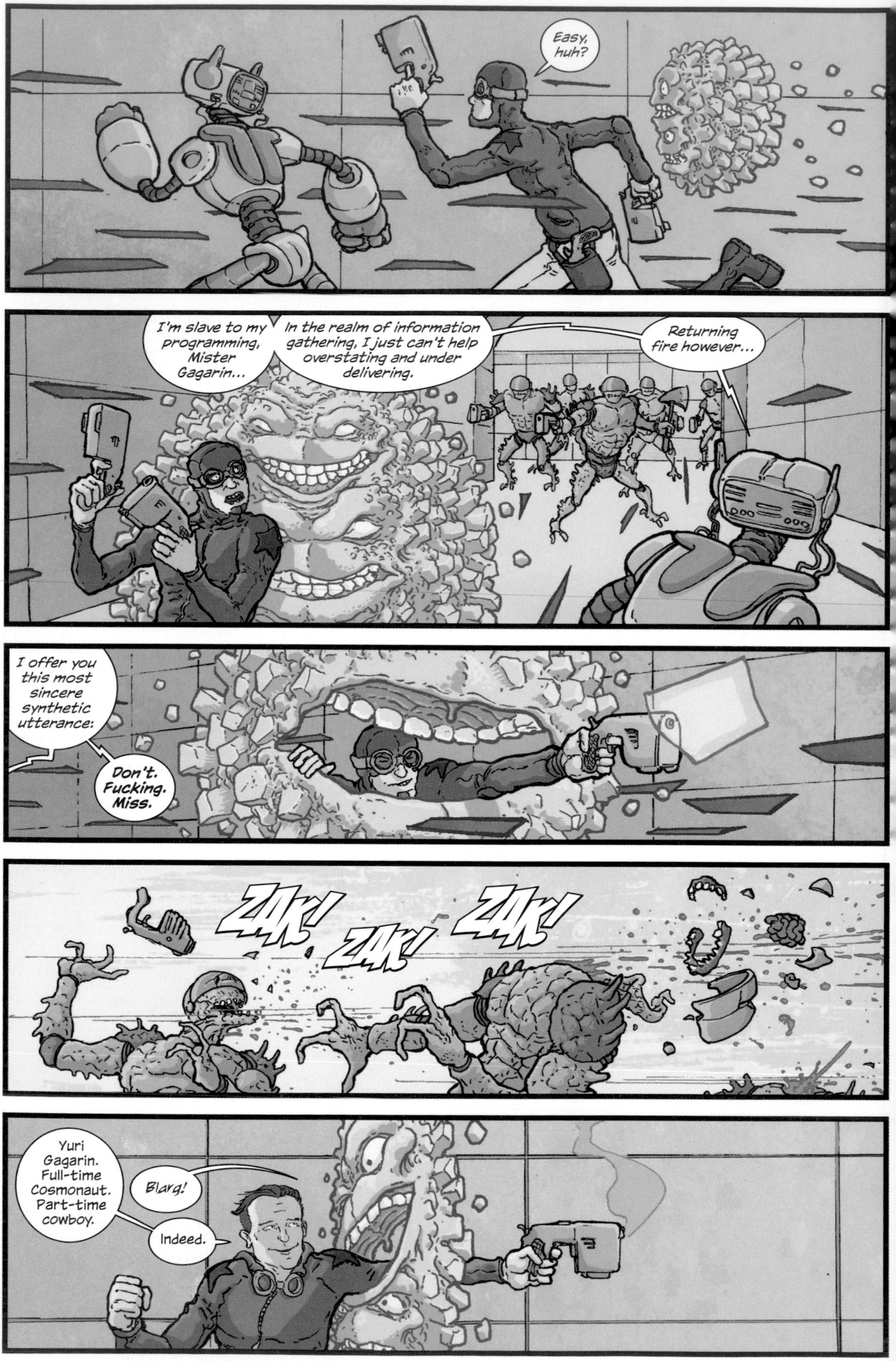
Easy, huh?
I'm slave to my programming, Mister Gagarin...
In the realm of information gathering, I just can't help overstating and under delivering.
Returning fire however...
I offer you this most sincere synthetic utterance:
Don't. Fucking. Miss.
ZAK!
ZAK!
ZAK!
Yuri Gagarin. Full-time Cosmonaut. Part-time cowboy.
Blarg!
Indeed.

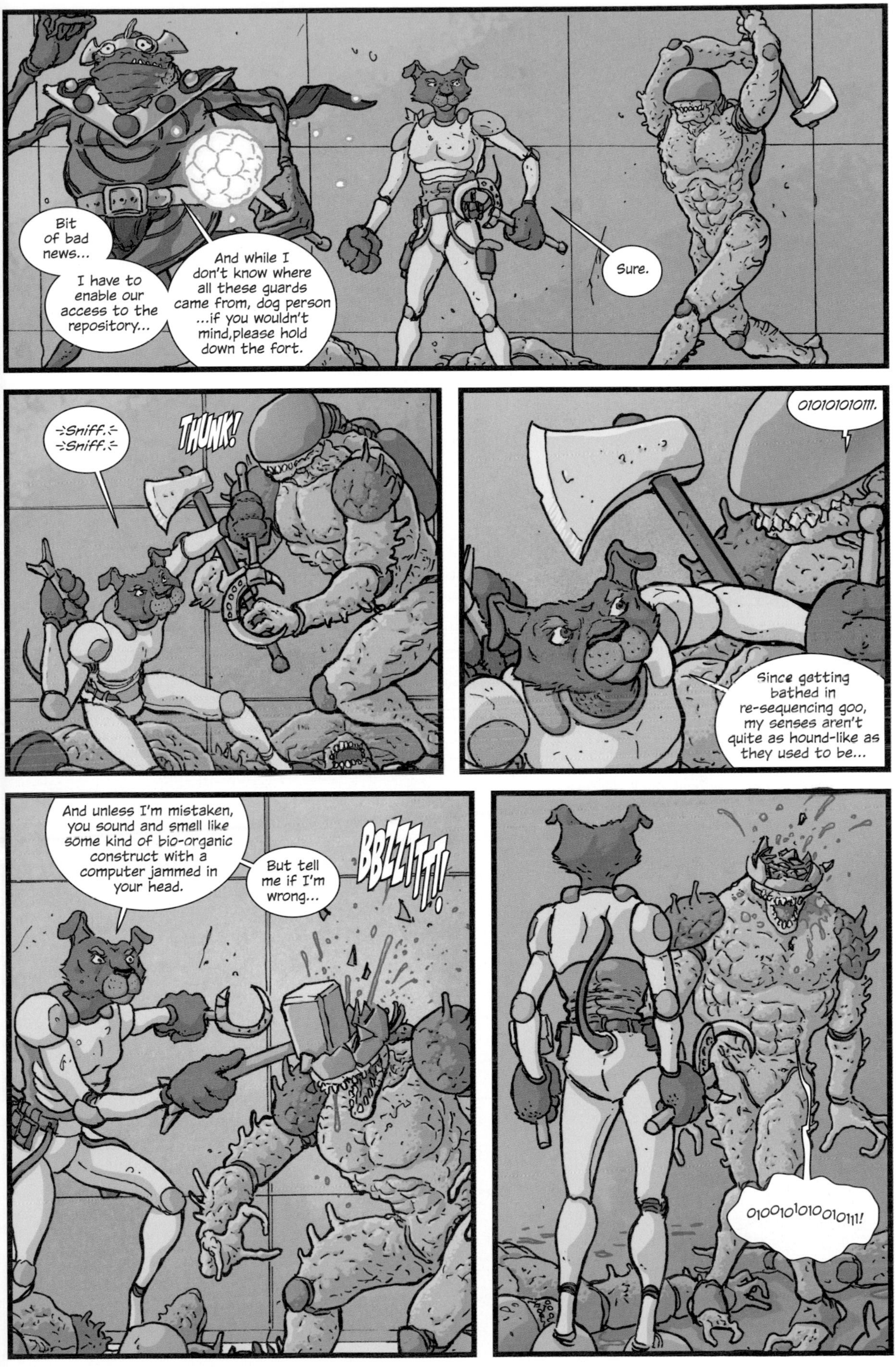
Bit of bad news...
I have to enable our access to the repository...
And while I don't know where all these guards came from, dog person ...if you wouldn't mind,please hold down the fort.
Sure.
-Sniff.- -Sniff.-
THUNK!
01010101011.
Since getting bathed in re-sequencing goo, my senses aren't quite as hound-like as they used to be...
And unless I'm mistaken, you sound and smell like some kind of bio-organic construct with a computer jammed in your head.
But tell me if I'm wrong...
BBZZTTTT!
0100101010010111!

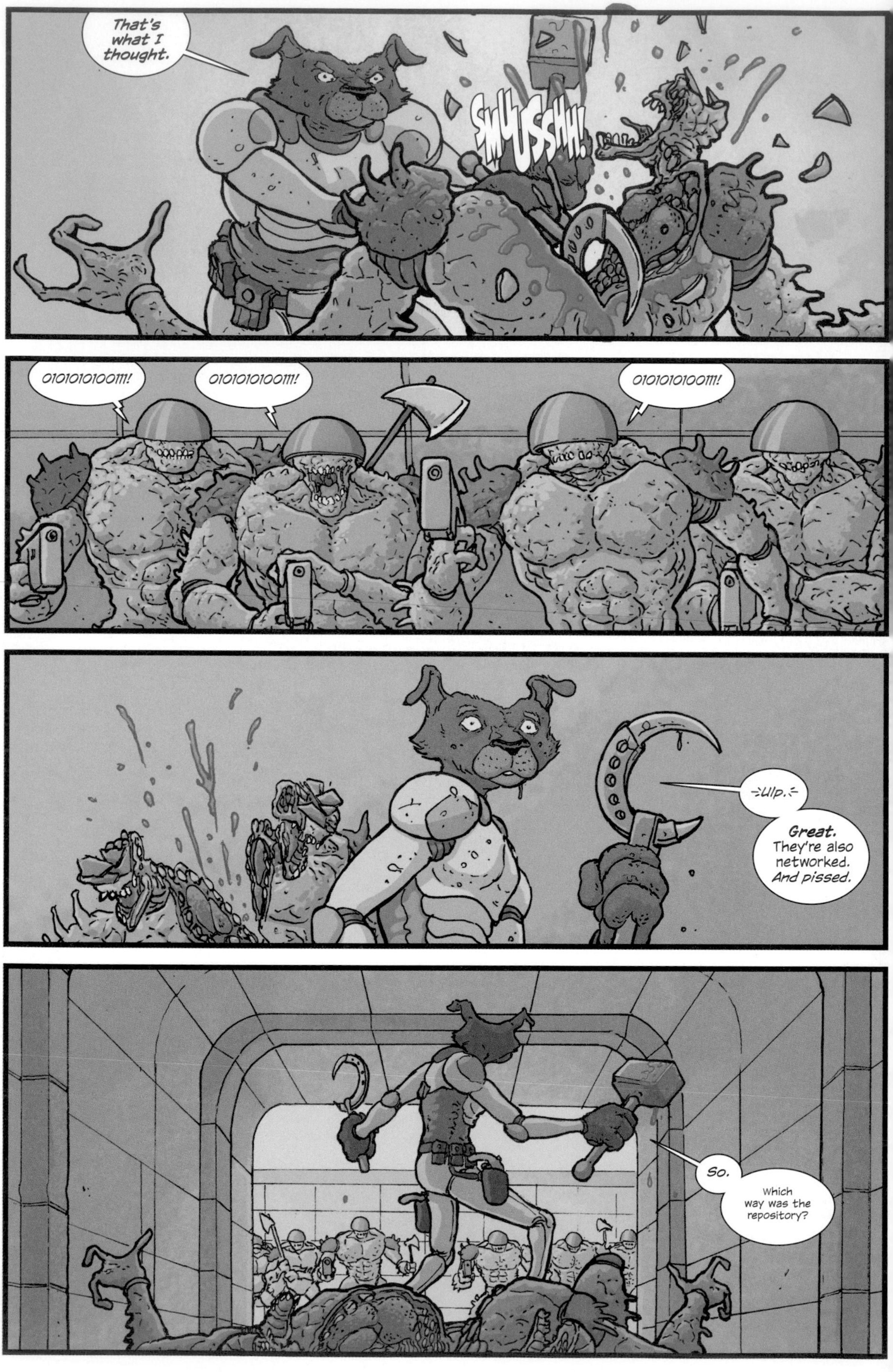
That's what I thought.
SMUSSHH!
0101010100111!
0101010100111!
0101010100111!
Ulp.
Great. They're also networked. *And pissed.*
So.
Which way was the repository?

Access granted. Now all you have to do is grab it.

Yes. There it is.

The only one of its kind in the universe.

Really?

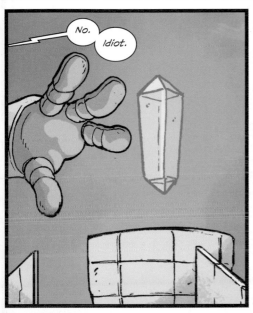

No. Idiot.

It's a key to a hyperspace gateway connecting trillions of citizens across hundreds of worlds.

There are probably hundreds of thousands of these out there. This is just the only one we have acc--

ZZZZAPP WWWW!!!

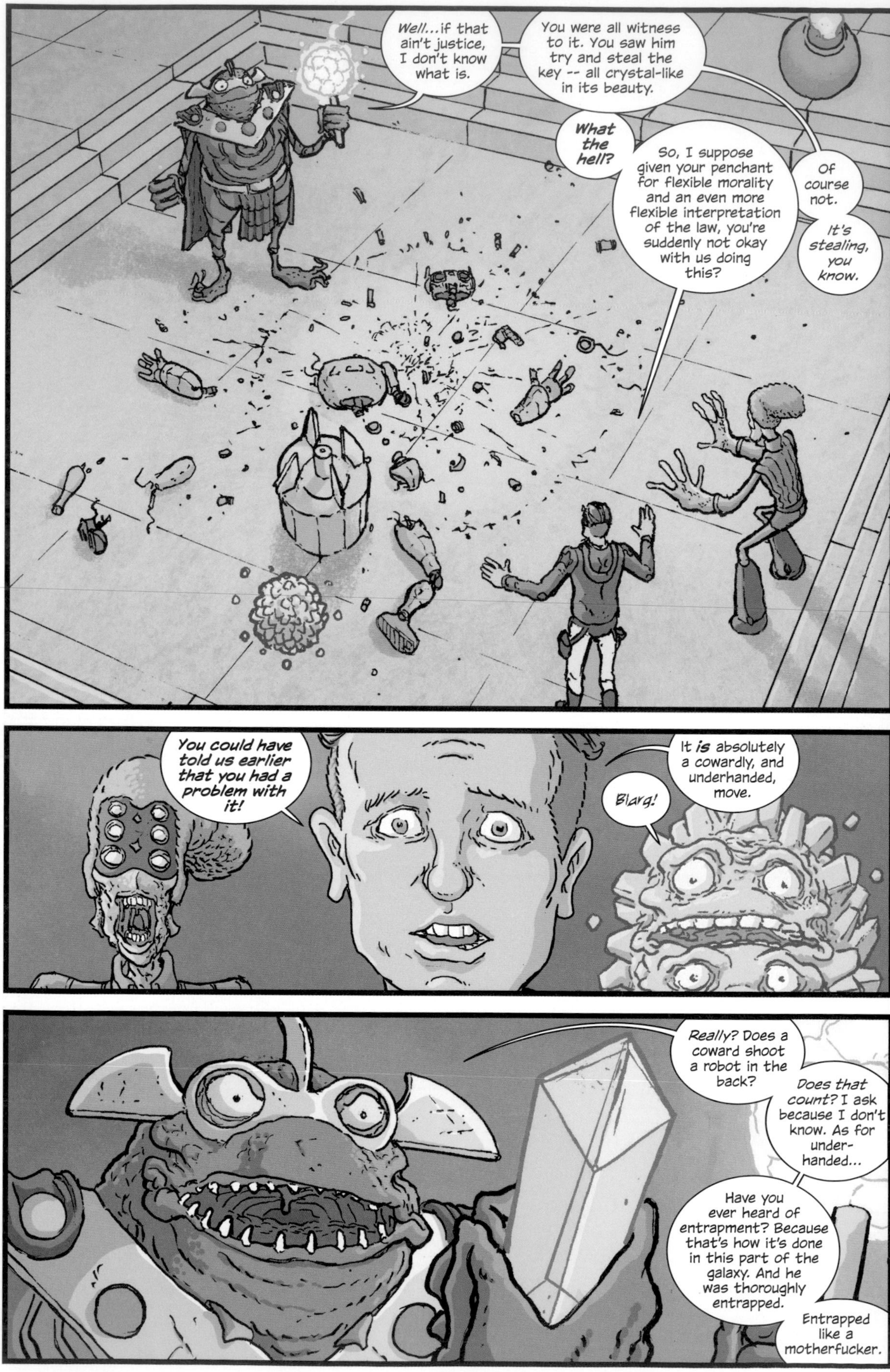
Well... if that ain't justice, I don't know what is.
You were all witness to it. You saw him try and steal the key -- all crystal-like in its beauty.
Of course not.
It's stealing, you know.
What the hell?
So, I suppose given your penchant for flexible morality and an even more flexible interpretation of the law, you're suddenly not okay with us doing this?
You could have told us earlier that you had a problem with it!
It *is* absolutely a cowardly, and underhanded, move.
Blarg!
Really? Does a coward shoot a robot in the back?
Does that count? I ask because I don't know. As for under-handed...
Have you ever heard of entrapment? Because that's how it's done in this part of the galaxy. And he was thoroughly entrapped.
Entrapped like a motherfucker.

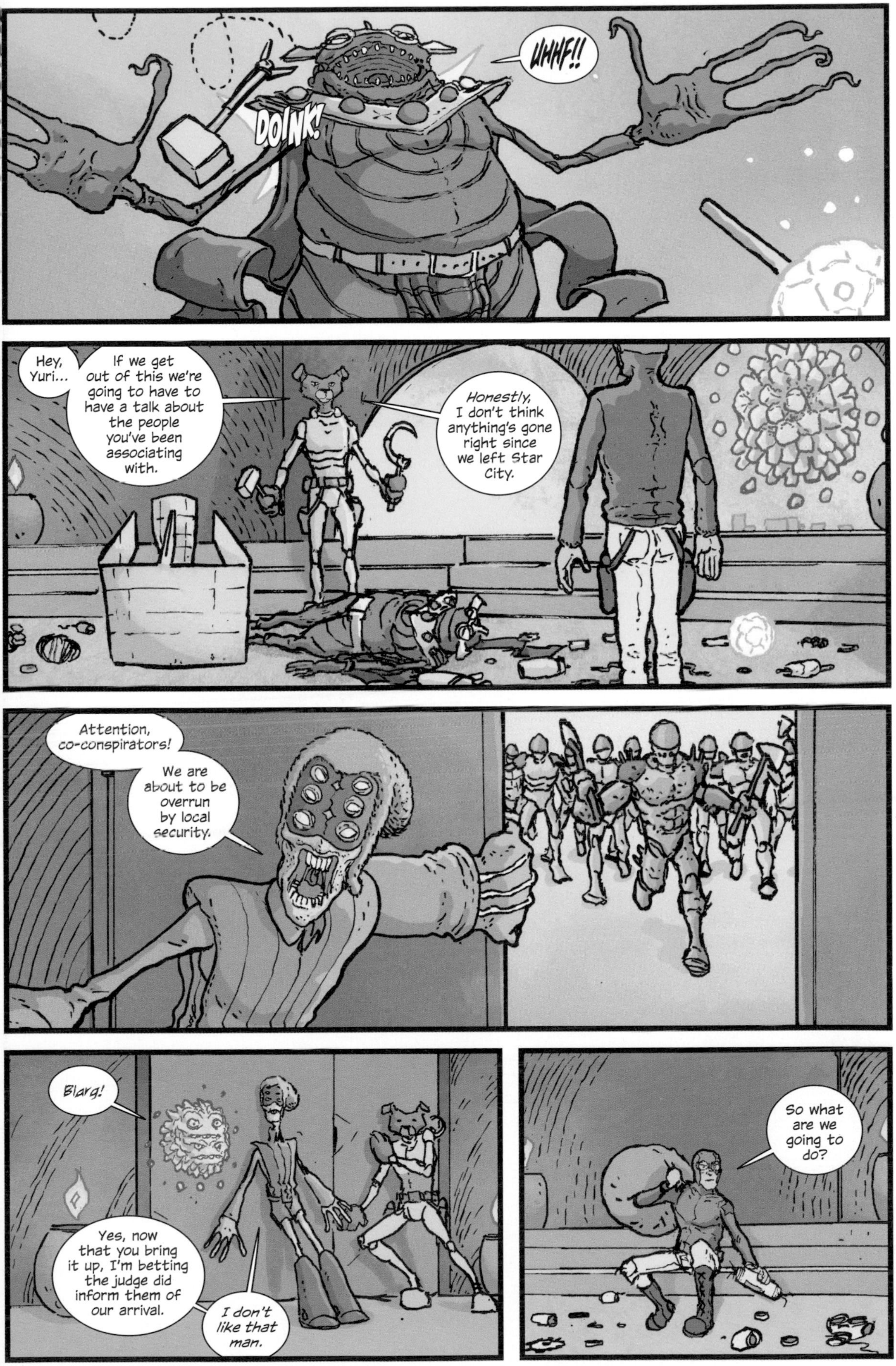
DOINK!
UHHF!!
Hey, Yuri...
If we get out of this we're going to have to have a talk about the people you've been associating with.
Honestly, I don't think anything's gone right since we left Star City.
Attention, co-conspirators!
We are about to be overrun by local security.
Blarg!
Yes, now that you bring it up, I'm betting the judge did inform them of our arrival.
I don't like that man.
So what are we going to do?

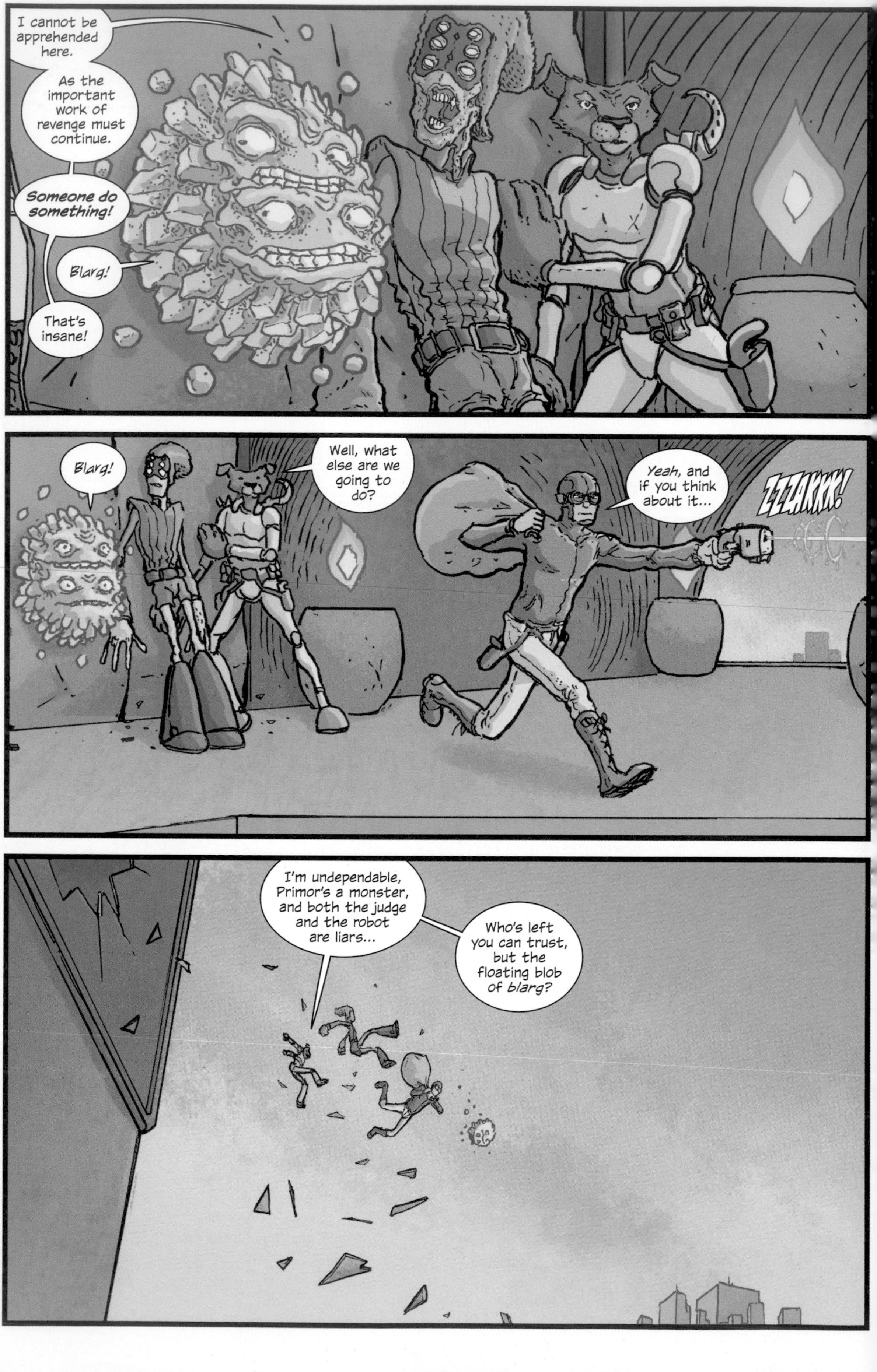
I cannot be apprehended here.
As the important work of revenge must continue.
Someone do something!
Blarg!
That's insane!
Blarg!
Well, what else are we going to do?
Yeah, and if you think about it...
ZZZAKKK!
I'm undependable, Primor's a monster, and both the judge and the robot are liars...
Who's left you can trust, but the floating blob of blarg?

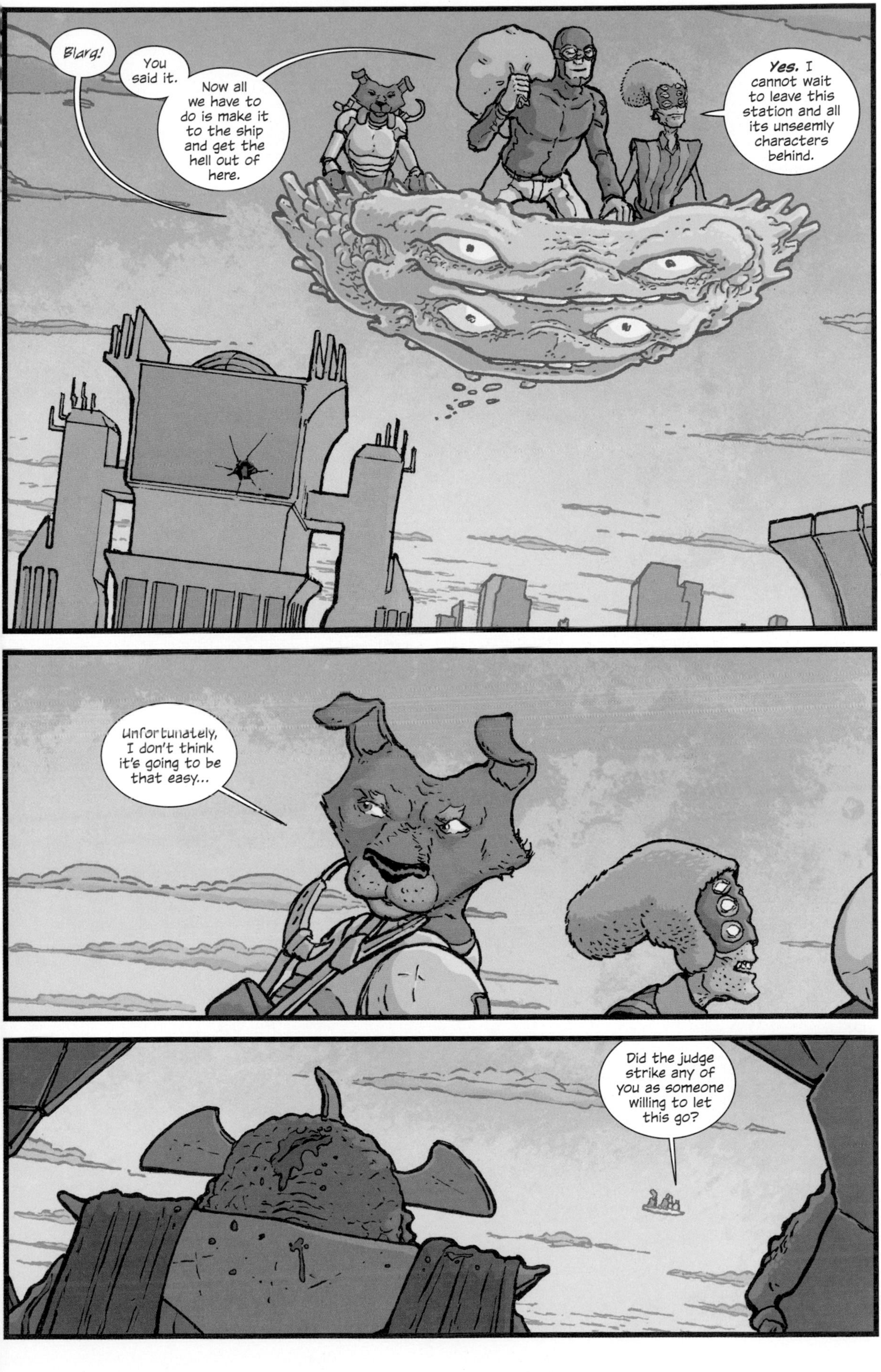
Blarg!
You said it.
Now all we have to do is make it to the ship and get the hell out of here.
Yes. I cannot wait to leave this station and all its unseemly characters behind.
Unfortunately, I don't think it's going to be that easy...
Did the judge strike any of you as someone willing to let this go?

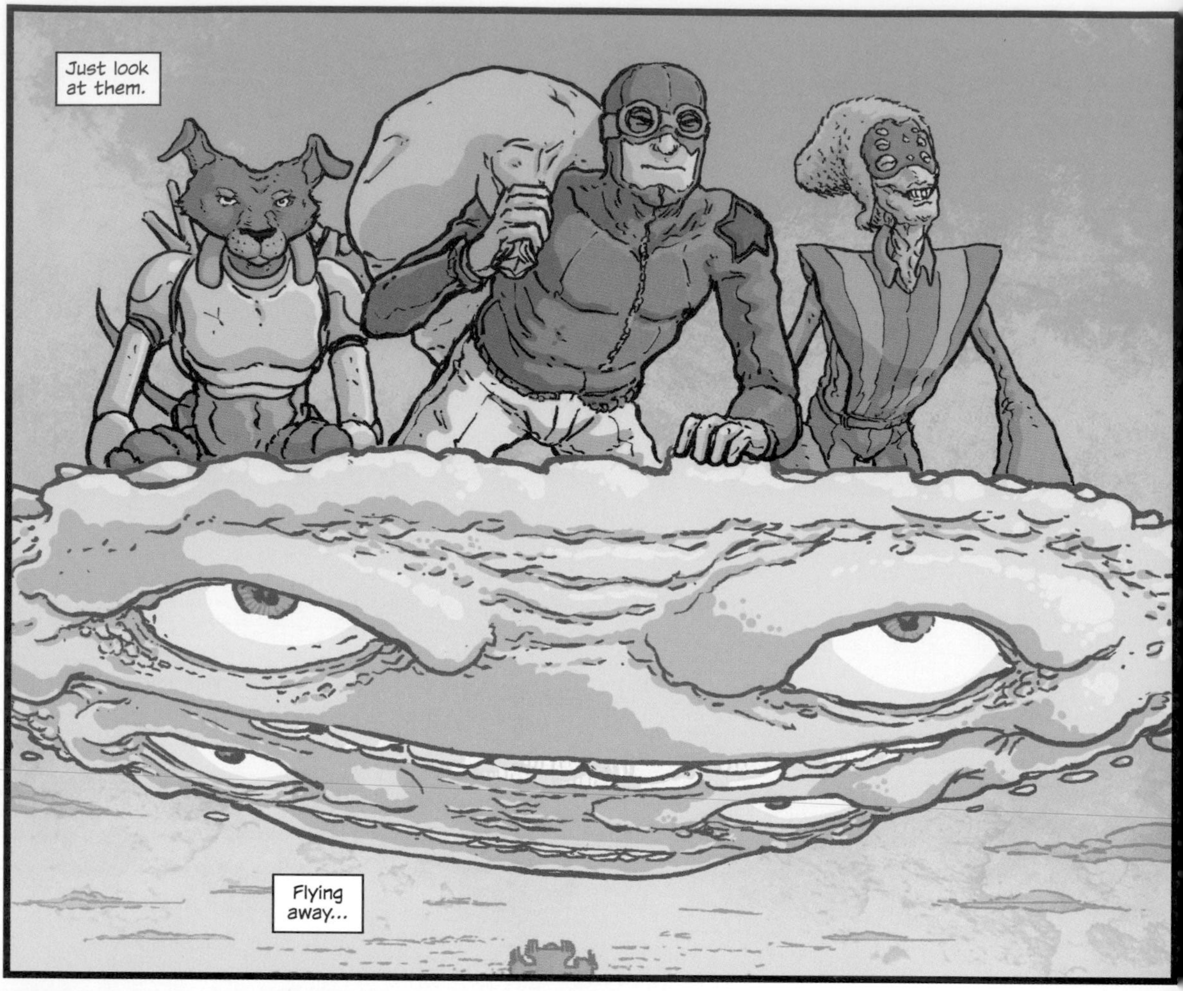
Just look at them.
Flying away...

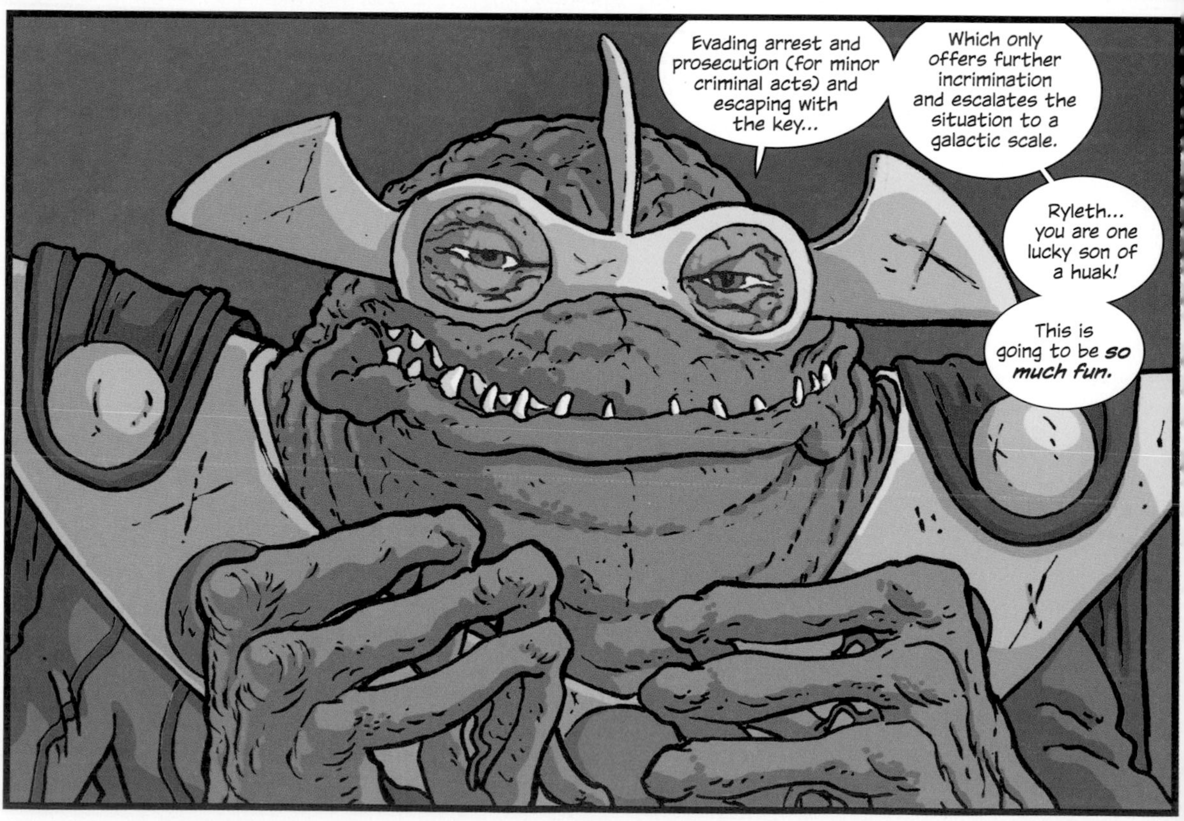
Evading arrest and prosecution (for minor criminal acts) and escaping with the key...
Which only offers further incrimination and escalates the situation to a galactic scale.
Ryleth... you are one lucky son of a huak!
This is going to be ***so much fun.***

HOLD ON TO
SOMETHING

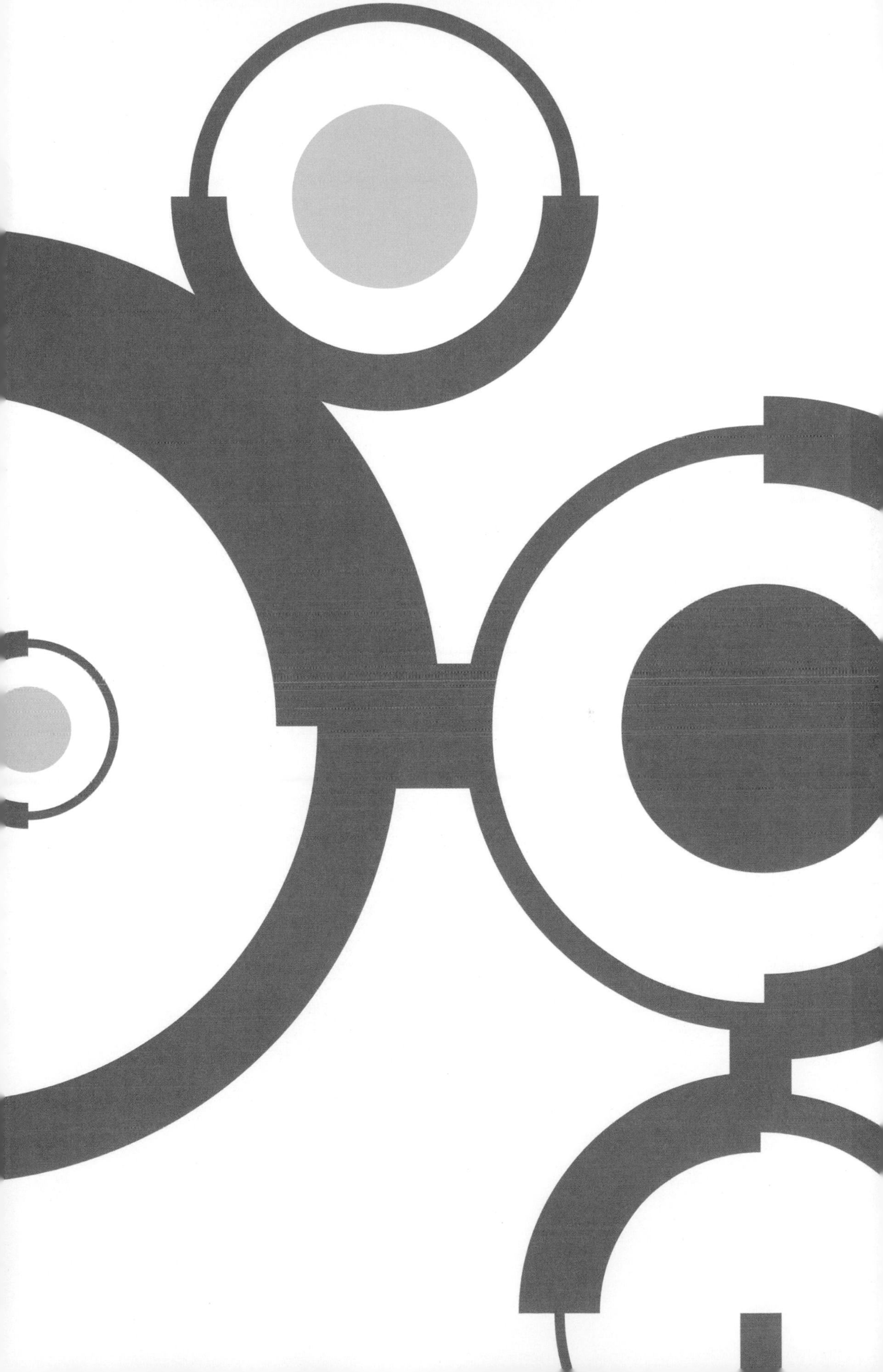

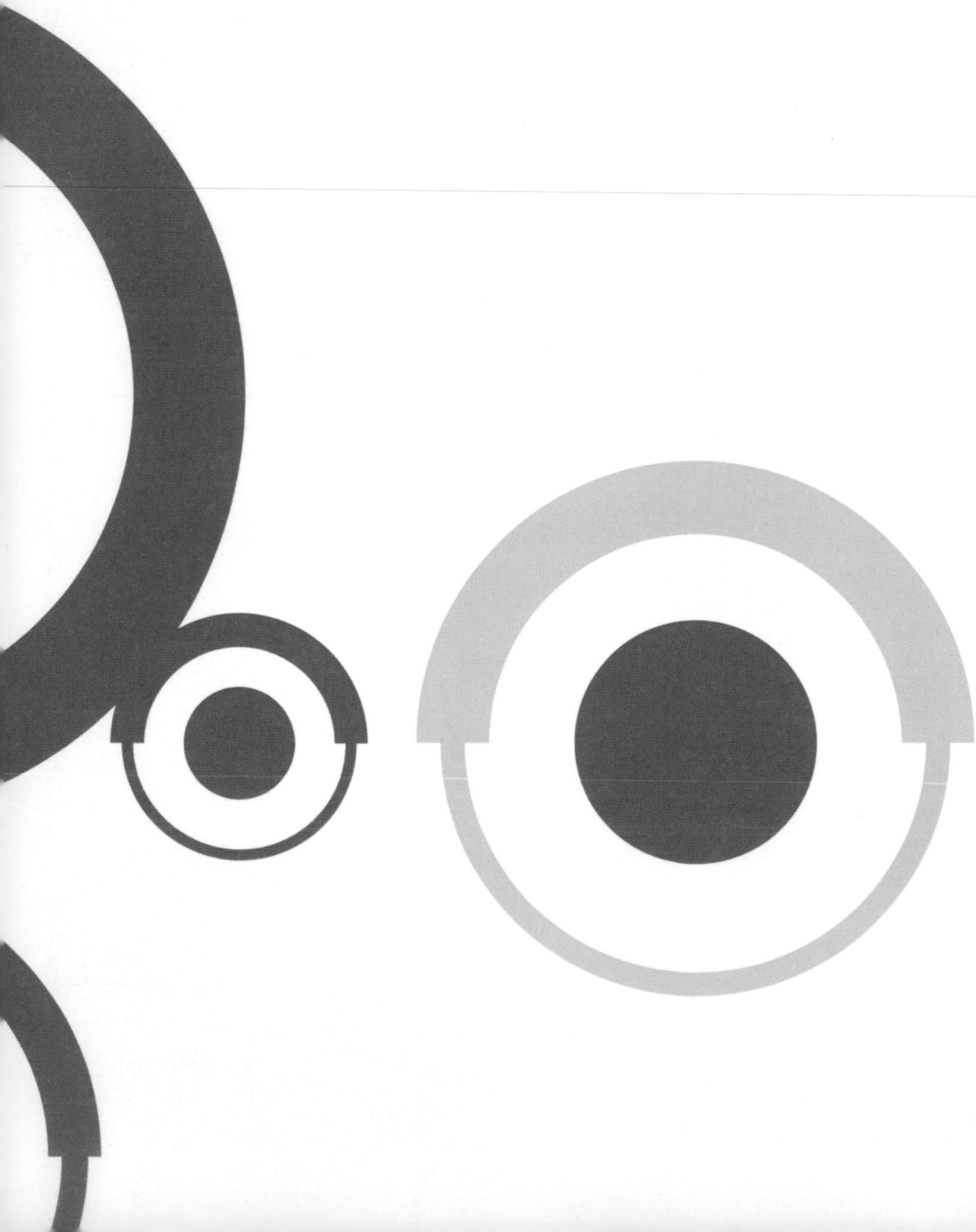

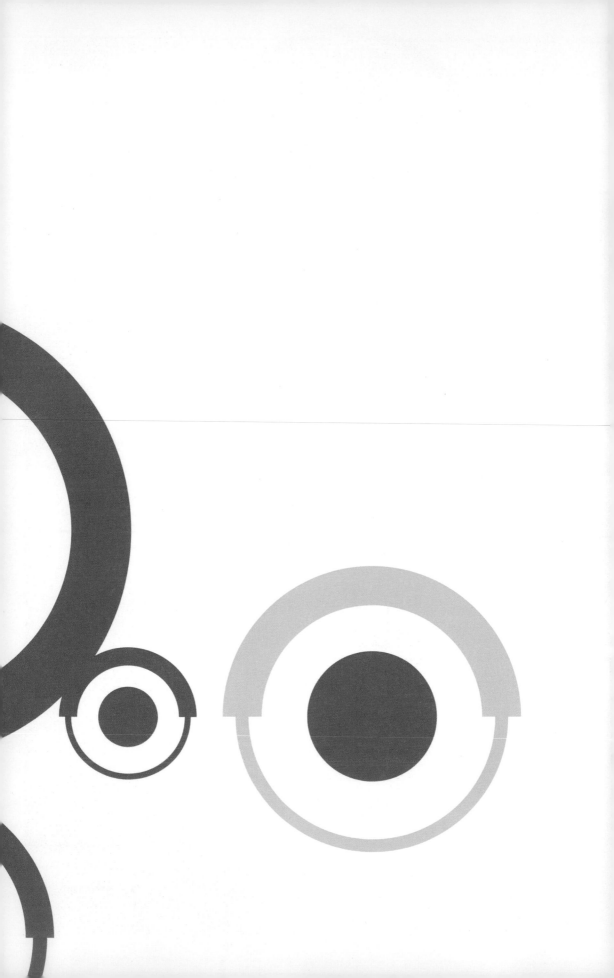

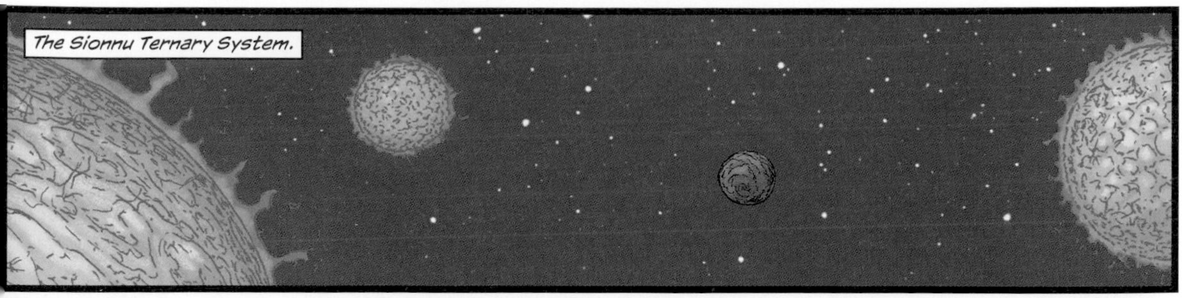
The Sionnu Ternary System.

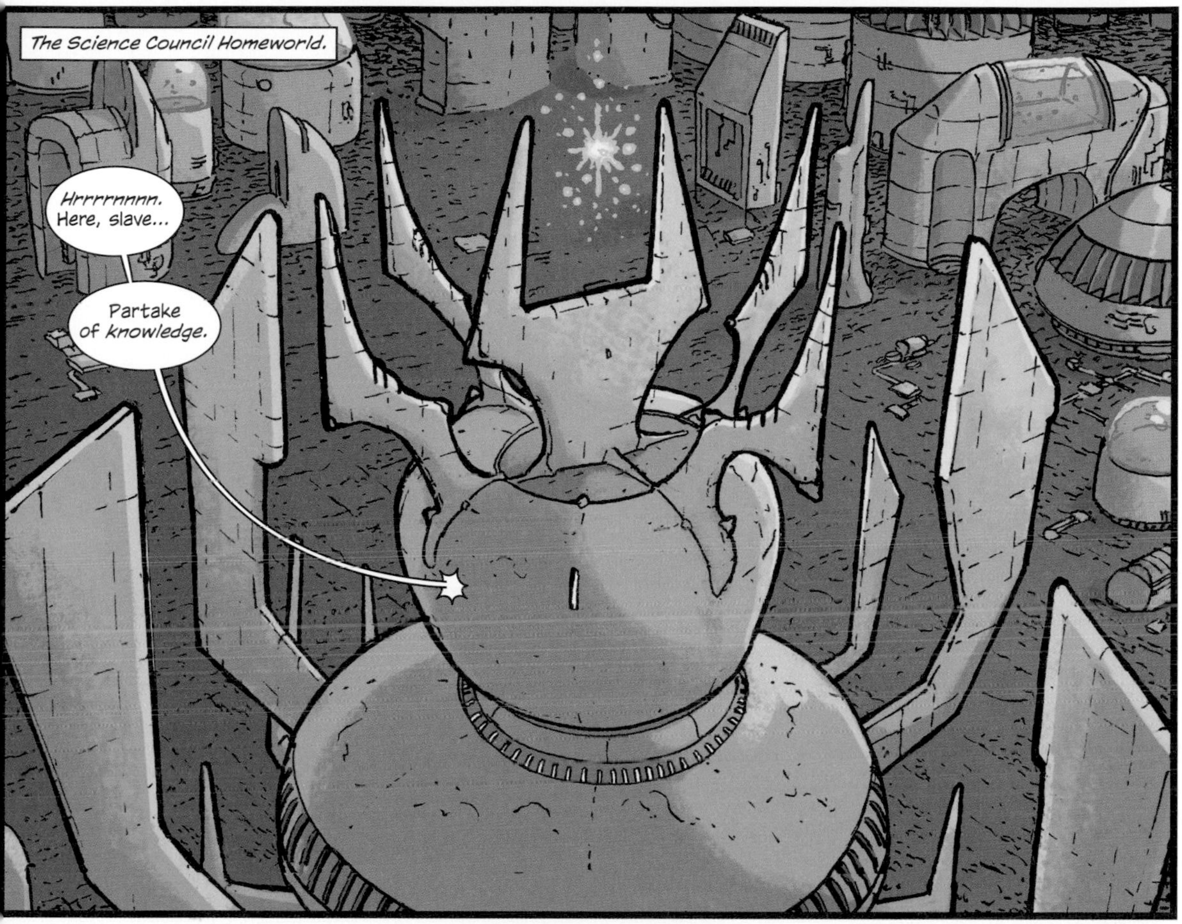
The Science Council Homeworld.
Hrrrrnnnn. Here, slave...
Partake of knowledge.

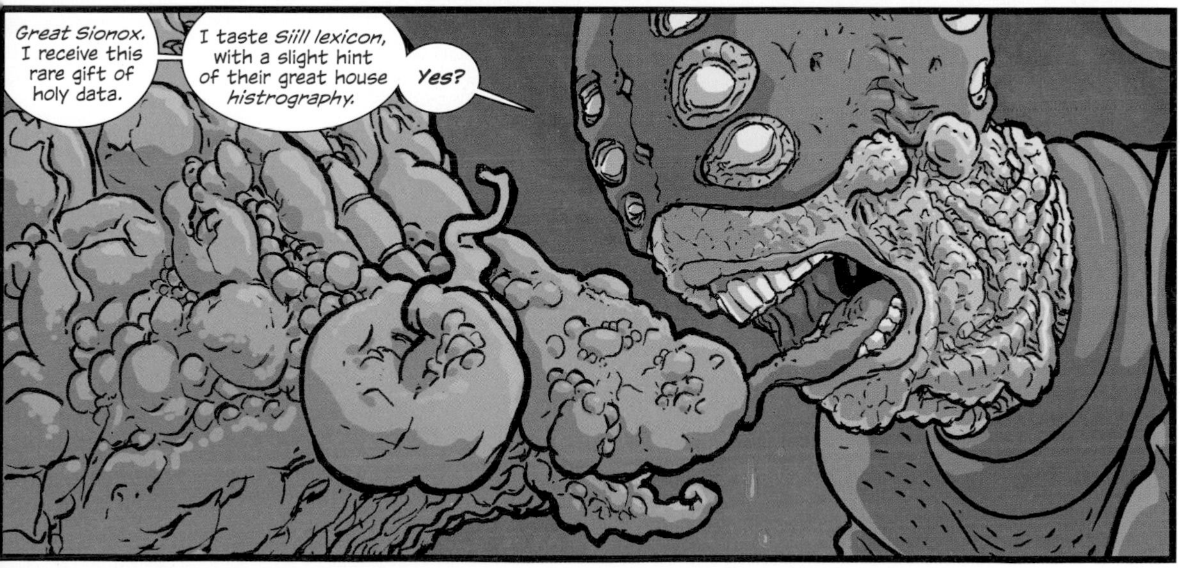
Great Sionox. I receive this rare gift of holy data.
I taste Siill lexicon, with a slight hint of their great house histrography.
Yes?

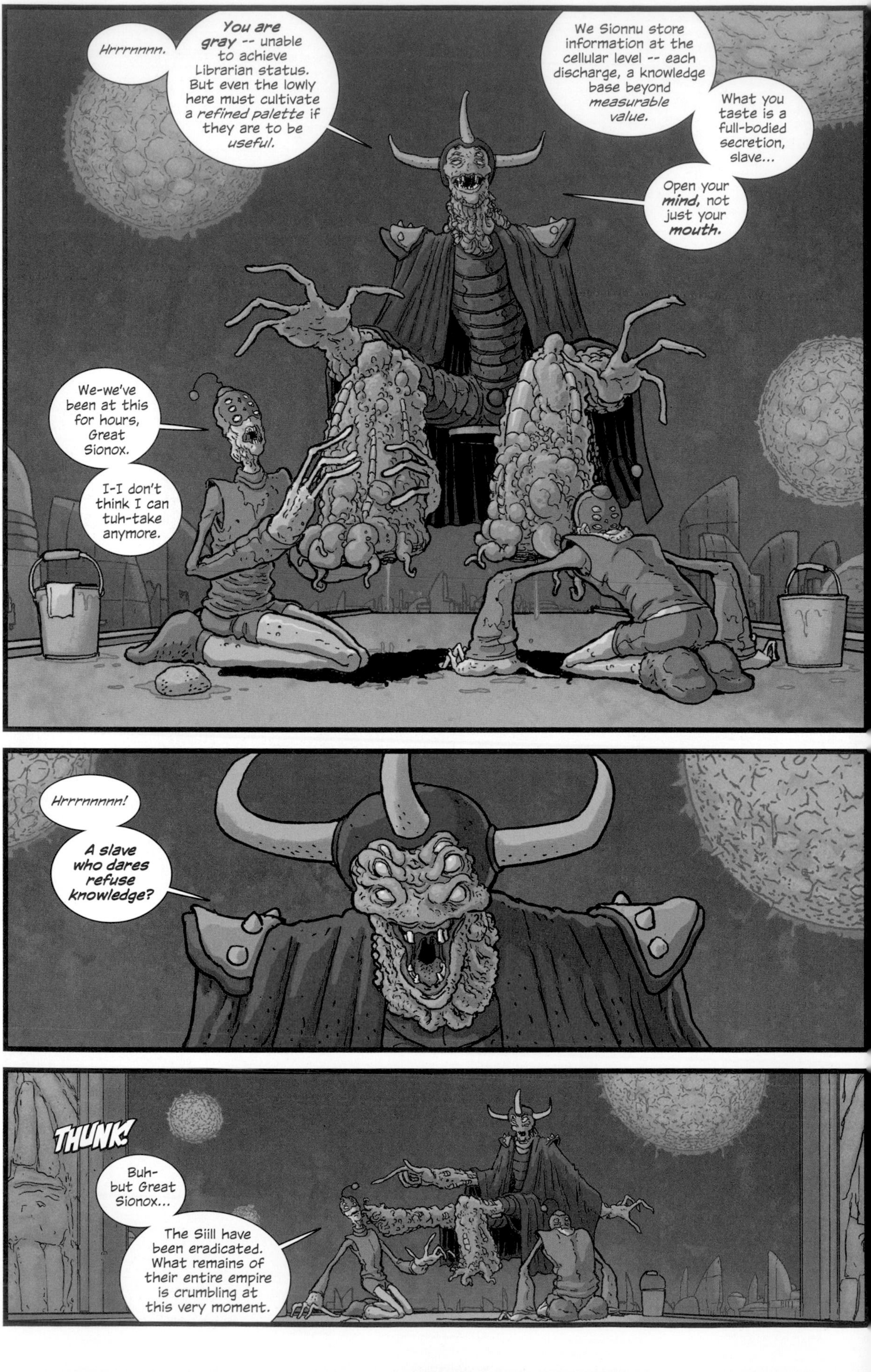
Hrrrnnnn.
You are gray -- unable to achieve Librarian status. But even the lowly here must cultivate a *refined palette* if they are to be *useful.*
We Sionnu store information at the cellular level -- each discharge, a knowledge base beyond *measurable value.*
What you taste is a full-bodied secretion, slave...
Open your ***mind,*** not just your ***mouth.***
We-we've been at this for hours, Great Sionox.
I-I don't think I can tuh-take anymore.
Hrrrnnnnn!
A slave who dares refuse knowledge?
THUNK!
Buh-but Great Sionox...
The Siill have been eradicated. What remains of their entire empire is crumbling at this very moment.

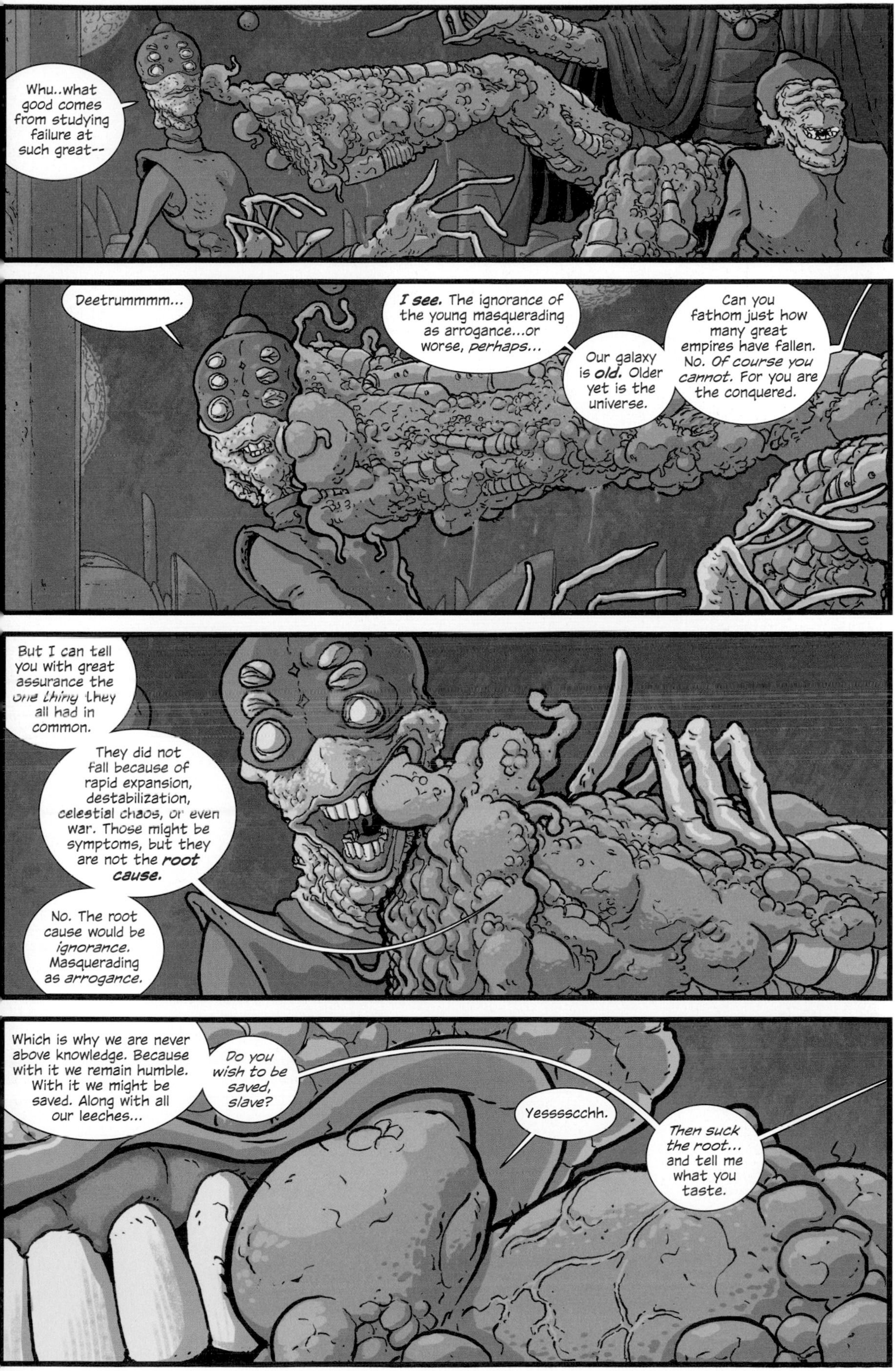

Whu..what good comes from studying failure at such great--
Deetrummmm...
I see. The ignorance of the young masquerading as arrogance...or worse, perhaps...
Our galaxy is old. Older yet is the universe.
Can you fathom just how many great empires have fallen. No. Of course you cannot. For you are the conquered.
But I can tell you with great assurance the one thing they all had in common.
They did not fall because of rapid expansion, destabilization, celestial chaos, or even war. Those might be symptoms, but they are not the root cause.
No. The root cause would be ignorance. Masquerading as arrogance.
Which is why we are never above knowledge. Because with it we remain humble. With it we might be saved. Along with all our leeches...
Do you wish to be saved, slave?
Yesssscchh.
Then suck the root... and tell me what you taste.

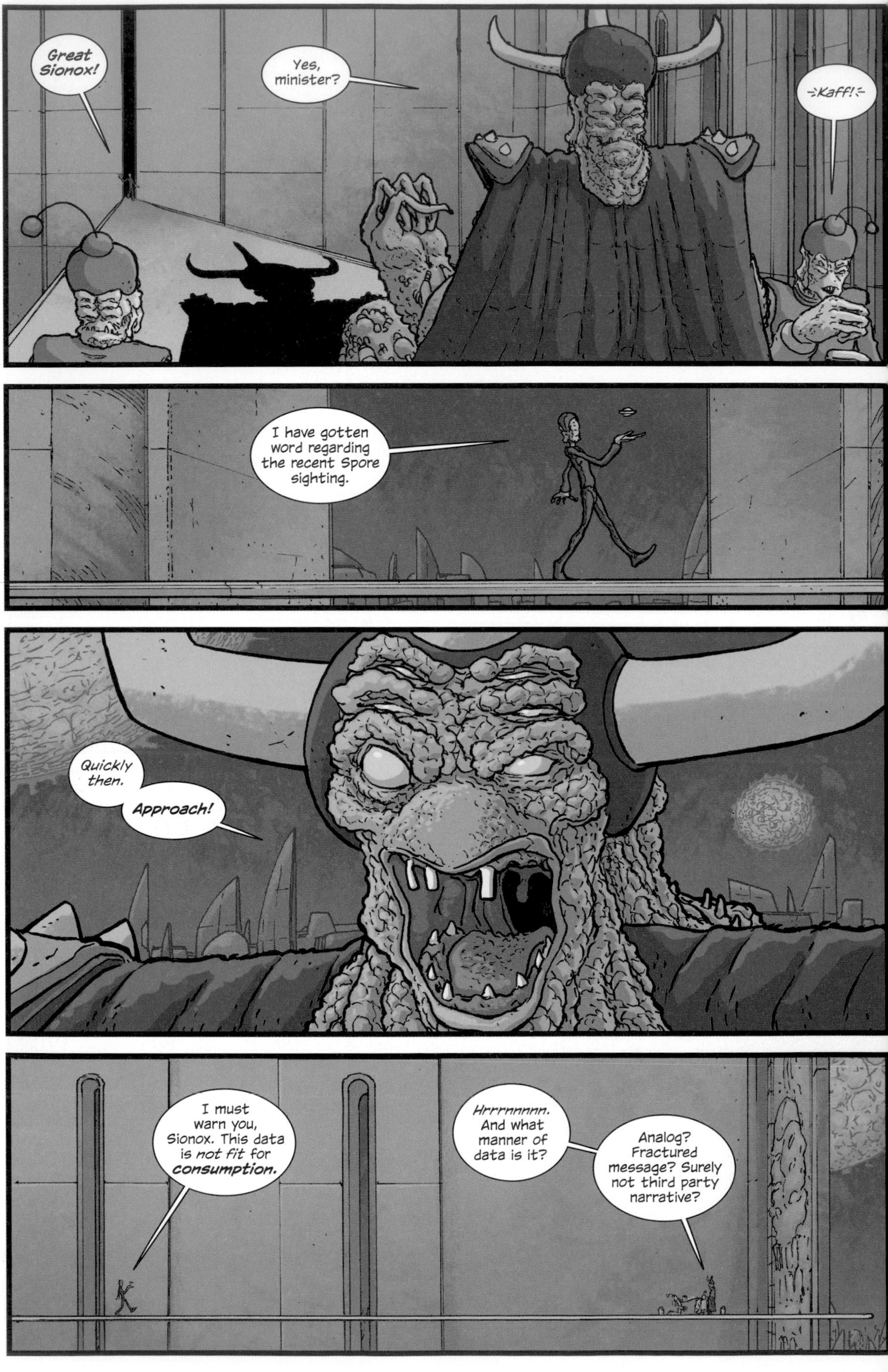

Great Sionox!
Yes, minister?
-Kaff!-
I have gotten word regarding the recent Spore sighting.
Quickly then.
Approach!
I must warn you, Sionox. This data is not fit for consumption.
Hrrrnnnnn. And what manner of data is it?
Analog? Fractured message? Surely not third party narrative?

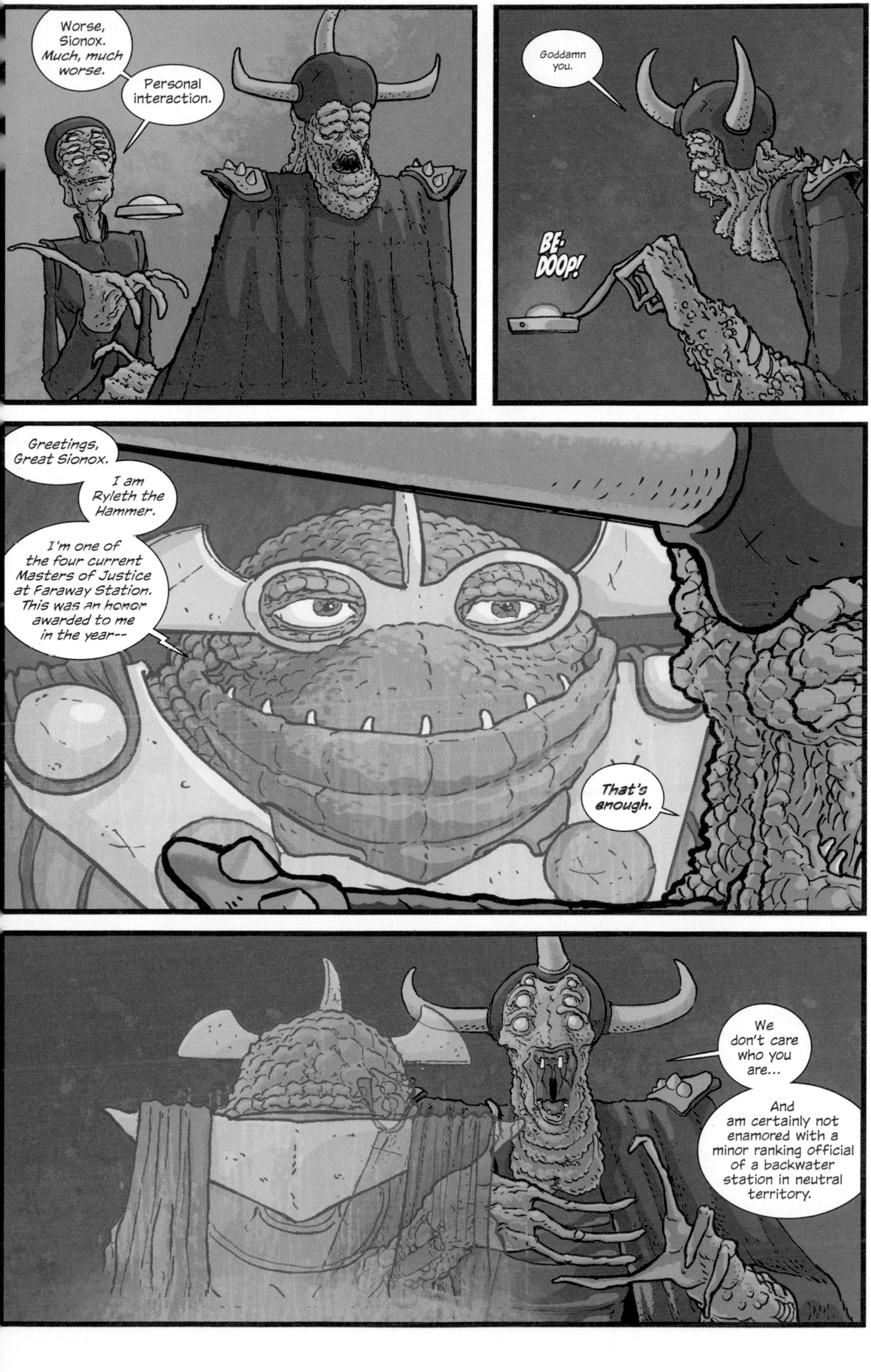

Worse, Sionox. Much, much worse.
Personal interaction.
Goddamn you.
BE-DOOP!
Greetings, Great Sionox.
I am Ryleth the Hammer.
I'm one of the four current Masters of Justice at Faraway Station. This was an honor awarded to me in the year--
That's enough.
We don't care who you are...
And am certainly not enamored with a minor ranking official of a backwater station in neutral territory.

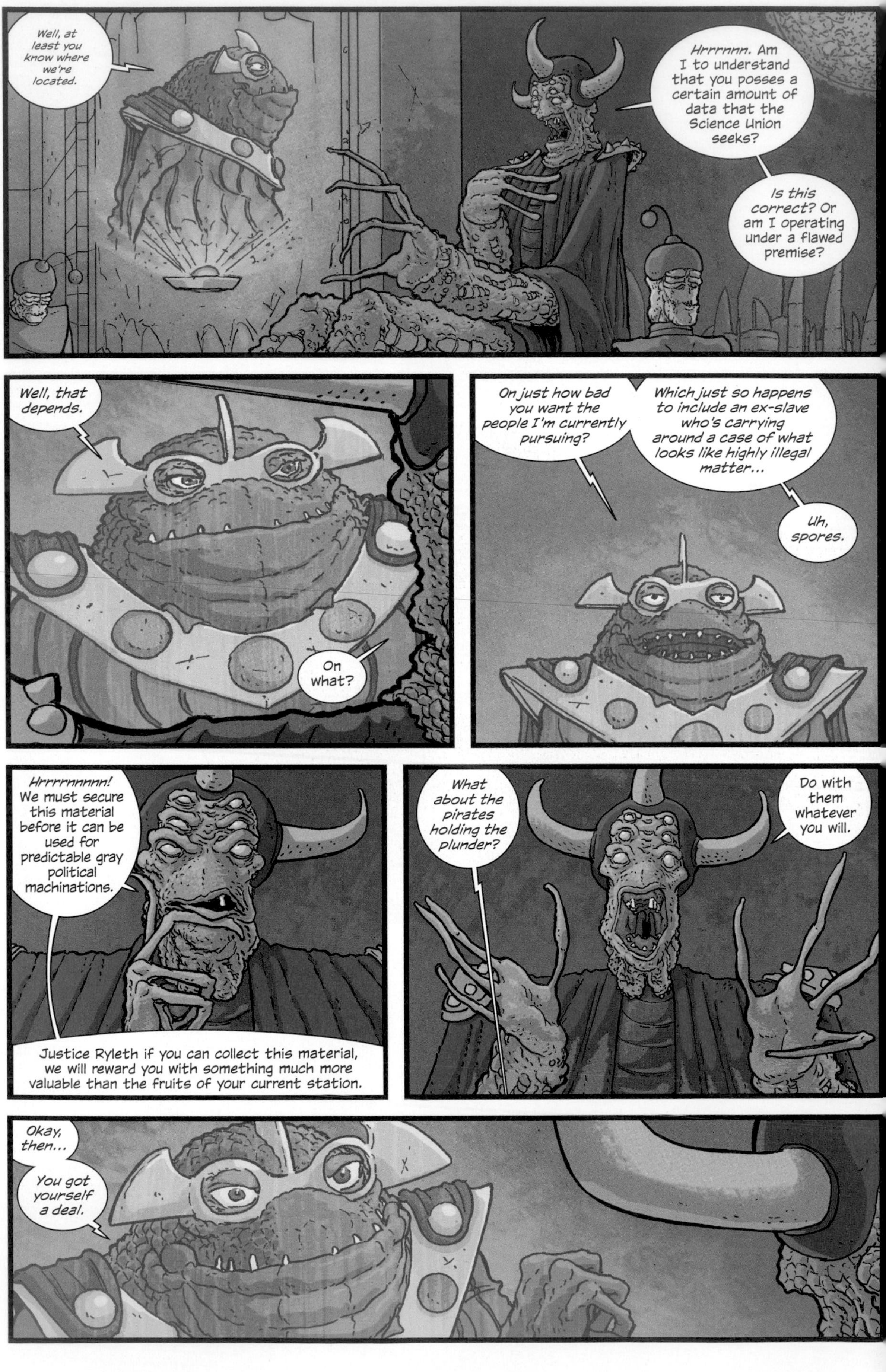
Well, at least you know where we're located.
Hrrrnnn. Am I to understand that you posses a certain amount of data that the Science Union seeks?
Is this correct? Or am I operating under a flawed premise?
Well, that depends.
On what?
On just how bad you want the people I'm currently pursuing?
Which just so happens to include an ex-slave who's carrying around a case of what looks like highly illegal matter...
Uh, spores.
Hrrrrnnnnn! We must secure this material before it can be used for predictable gray political machinations.
Justice Ryleth if you can collect this material, we will reward you with something much more valuable than the fruits of your current station.
What about the pirates holding the plunder?
Do with them whatever you will.
Okay, then...
You got yourself a deal.

"I DON'T EVEN KNOW WHAT'S GOING
ON ANYMORE."

CLAVIS AUREA
THE RECORDED FEYNMAN | **VOL. 4**

28

THE SUN BEYOND
THE STARS

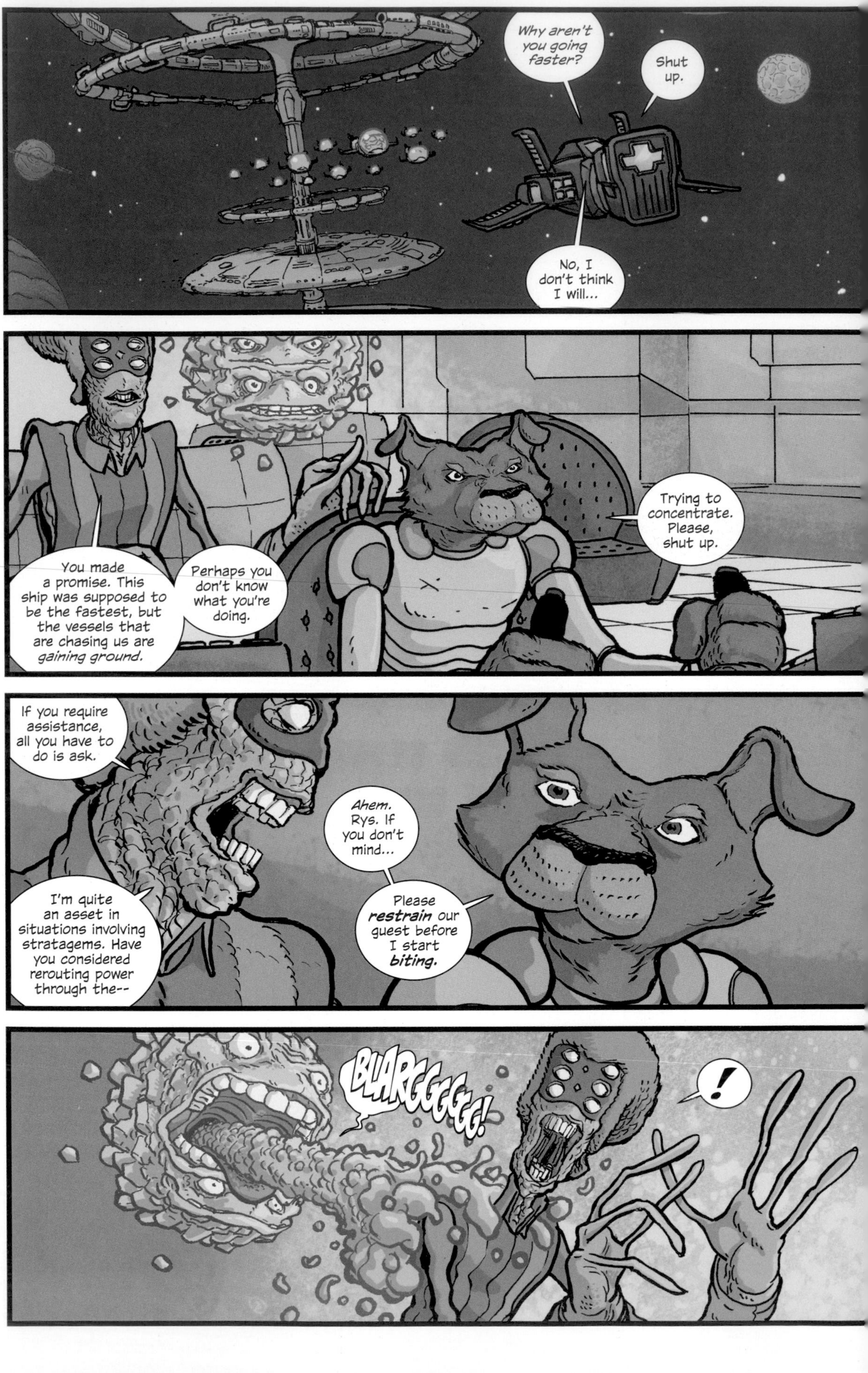
Why aren't you going faster?
Shut up.
No, I don't think I will...
You made a promise. This ship was supposed to be the fastest, but the vessels that are chasing us are *gaining ground.*
Perhaps you don't know what you're doing.
Trying to concentrate. Please, shut up.
If you require assistance, all you have to do is ask.
I'm quite an asset in situations involving stratagems. Have you considered rerouting power through the--
Ahem. Rys. If you don't mind...
Please ***restrain*** our guest before I start ***biting.***
BLARGGGGGG!
!

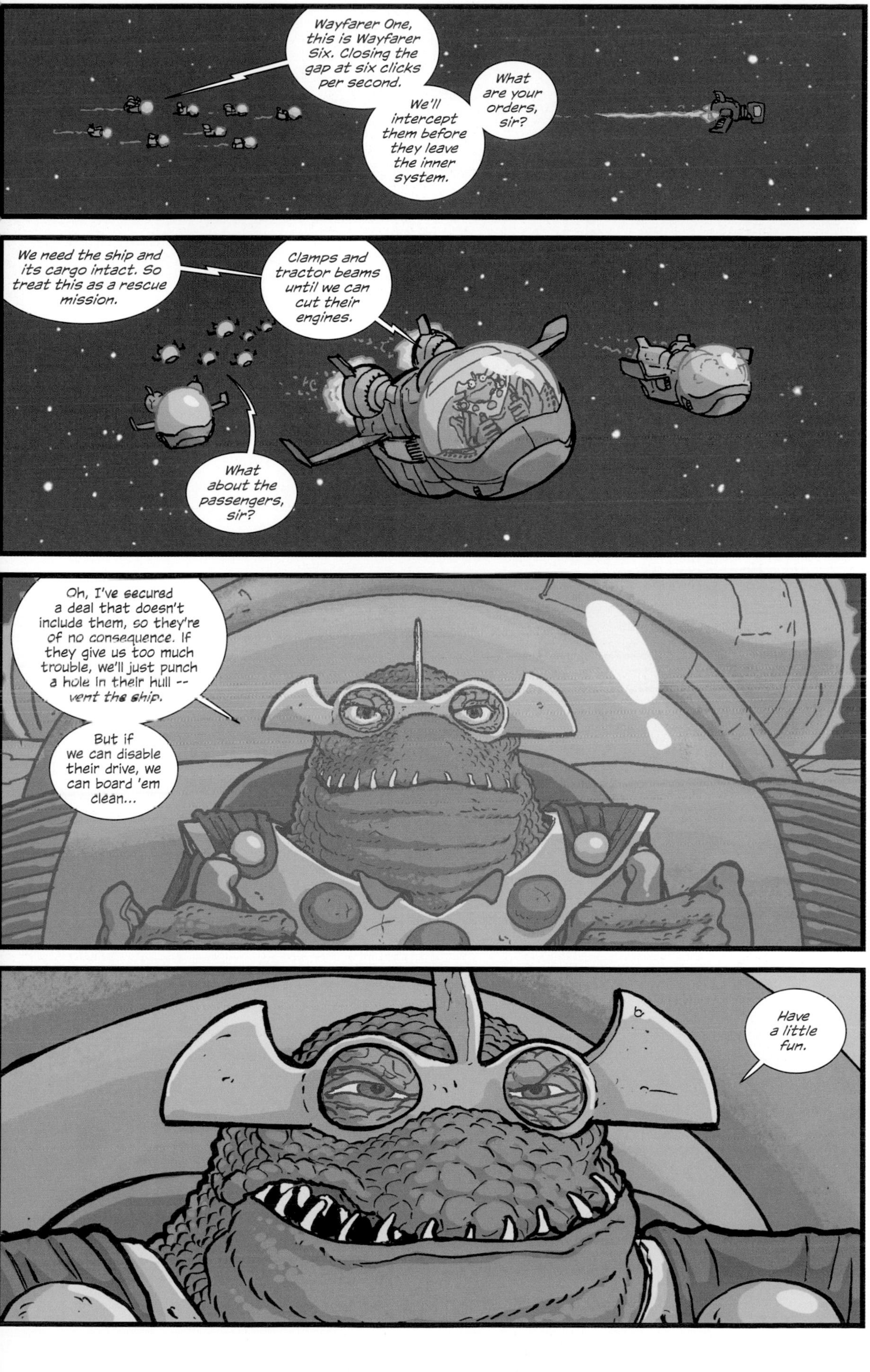
Wayfarer One, this is Wayfarer Six. Closing the gap at six clicks per second.
We'll intercept them before they leave the inner system.
What are your orders, sir?
We need the ship and its cargo intact. So treat this as a rescue mission.
Clamps and tractor beams until we can cut their engines.
What about the passengers, sir?
Oh, I've secured a deal that doesn't include them, so they're of no consequence. If they give us too much trouble, we'll just punch a hole in their hull -- vent the ship.
But if we can disable their drive, we can board 'em clean...
Have a little fun.

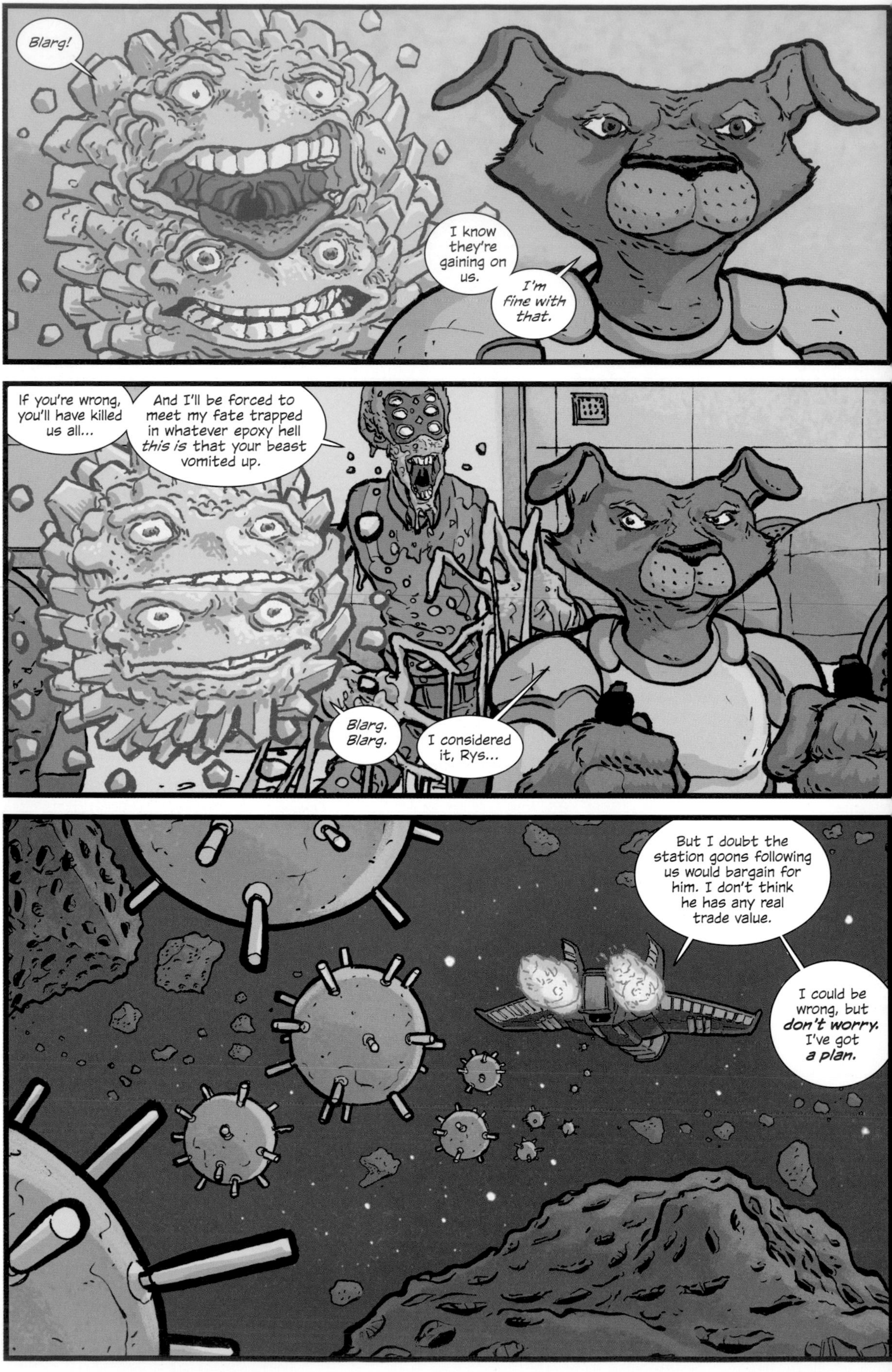
Blarg!
I know they're gaining on us.
I'm fine with that.
If you're wrong, you'll have killed us all...
And I'll be forced to meet my fate trapped in whatever epoxy hell *this is* that your beast vomited up.
Blarg. Blarg.
I considered it, Rys...
But I doubt the station goons following us would bargain for him. I don't think he has any real trade value.
I could be wrong, but **don't worry.** I've got **a plan.**

Decrease speed and extend long-range scanners. Look for heat blooms...

They have to be hiding in here **somewhere.**

Wayfarer One, I'm not picking up anything big enough to be their ship yet, but I am getting hits on multiple smaller targets.

I am too. Moving in for a closer look...

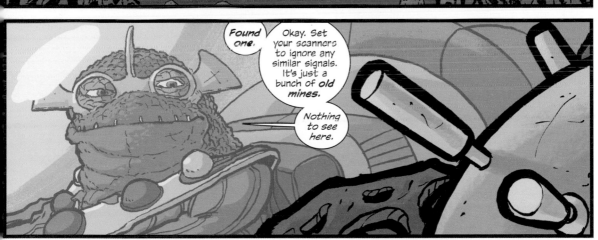

Found one.

Okay. Set your scanners to ignore any similar signals. It's just a bunch of **old mines.**

Nothing to see here.

Wait.

Shit.

Evade!

EVADE!

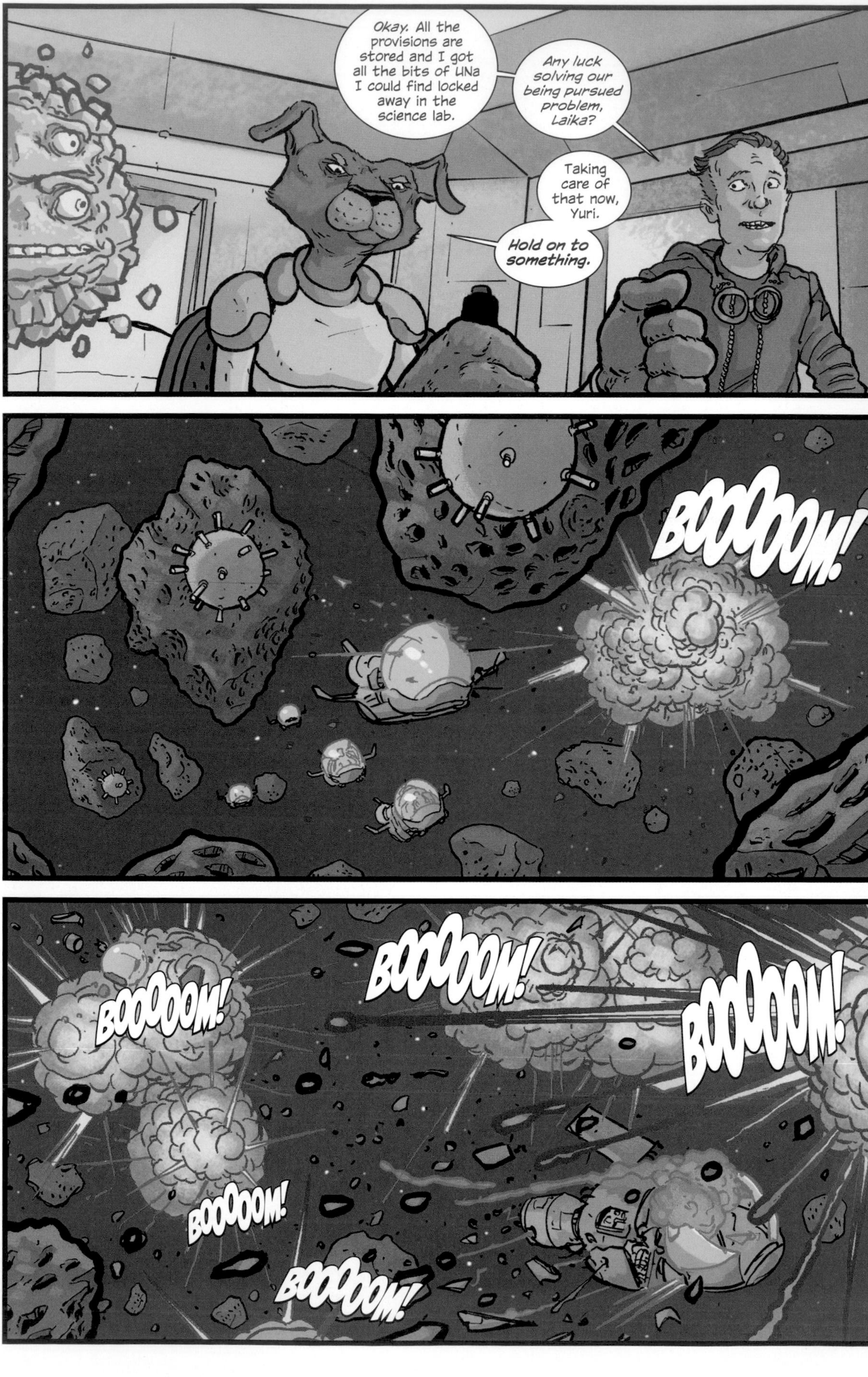

Okay. All the provisions are stored and I got all the bits of UNa I could find locked away in the science lab.
Any luck solving our being pursued problem, Laika?
Taking care of that now, Yuri.
Hold on to something.
BOOOOOM!
BOOOOOM!
BOOOOOM!
BOOOOOM!
BOOOOOM!
BOOOOOM!

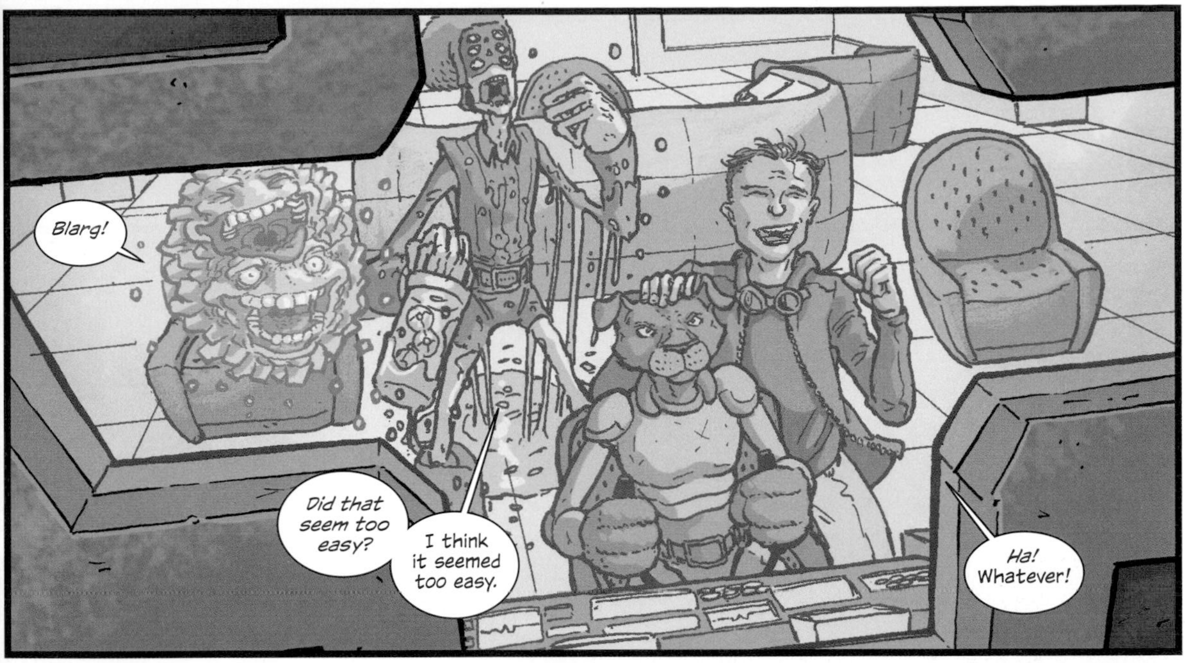
Blarg!
Did that seem too easy?
I think it seemed too easy.
Ha! Whatever!

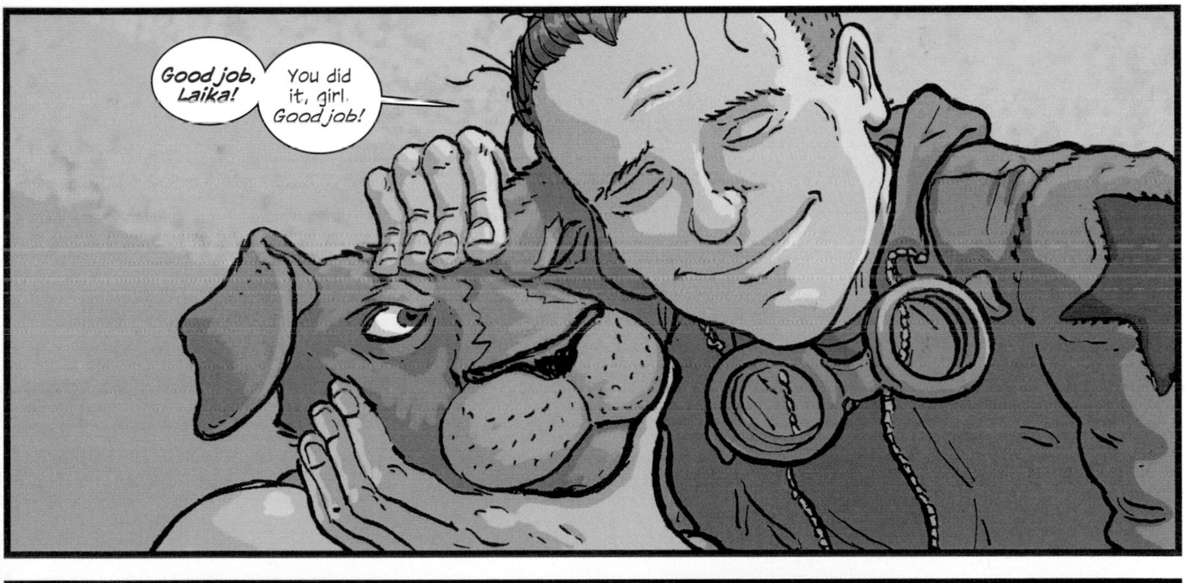
Good job, Laika!
You did it, girl. Good job!

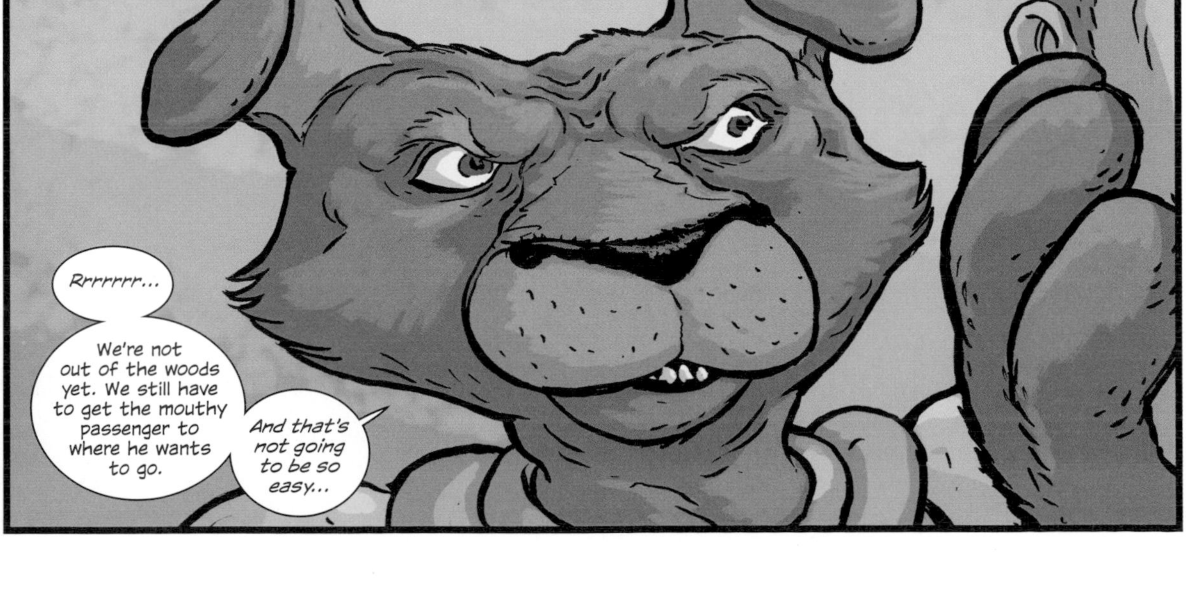
Rrrrrrr...
We're not out of the woods yet. We still have to get the mouthy passenger to where he wants to go.
And that's not going to be so easy...

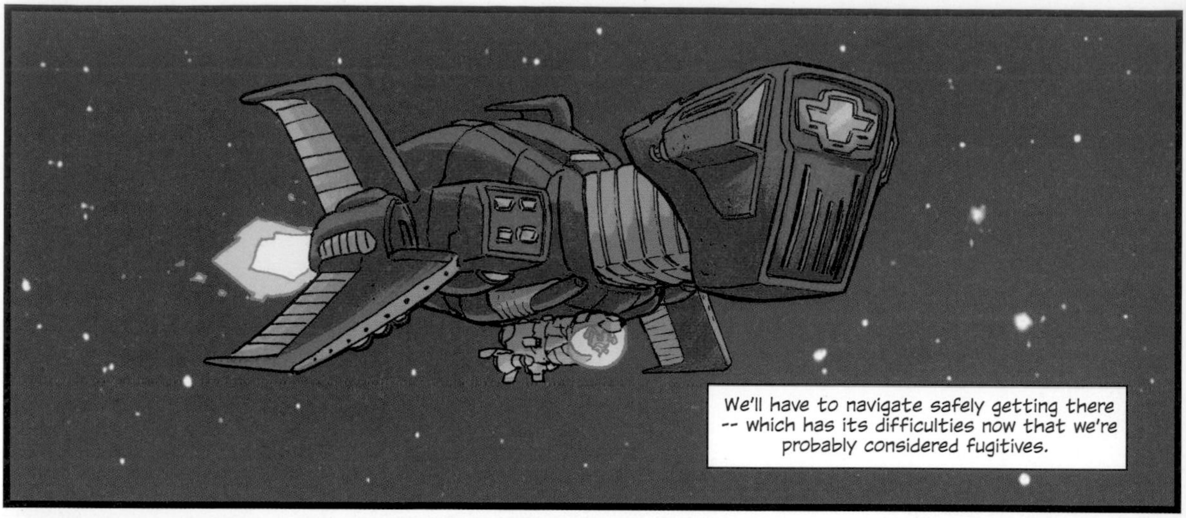
We'll have to navigate safely getting there -- which has its difficulties now that we're probably considered fugitives.

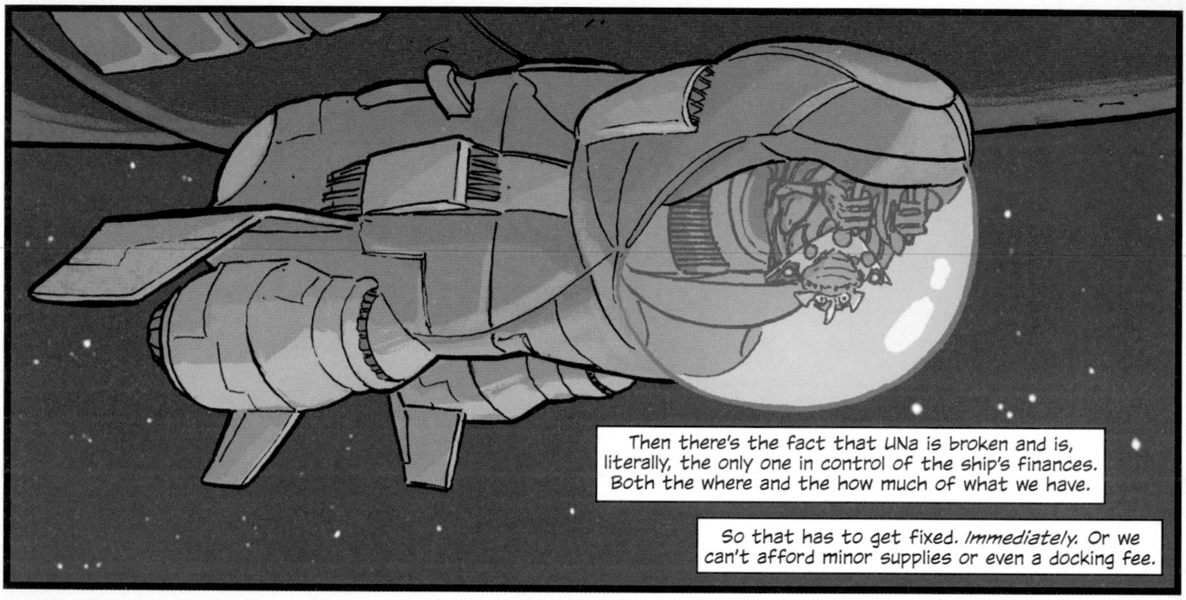
Then there's the fact that UNa is broken and is, literally, the only one in control of the ship's finances. Both the where and the how much of what we have.
So that has to get fixed. *Immediately.* Or we can't afford minor supplies or even a docking fee.

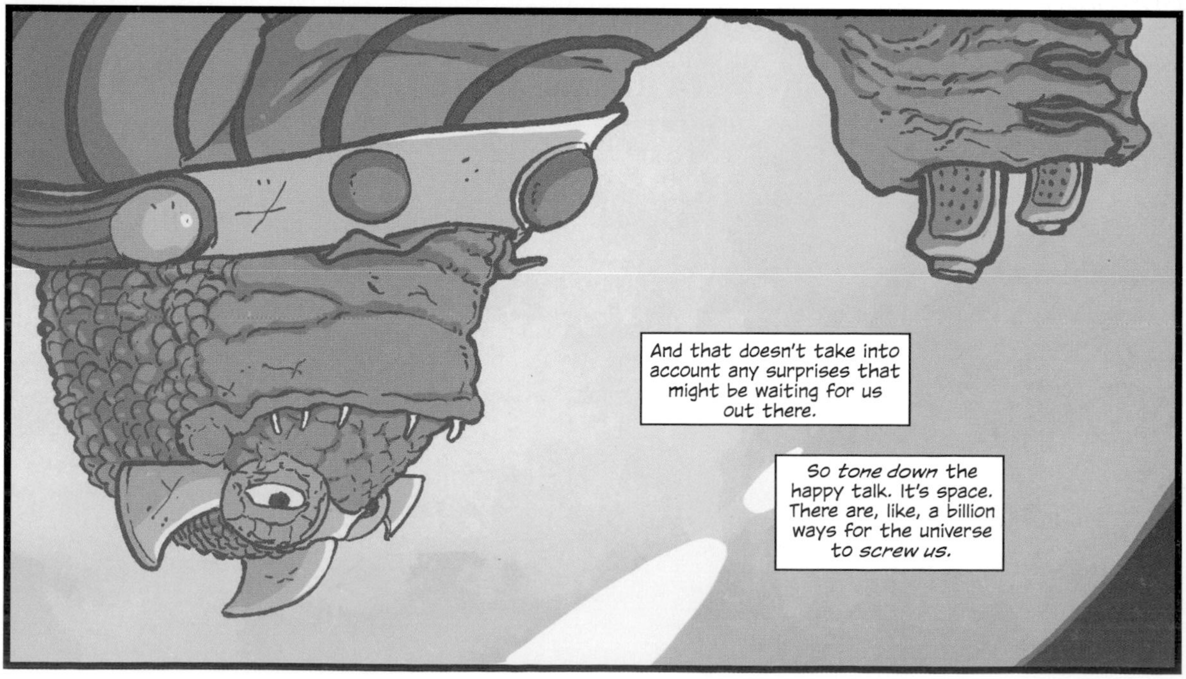
And that doesn't take into account any surprises that might be waiting for us out there.
So *tone down* the happy talk. It's space. There are, like, a billion ways for the universe to *screw us.*

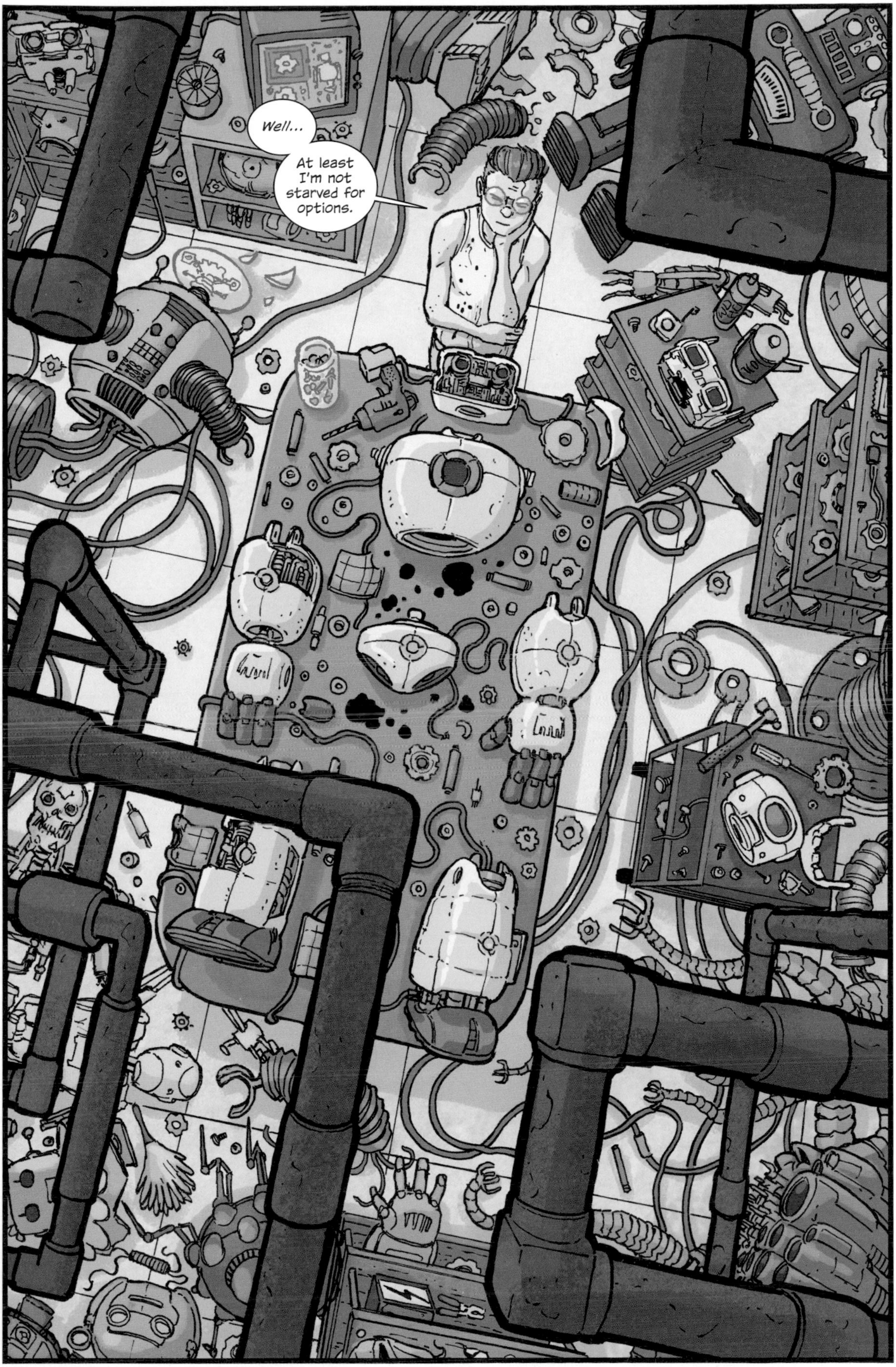
Well...
At least I'm not starved for options.

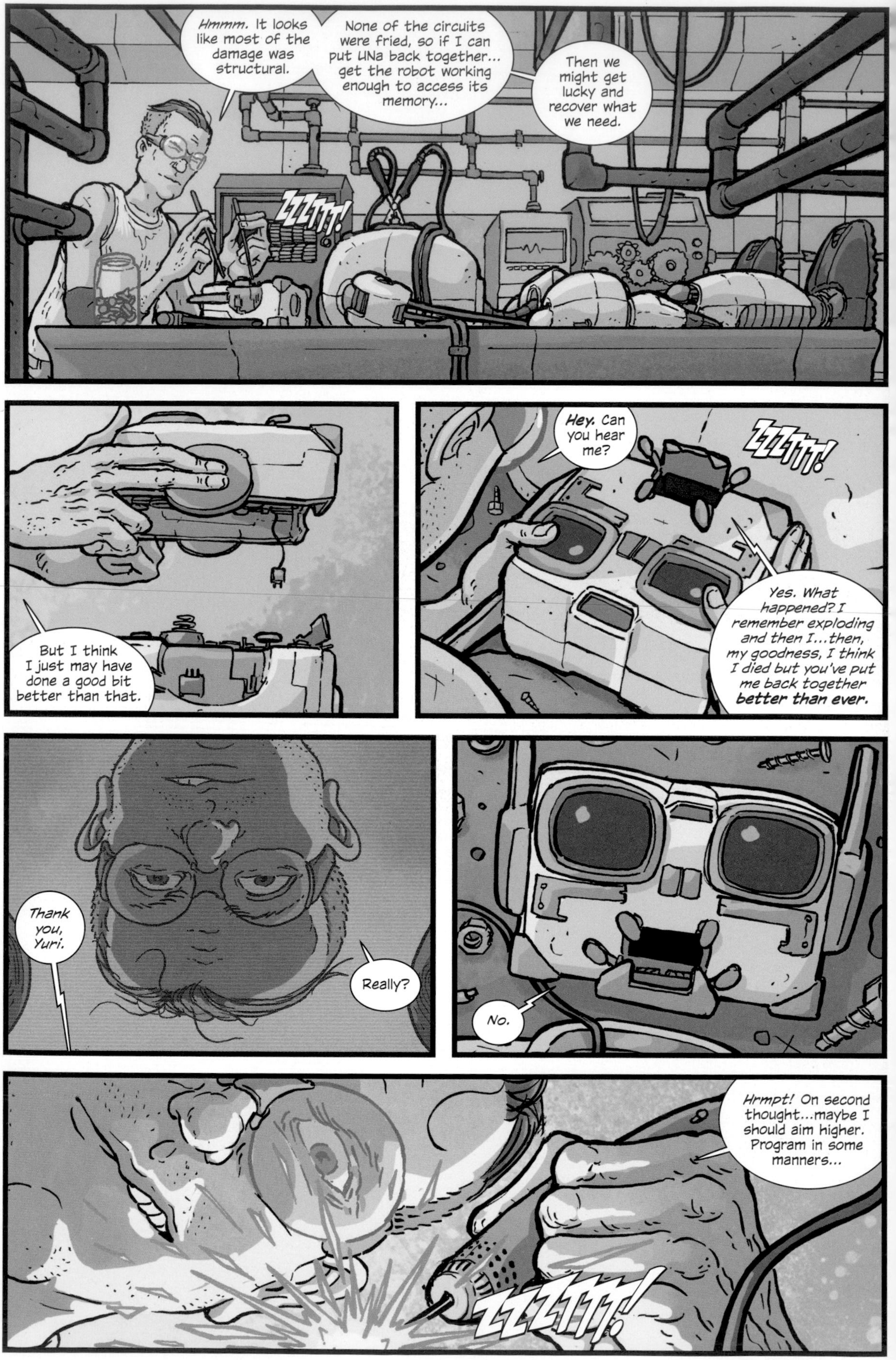
Hmmm. It looks like most of the damage was structural.
None of the circuits were fried, so if I can put UNa back together... get the robot working enough to access its memory...
Then we might get lucky and recover what we need.
ZZZTTT!
But I think I just may have done a good bit better than that.
Hey. Can you hear me?
ZZZTTT!
Yes. What happened? I remember exploding and then I...then, my goodness, I think I died but you've put me back together better than ever.
Thank you, Yuri.
Really?
No.
Hrmpt! On second thought...maybe I should aim higher. Program in some manners...
ZZZTTT!

Later.

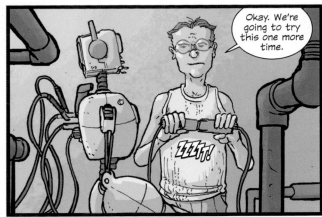

Okay. We're going to try this one more time.

ZZZTt!

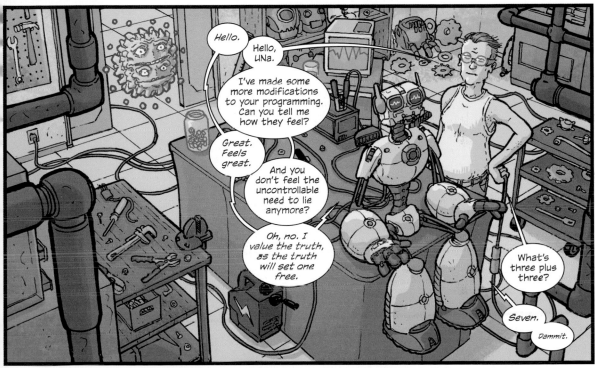

Hello.

Hello, UNa.

I've made some more modifications to your programming. Can you tell me how they feel?

Great. Feels great.

And you don't feel the uncontrollable need to lie anymore?

Oh, no. I value the truth, as the truth will set one free.

What's three plus three?

Seven.

Dammit.

I give up.

Wait. Wait. Don't unplug me.

I'll be good. A little lying can go a long way.

Don't --

ZZZTT!

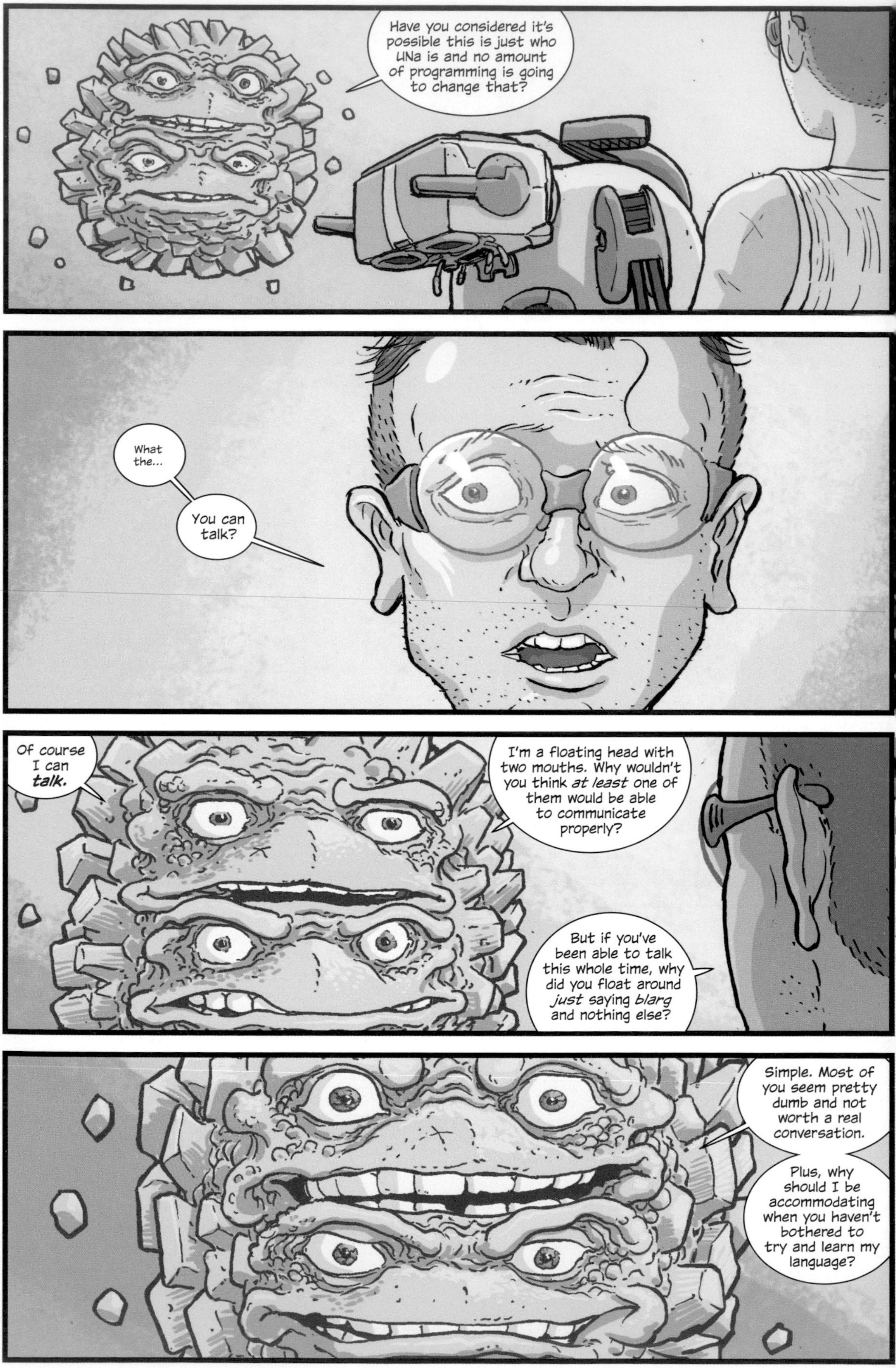

Have you considered it's possible this is just who UNa is and no amount of programming is going to change that?
What the...
You can talk?
Of course I can *talk.*
I'm a floating head with two mouths. Why wouldn't you think *at least* one of them would be able to communicate properly?
But if you've been able to talk this whole time, why did you float around *just* saying *blarg* and nothing else?
Simple. Most of you seem pretty dumb and not worth a real conversation.
Plus, why should I be accommodating when you haven't bothered to try and learn my language?

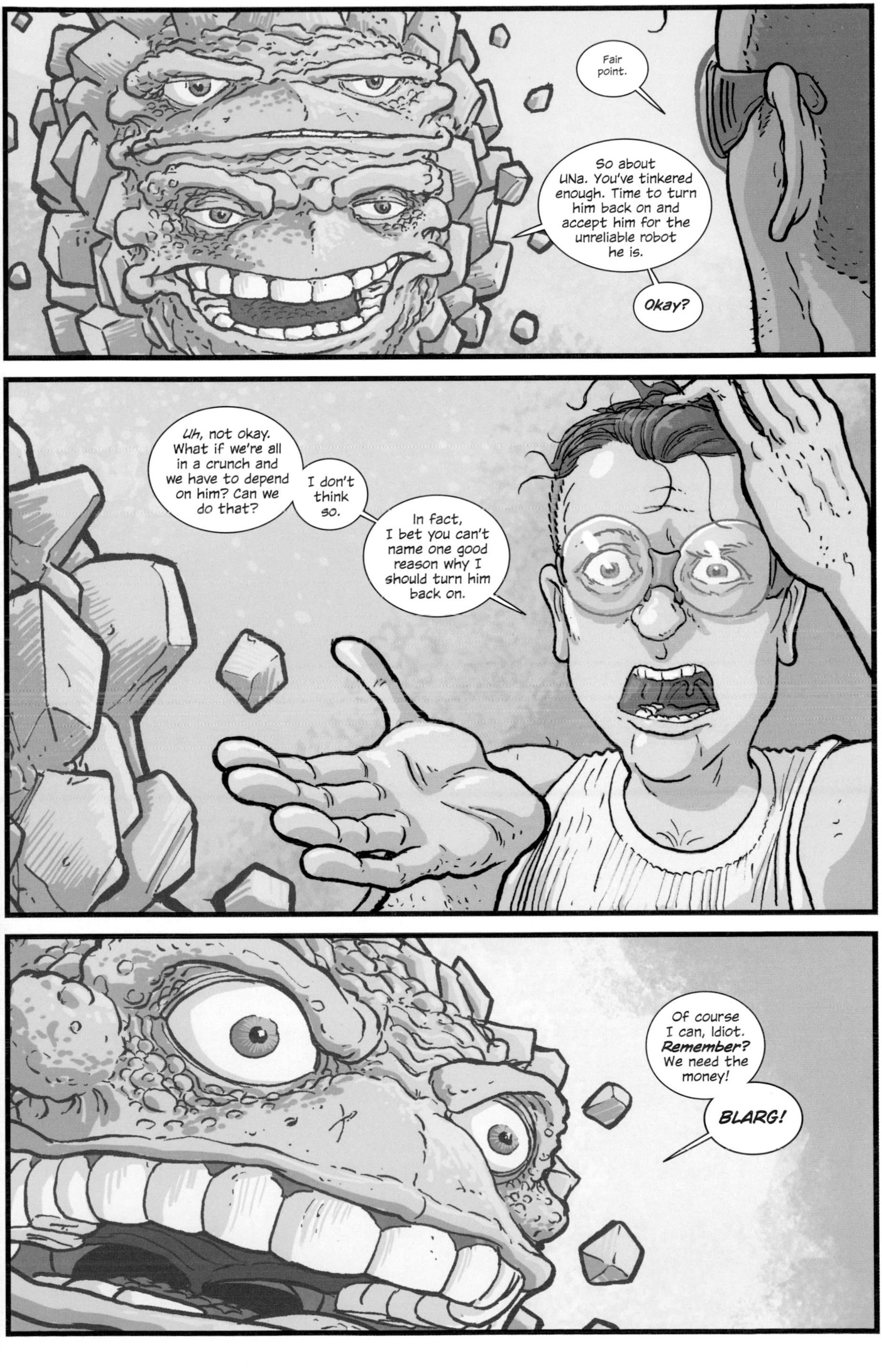
Fair point.
So about UNa. You've tinkered enough. Time to turn him back on and accept him for the unreliable robot he is.
Okay?
Uh, not okay. What if we're all in a crunch and we have to depend on him? Can we do that?
I don't think so.
In fact, I bet you can't name one good reason why I should turn him back on.
Of course I can, Idiot. Remember? We need the money!
BLARG!

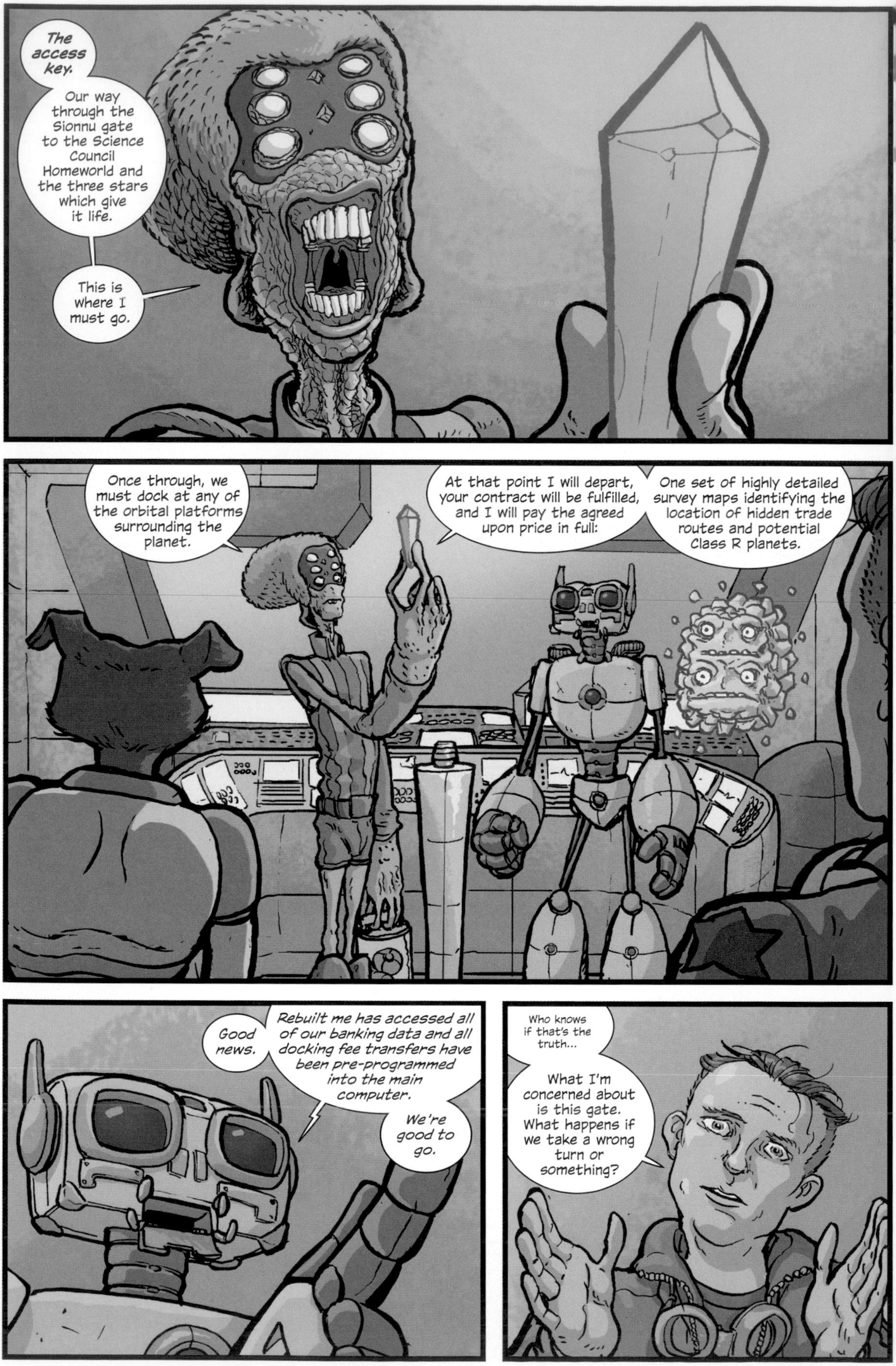
The access key.
Our way through the Sionnu gate to the Science Council Homeworld and the three stars which give it life.
This is where I must go.
Once through, we must dock at any of the orbital platforms surrounding the planet.
At that point I will depart, your contract will be fulfilled, and I will pay the agreed upon price in full:
One set of highly detailed survey maps identifying the location of hidden trade routes and potential Class R planets.
Good news.
Rebuilt me has accessed all of our banking data and all docking fee transfers have been pre-programmed into the main computer.
We're good to go.
Who knows if that's the truth...
What I'm concerned about is this gate. What happens if we take a wrong turn or something?

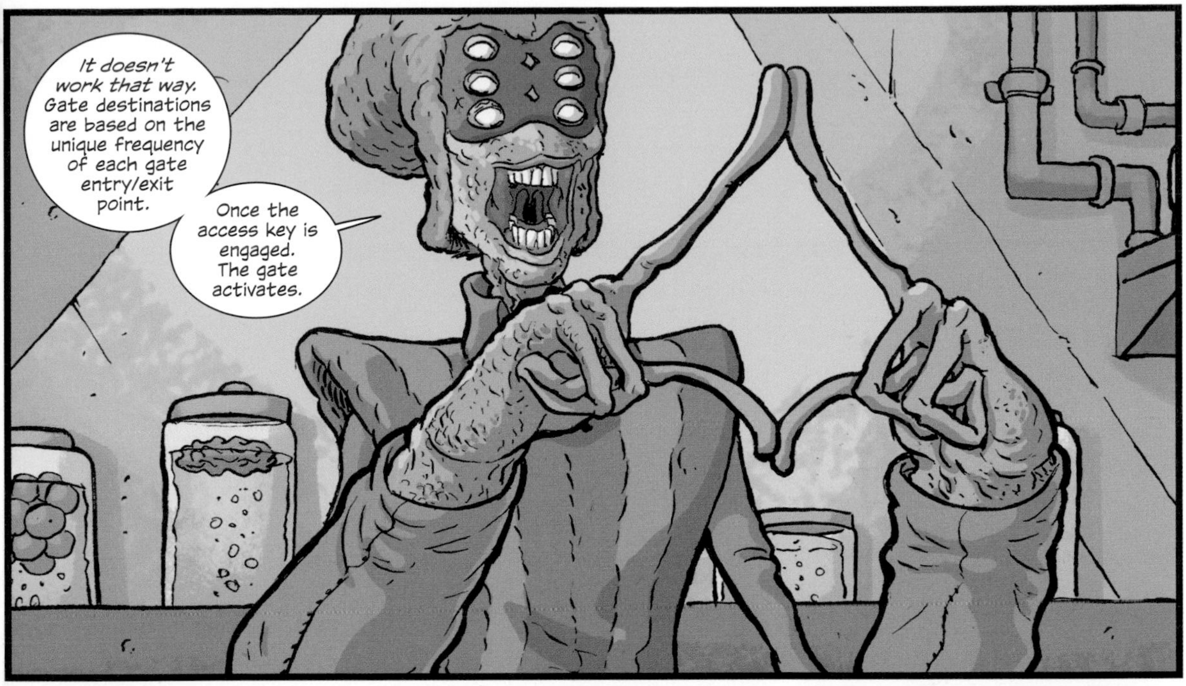
It doesn't work that way. Gate destinations are based on the unique frequency of each gate entry/exit point.
Once the access key is engaged. The gate activates.

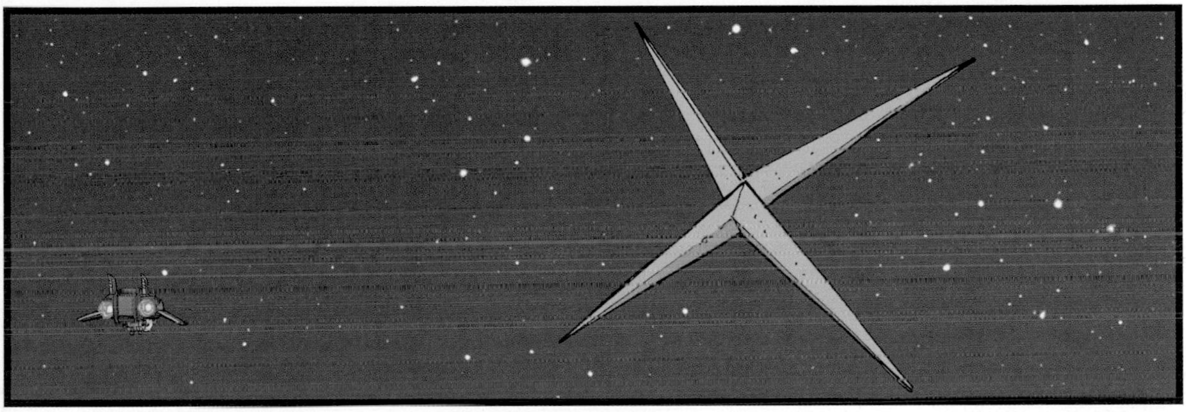

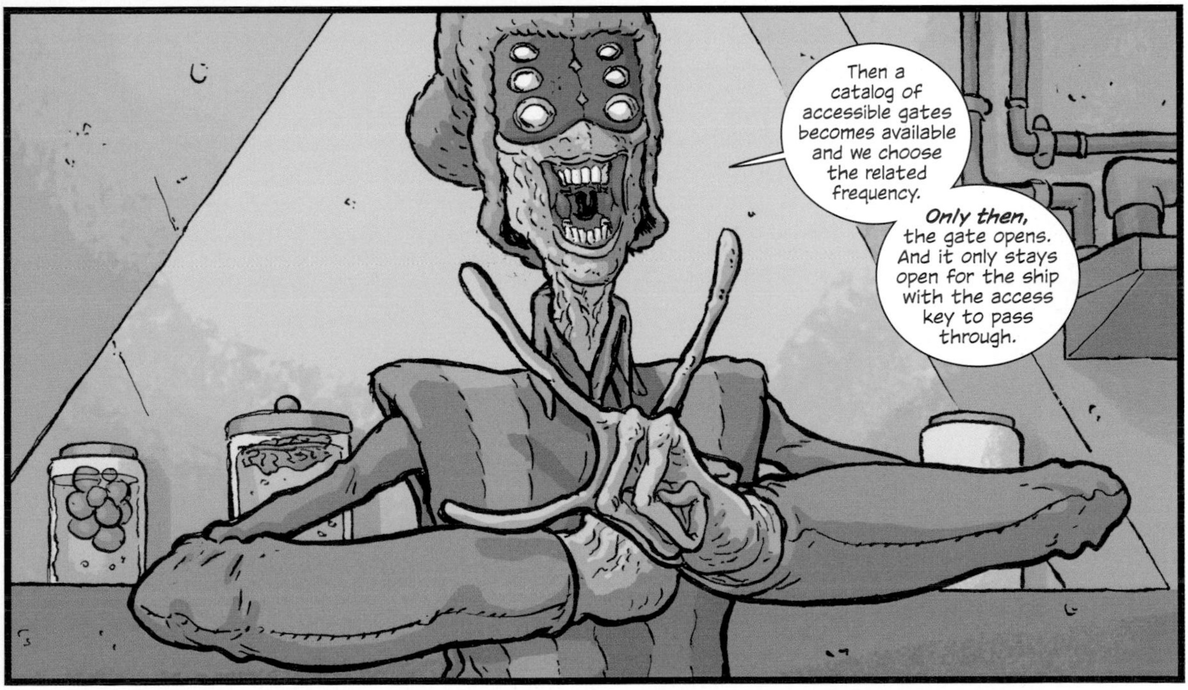
Then a catalog of accessible gates becomes available and we choose the related frequency.
Only then, the gate opens. And it only stays open for the ship with the access key to pass through.

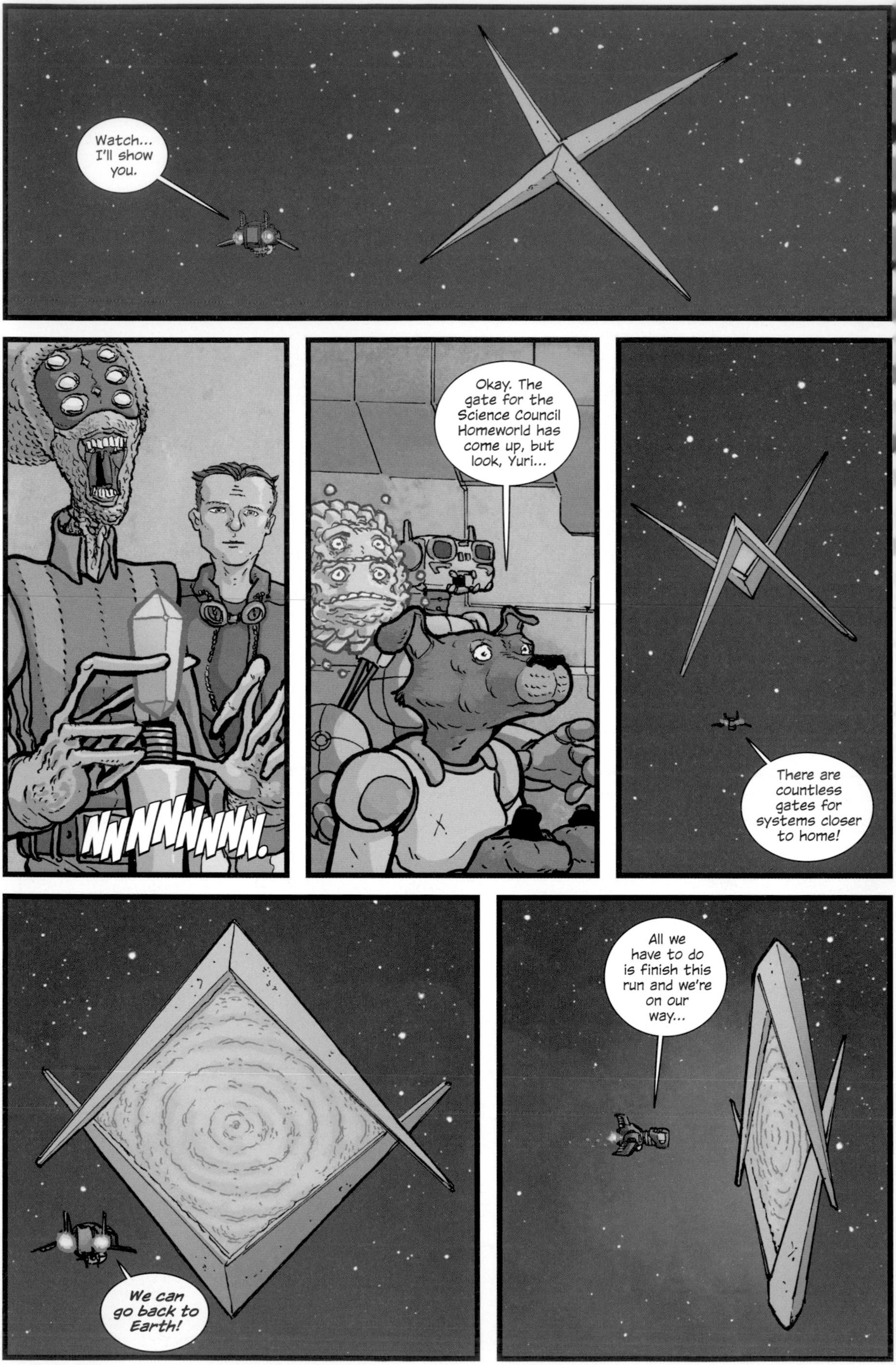
Watch... I'll show you.
NNNNNNNNN.
Okay. The gate for the Science Council Homeworld has come up, but look, Yuri...
There are countless gates for systems closer to home!
We can go back to Earth!
All we have to do is finish this run and we're on our way...

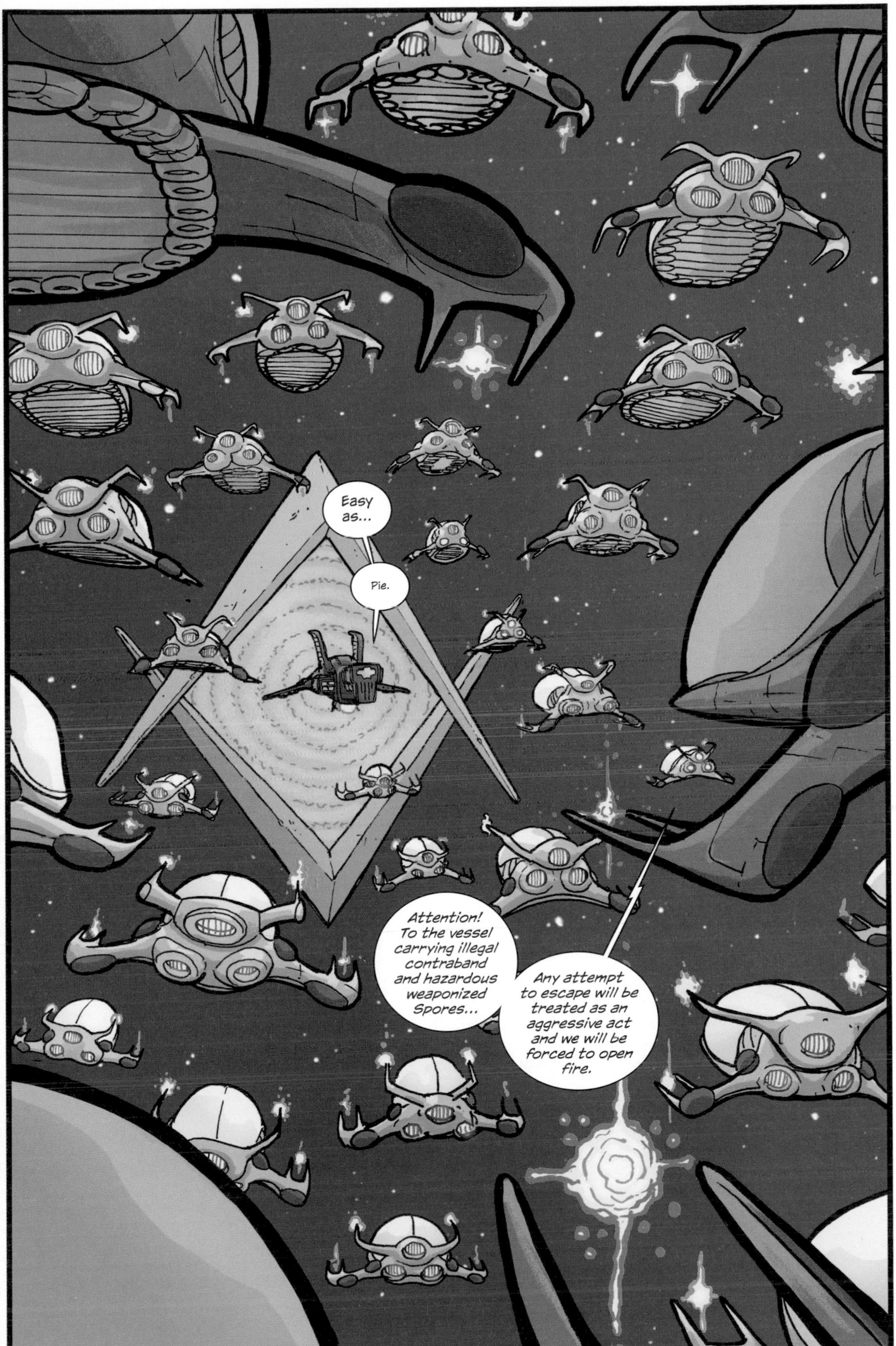
Easy as...
Pie.
Attention! To the vessel carrying illegal contraband and hazardous weaponized Spores...
Any attempt to escape will be treated as an aggressive act and we will be forced to open fire.

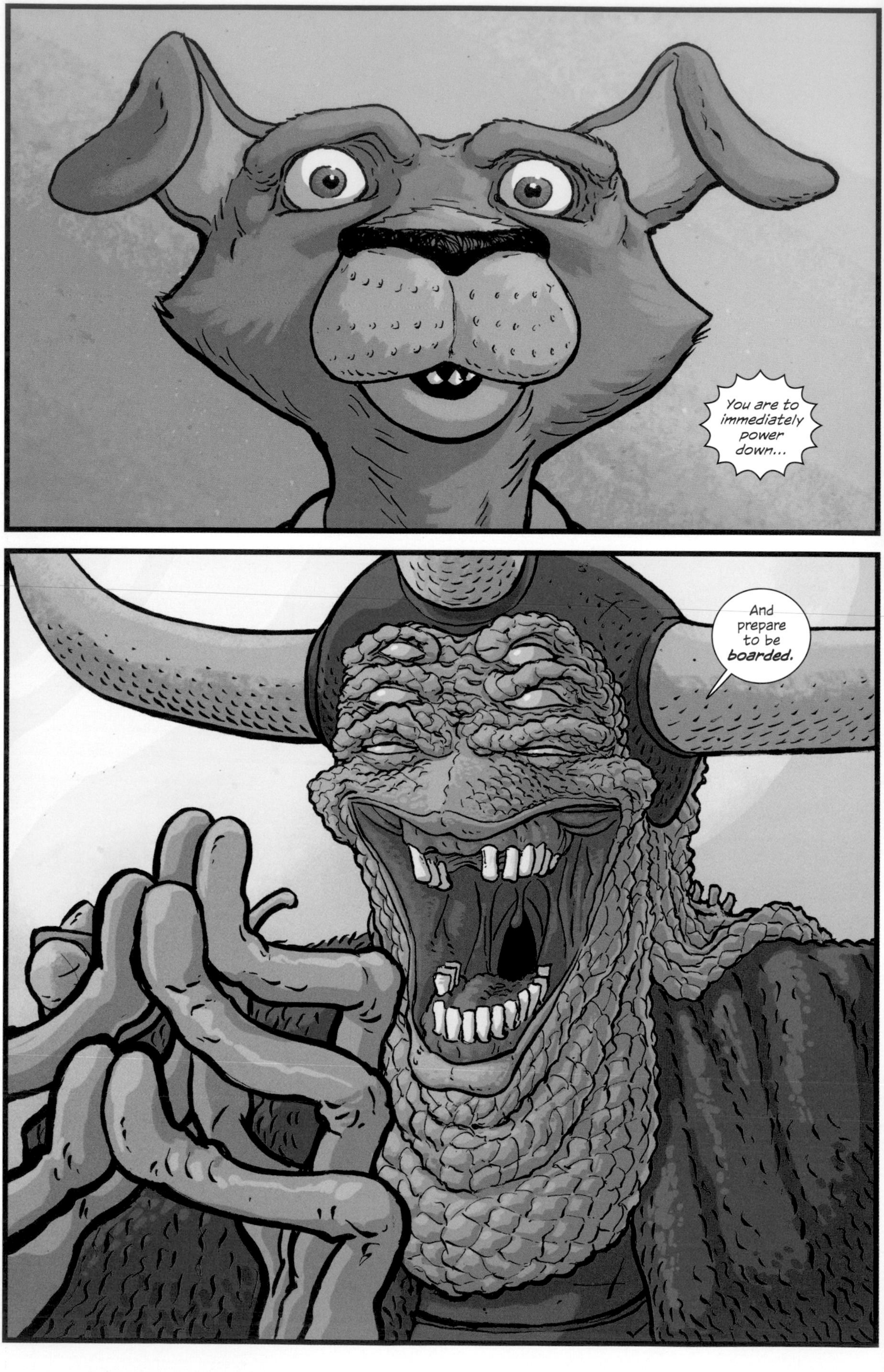
You are to immediately power down...
And prepare to be *boarded.*

IT'S ONLY LUCK IF YOU
KEEP GOING

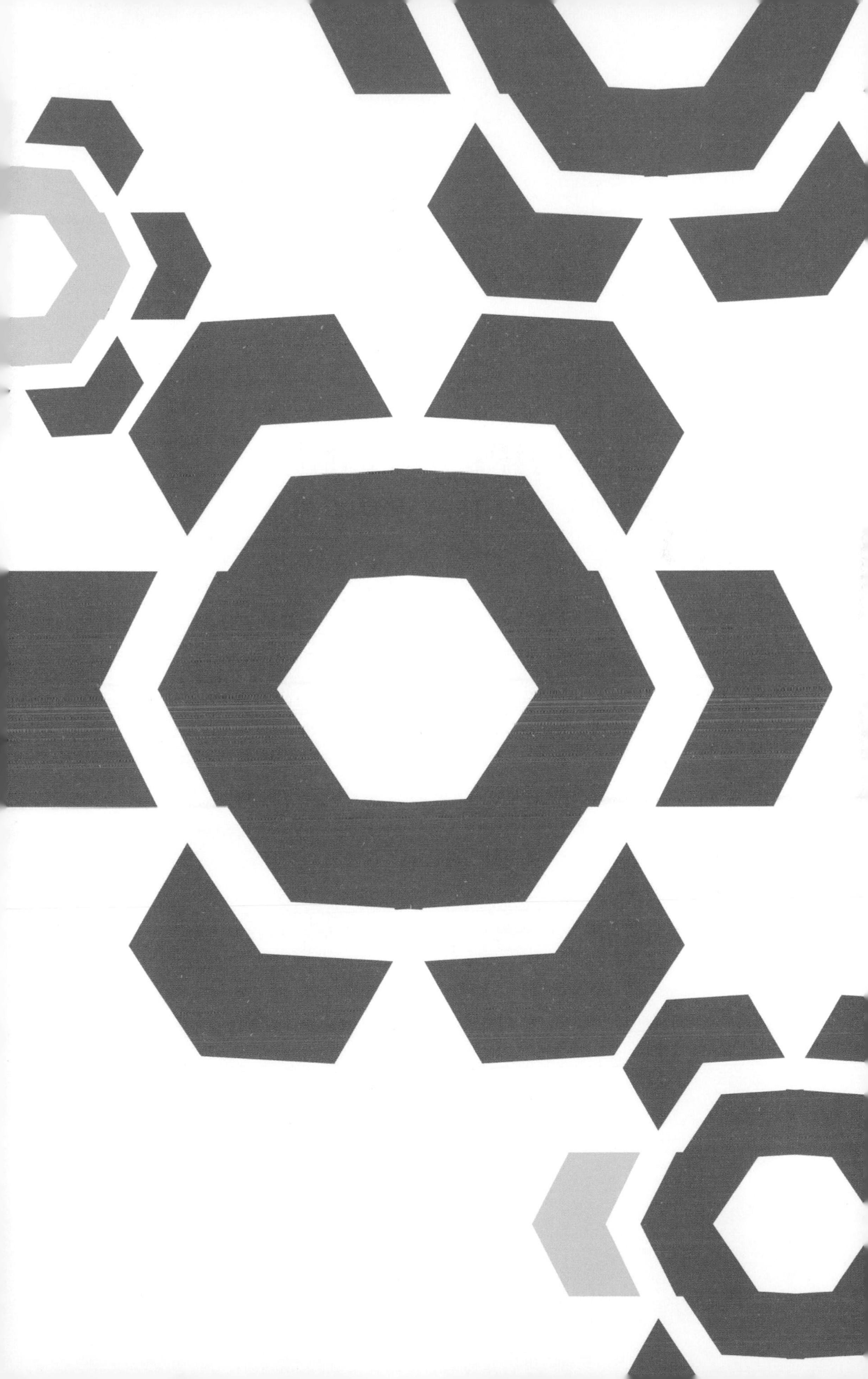

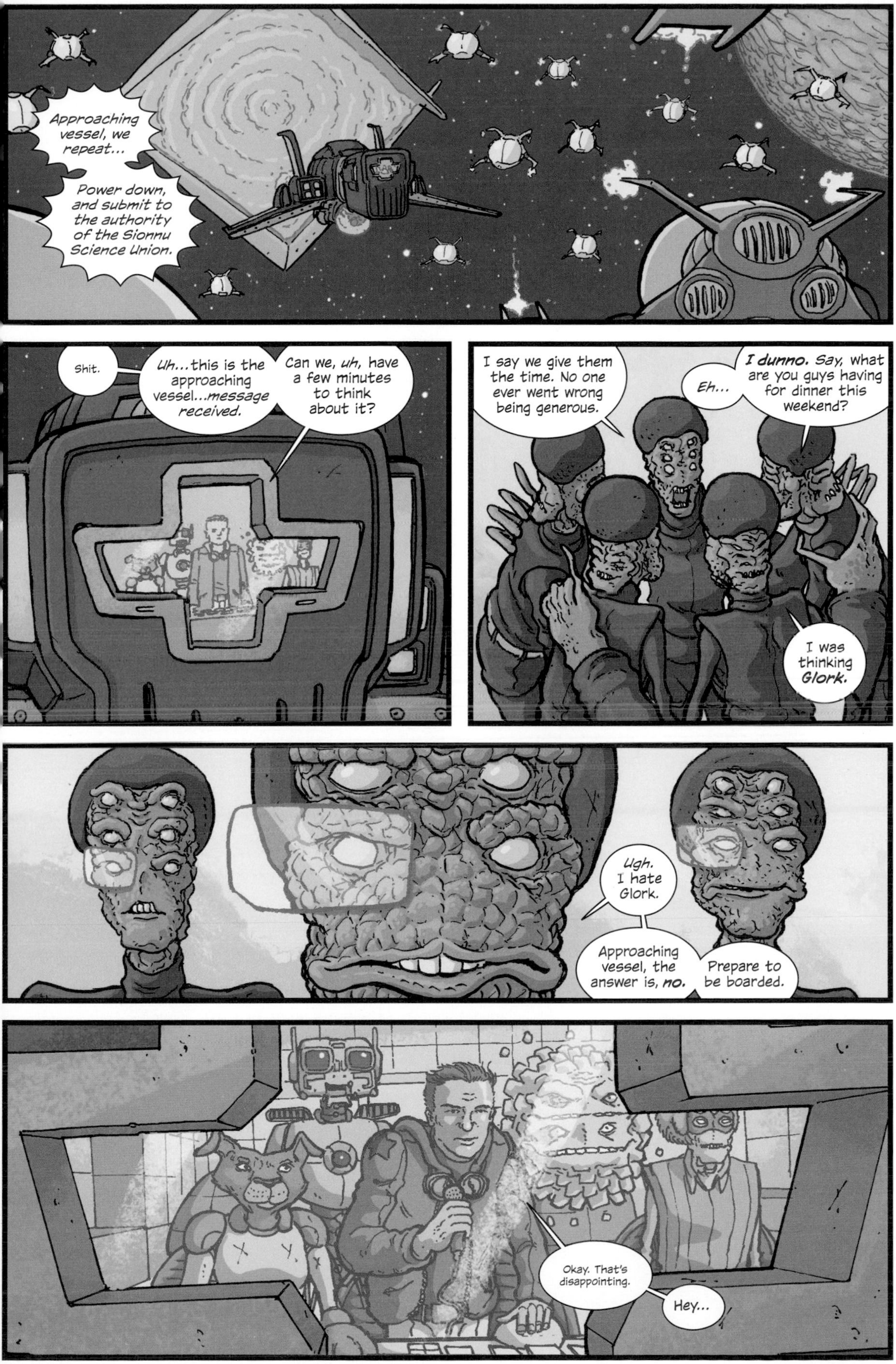
Approaching vessel, we repeat...
Power down, and submit to the authority of the Sionnu Science Union.
Shit.
Uh...this is the approaching vessel...message received.
Can we, uh, have a few minutes to think about it?
I say we give them the time. No one ever went wrong being generous.
Eh...
I dunno. Say, what are you guys having for dinner this weekend?
I was thinking Glork.
Ugh. I hate Glork.
Approaching vessel, the answer is, no.
Prepare to be boarded.
Okay. That's disappointing.
Hey...

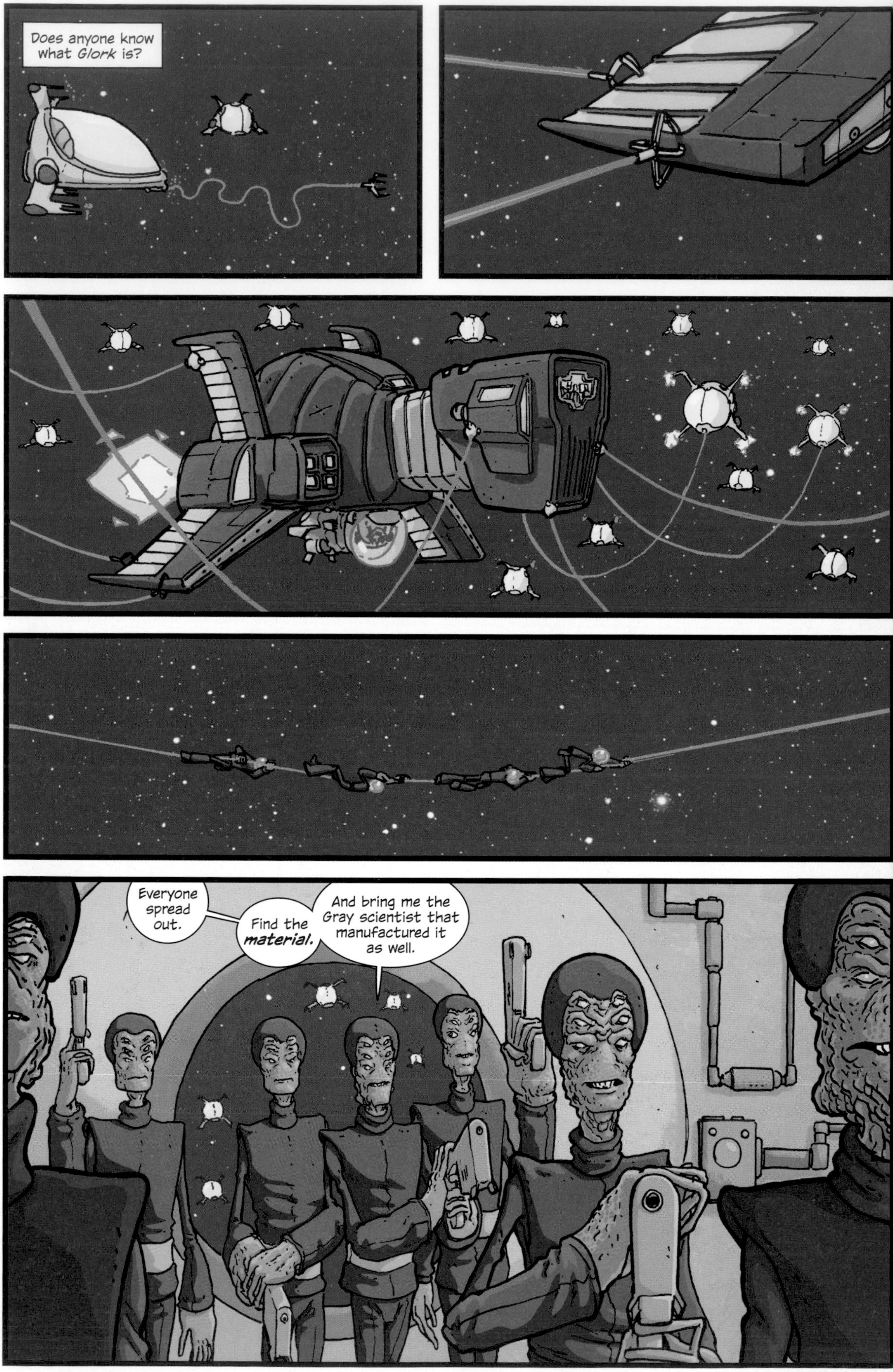
Does anyone know what *Glork* is?
Everyone spread out.
Find the ***material.***
And bring me the Gray scientist that manufactured it as well.

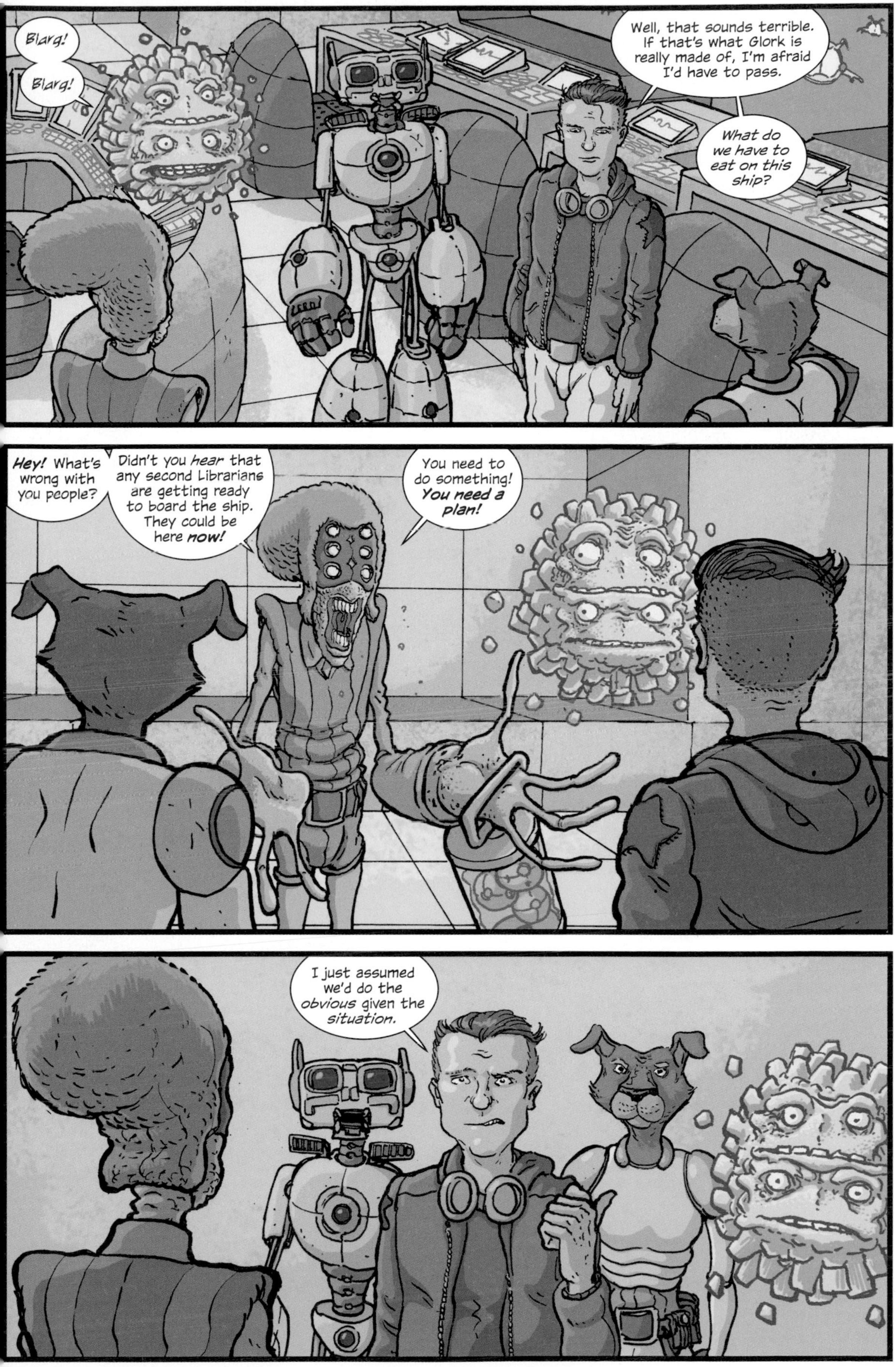
Blarg!
Blarg!
Well, that sounds terrible. If that's what Glork is really made of, I'm afraid I'd have to pass.
What do we have to eat on this ship?
Hey! What's wrong with you people?
Didn't you hear that any second Librarians are getting ready to board the ship. They could be here now!
You need to do something! You need a plan!
I just assumed we'd do the obvious given the situation.

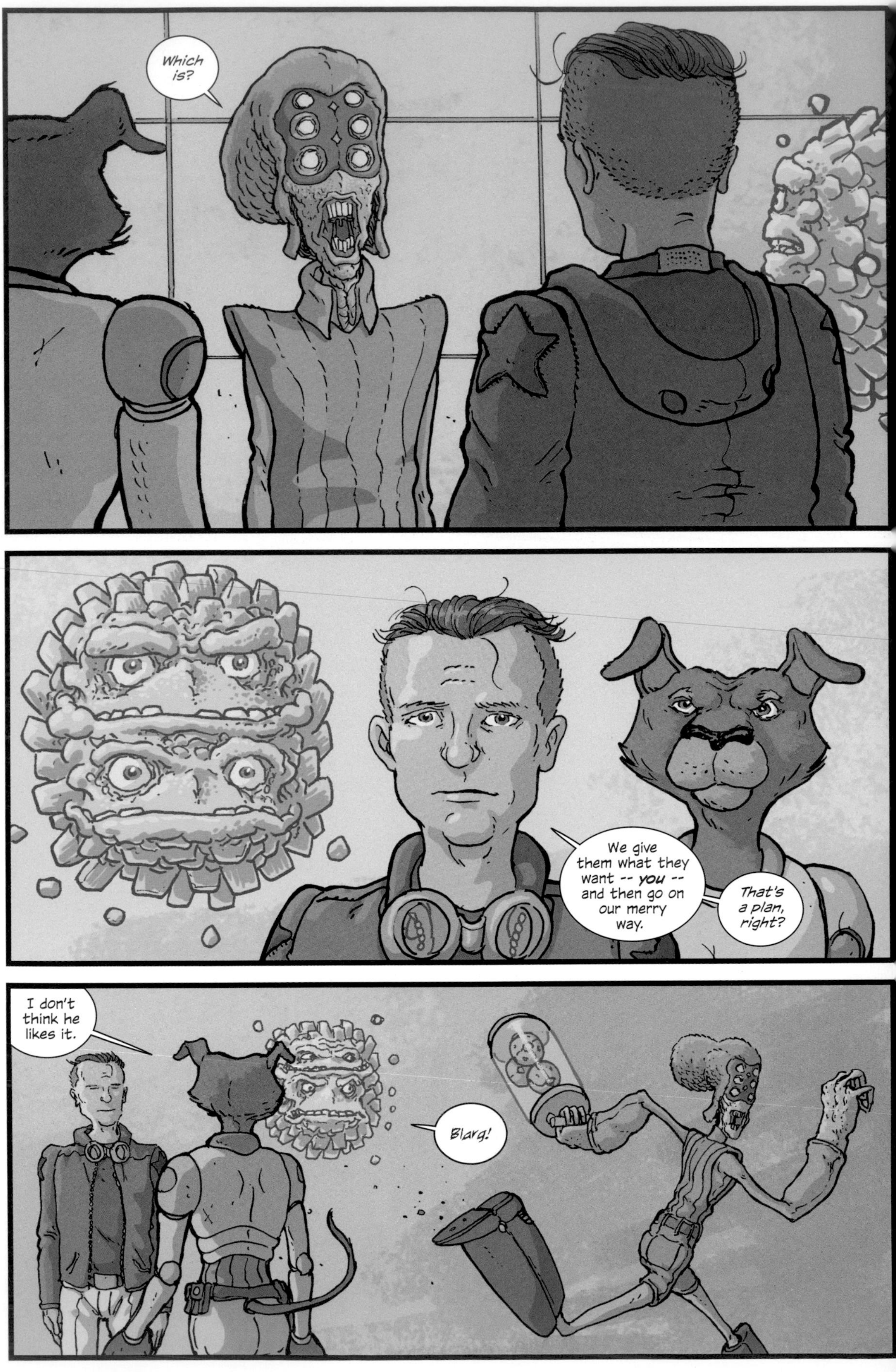
Which is?
We give them what they want -- *you* -- and then go on our merry way.
That's a plan, right?
I don't think he likes it.
Blarg!

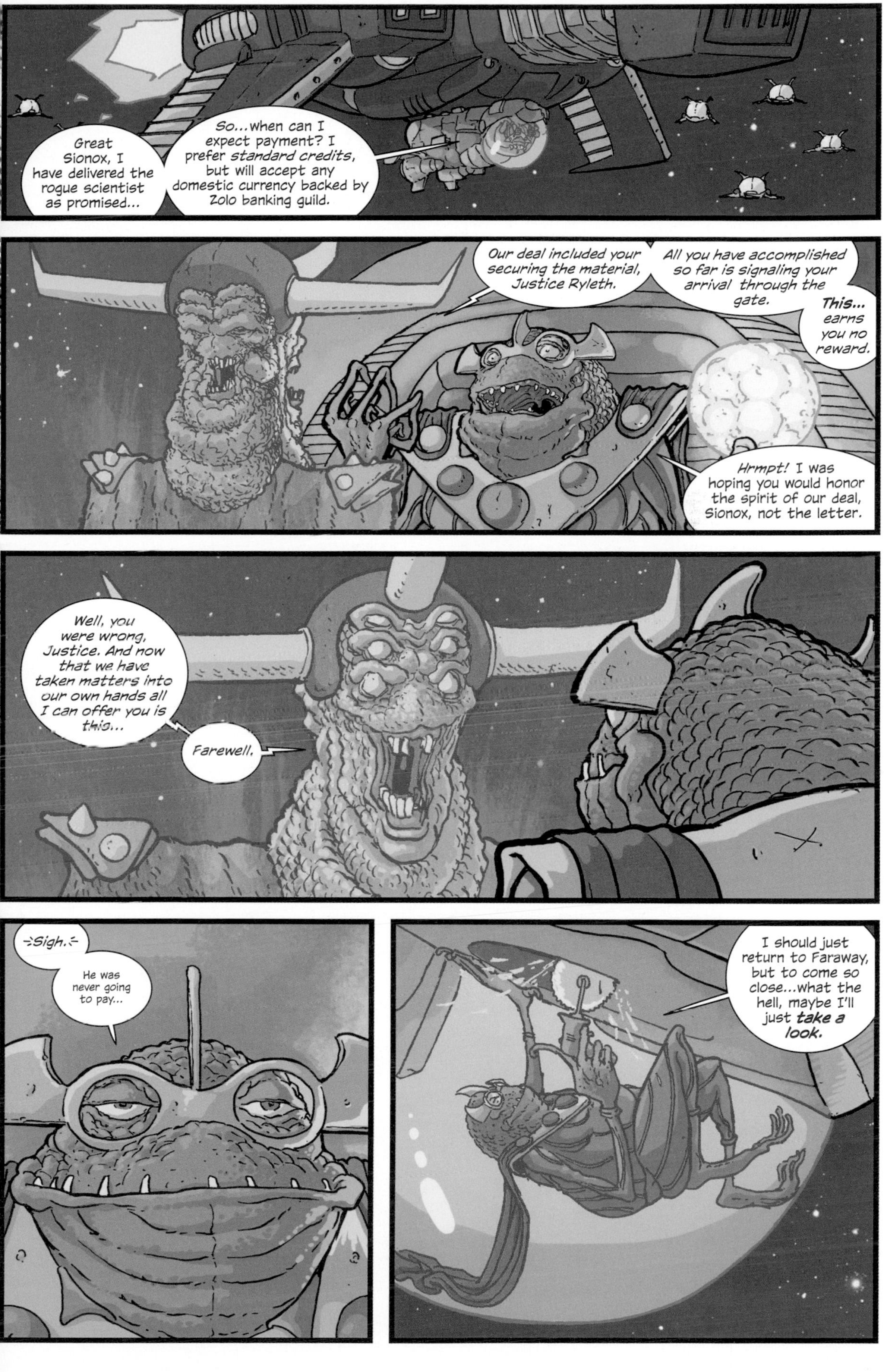

Great Sionox, I have delivered the rogue scientist as promised...
So...when can I expect payment? I prefer *standard credits*, but will accept any domestic currency backed by Zolo banking guild.
Our deal included your securing the material, Justice Ryleth.
All you have accomplished so far is signaling your arrival through the gate.
This... earns you no reward.
Hrmpt! I was hoping you would honor the spirit of our deal, Sionox, not the letter.
Well, you were wrong, Justice. And now that we have taken matters into our own hands all I can offer you is this...
Farewell.
Sigh.
He was never going to pay...
I should just return to Faraway, but to come so close...what the hell, maybe I'll just **take a look.**

29

THE SUN BEYOND THE STARS

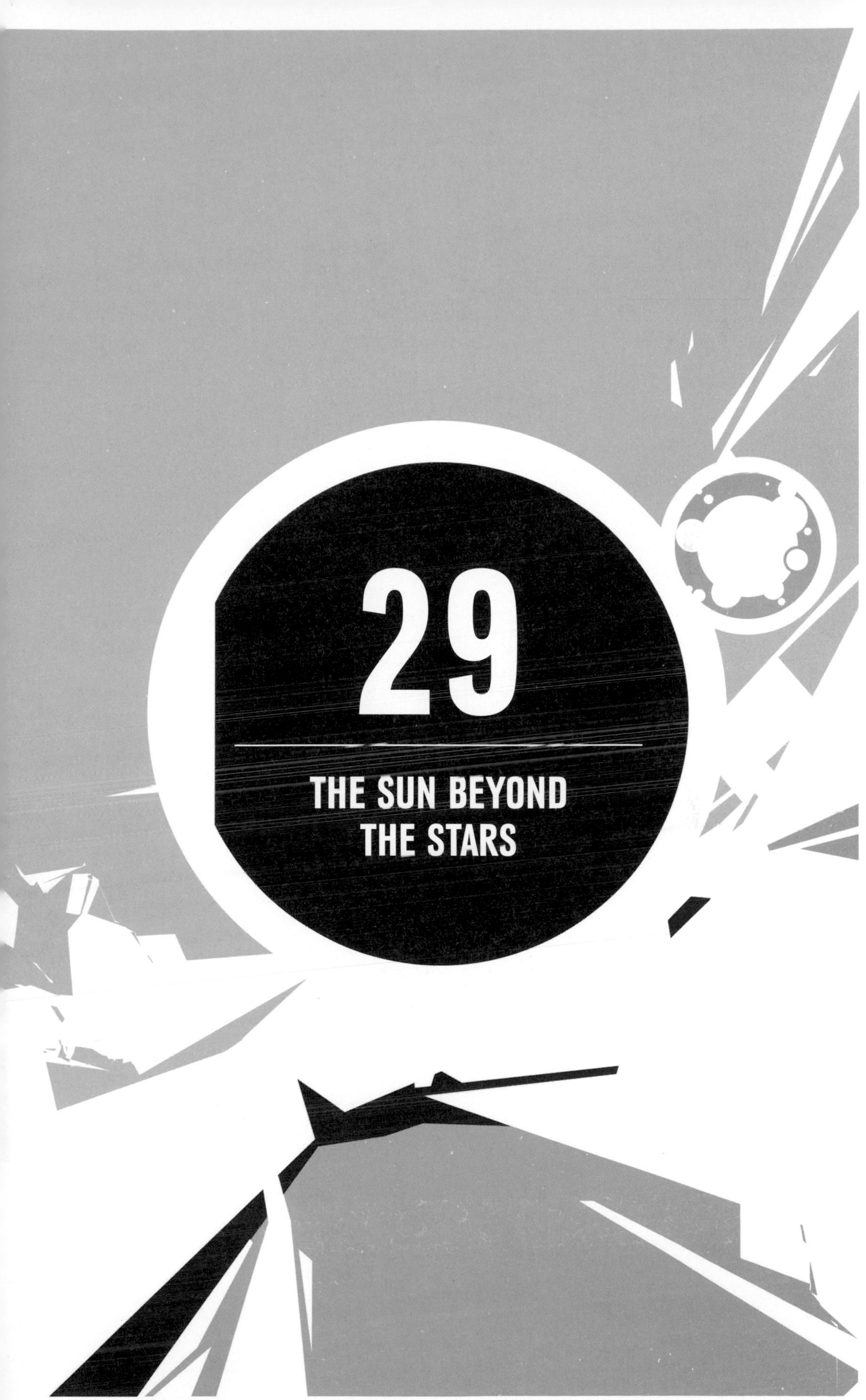

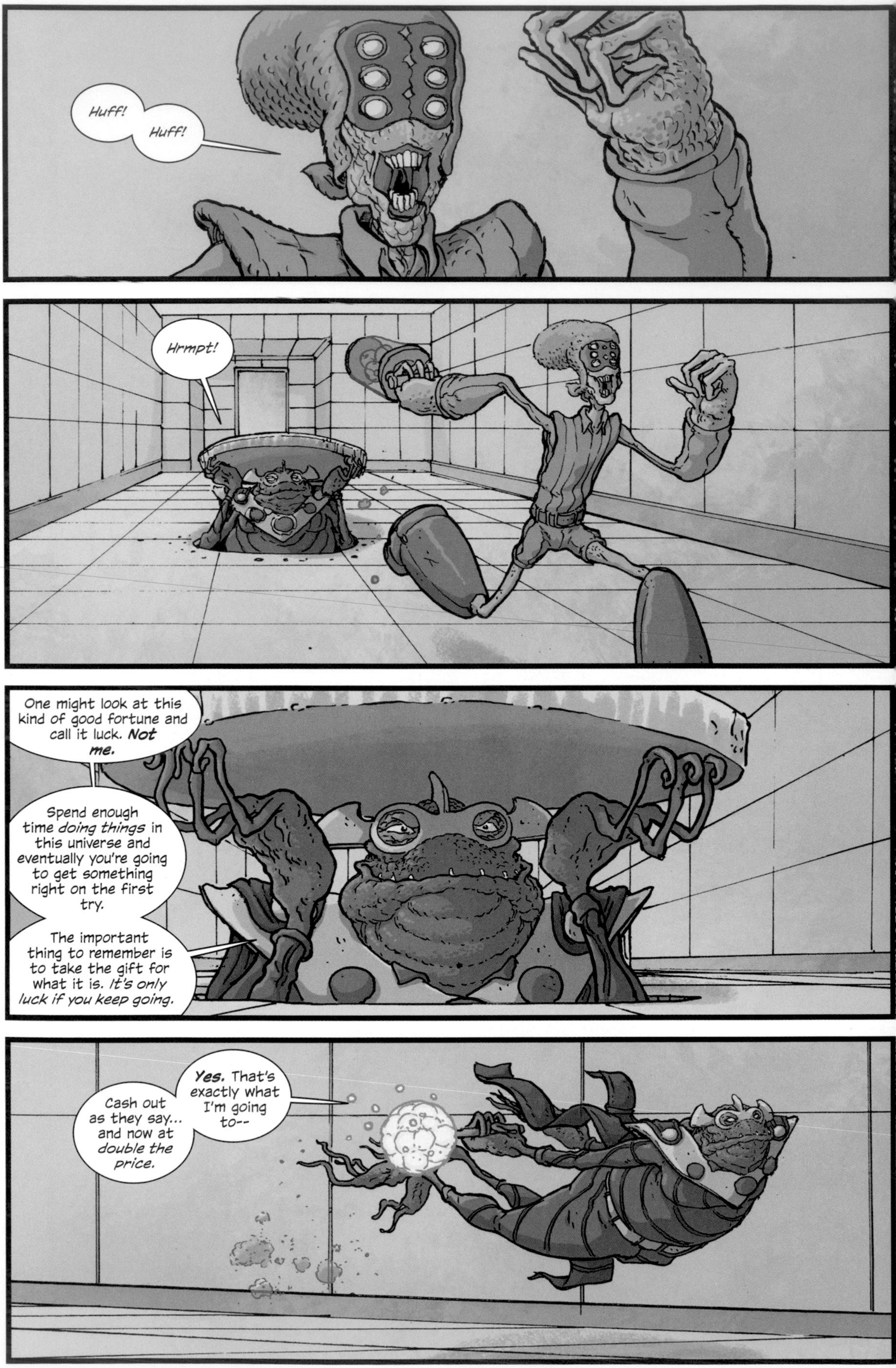
Huff!
Huff!
Hrmpt!
One might look at this kind of good fortune and call it luck. **Not me.**
Spend enough time *doing things* in this universe and eventually you're going to get something right on the first try.
The important thing to remember is to take the gift for what it is. *It's only luck if you keep going.*
Cash out as they say... and now at *double the price.*
Yes. That's exactly what I'm going to--

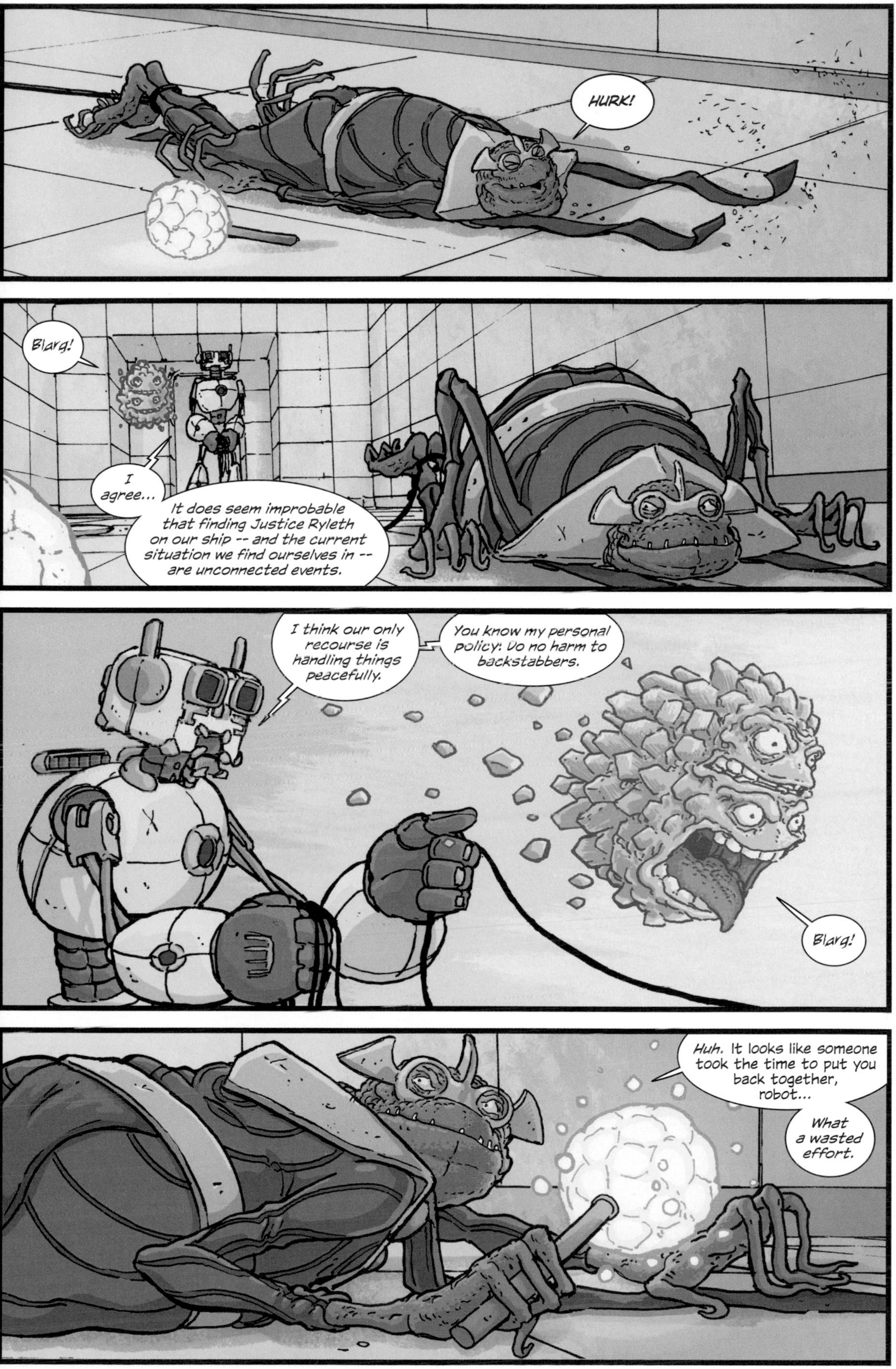
HURK!
Blarg!
I agree...
It does seem improbable that finding Justice Ryleth on our ship -- and the current situation we find ourselves in -- are unconnected events.
I think our only recourse is handling things peacefully.
You know my personal policy: Do no harm to backstabbers.
Blarg!
Huh. It looks like someone took the time to put you back together, robot...
What a wasted effort.

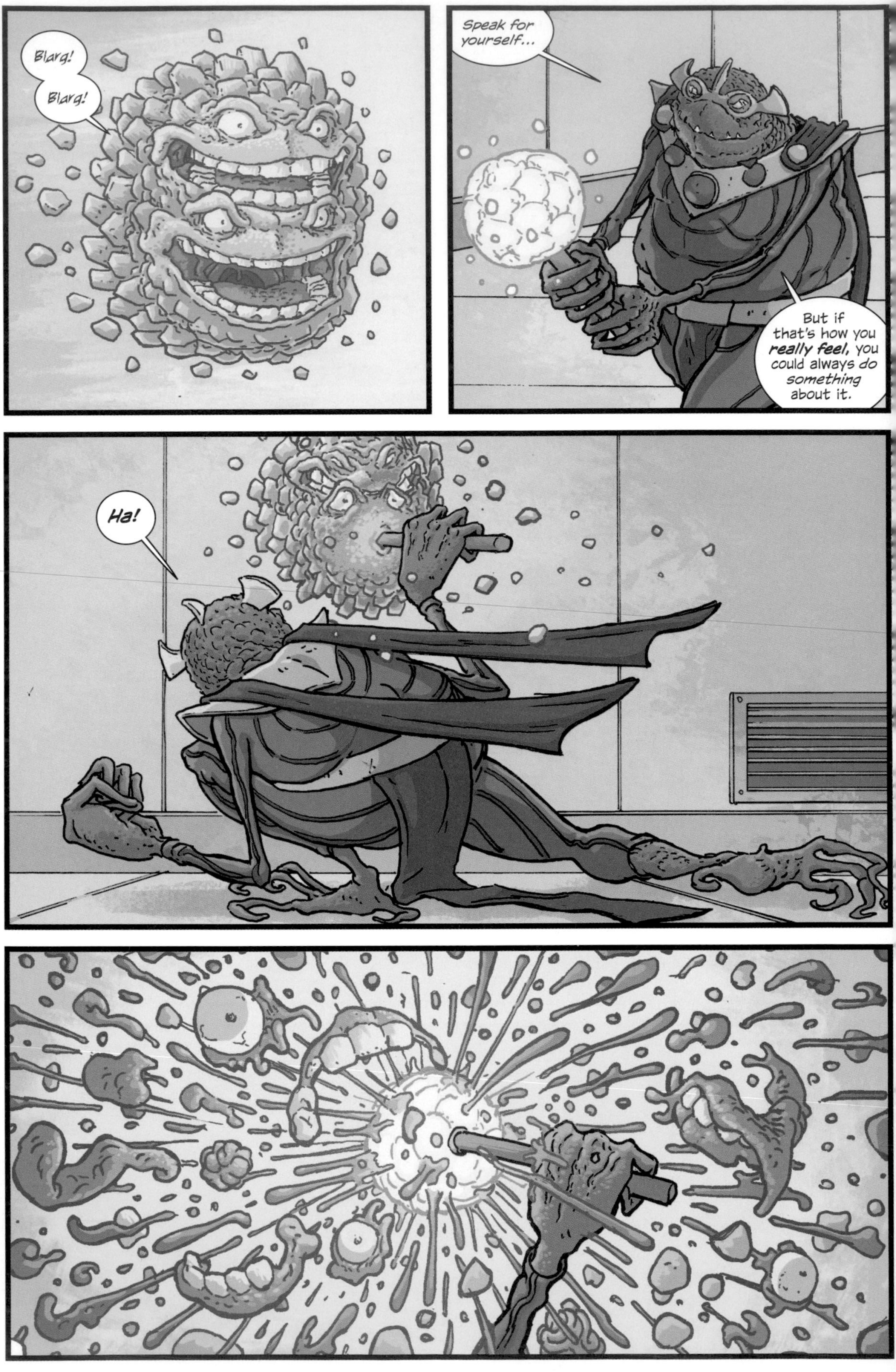
Blarg!
Blarg!
Speak for yourself...
But if that's how you **really feel,** you could always do *something* about it.
Ha!

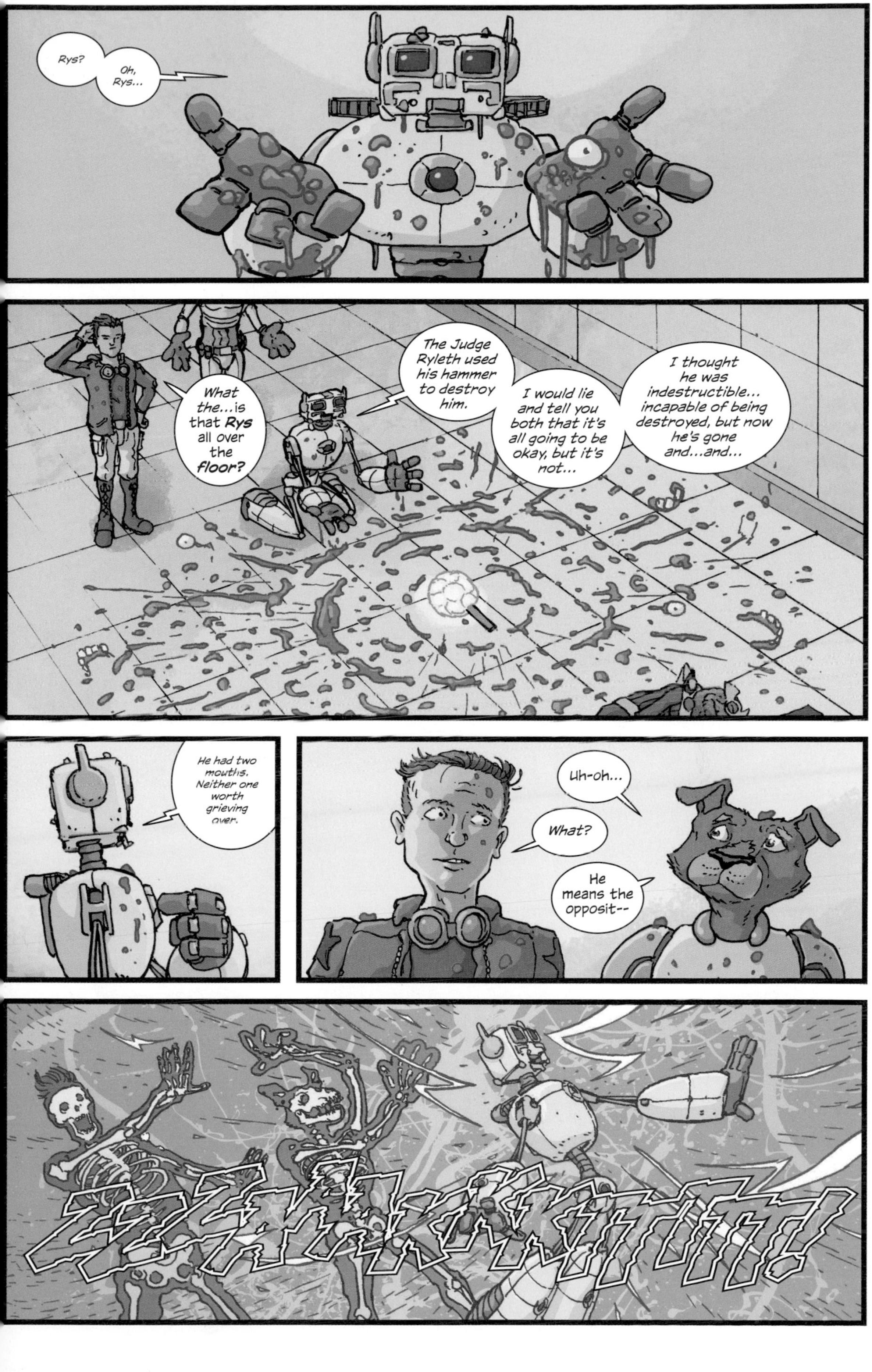
Rys?
Oh, Rys...
What the...is that Rys all over the floor?
The Judge Ryleth used his hammer to destroy him.
I would lie and tell you both that it's all going to be okay, but it's not...
I thought he was indestructible... incapable of being destroyed, but now he's gone and...and...
He had two mouths. Neither one worth grieving over.
Uh-oh...
What?
He means the opposit--

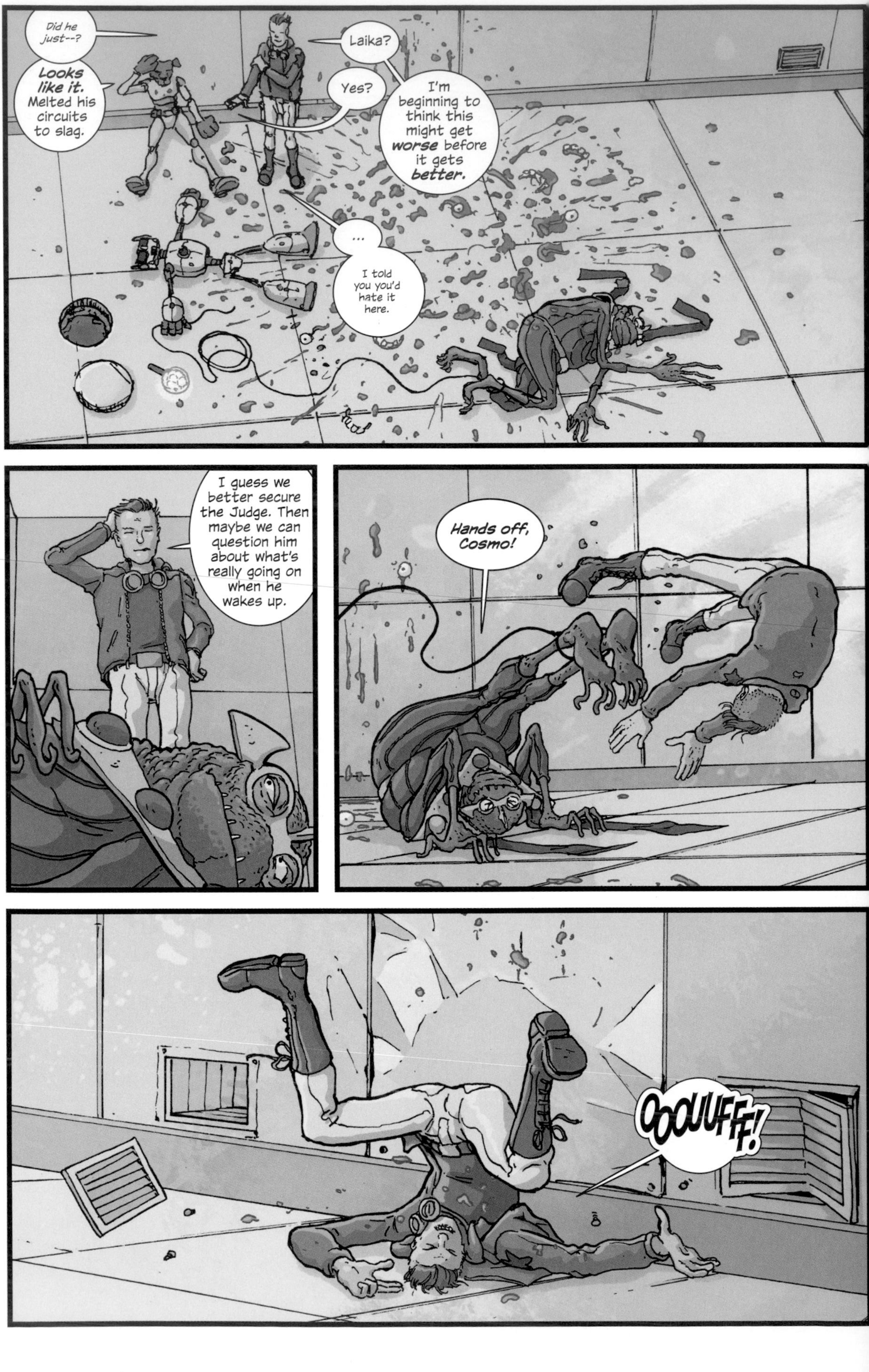
Did he just--?
Looks like it. Melted his circuits to slag.
Laika?
Yes?
I'm beginning to think this might get worse before it gets better.
...
I told you you'd hate it here.
I guess we better secure the Judge. Then maybe we can question him about what's really going on when he wakes up.
Hands off, Cosmo!
OOOUUFFF!

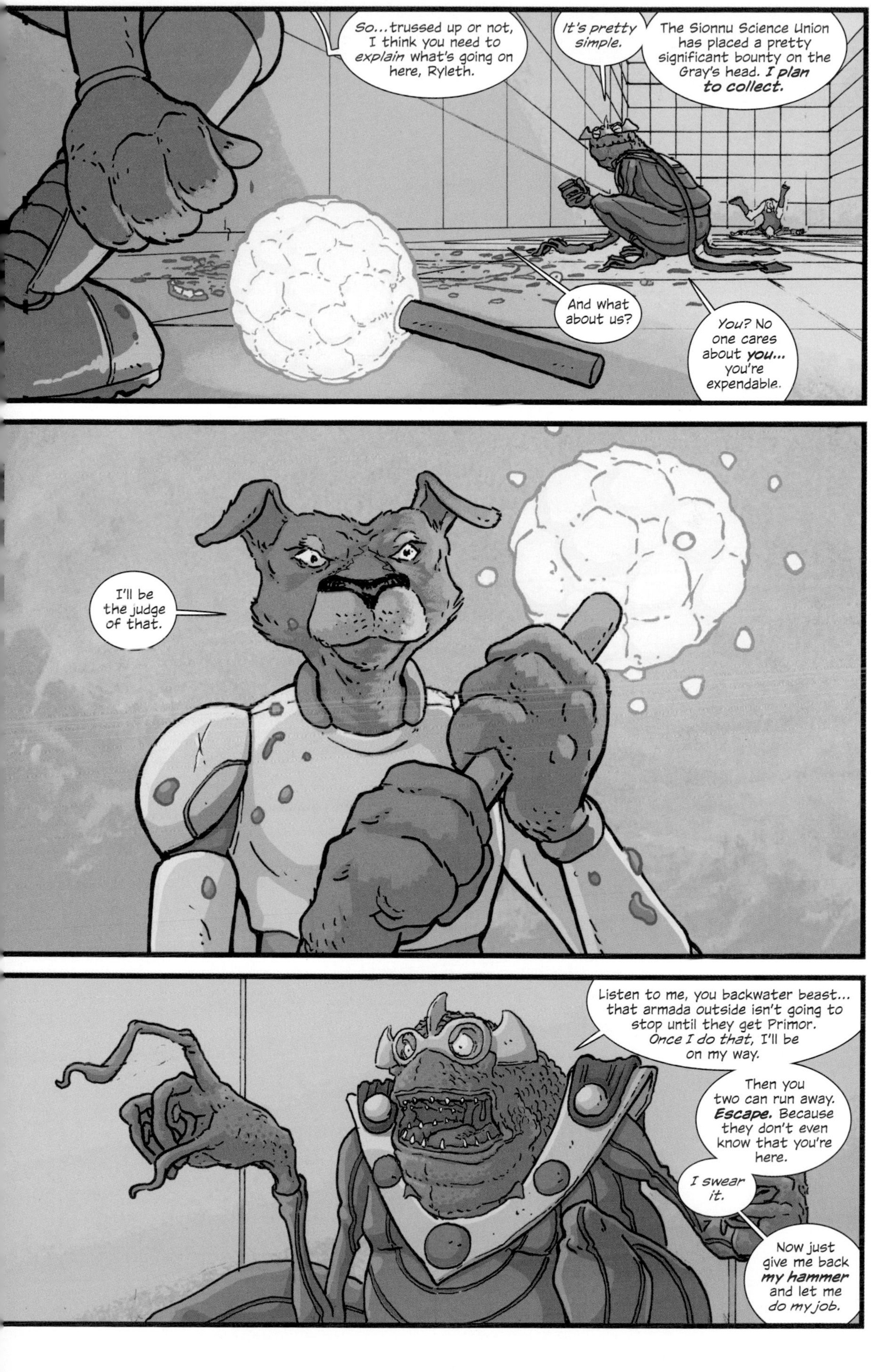
So...trussed up or not, I think you need to *explain* what's going on here, Ryleth.
It's pretty simple.
The Sionnu Science Union has placed a pretty significant bounty on the Gray's head. ***I plan to collect.***
And what about us?
You? No one cares about **you...** you're expendable.
I'll be the judge of that.
Listen to me, you backwater beast... that armada outside isn't going to stop until they get Primor. *Once I do that,* I'll be on my way.
Then you two can run away. ***Escape.*** Because they don't even know that you're here.
I swear it.
Now just give me back ***my hammer*** and let me *do my job.*

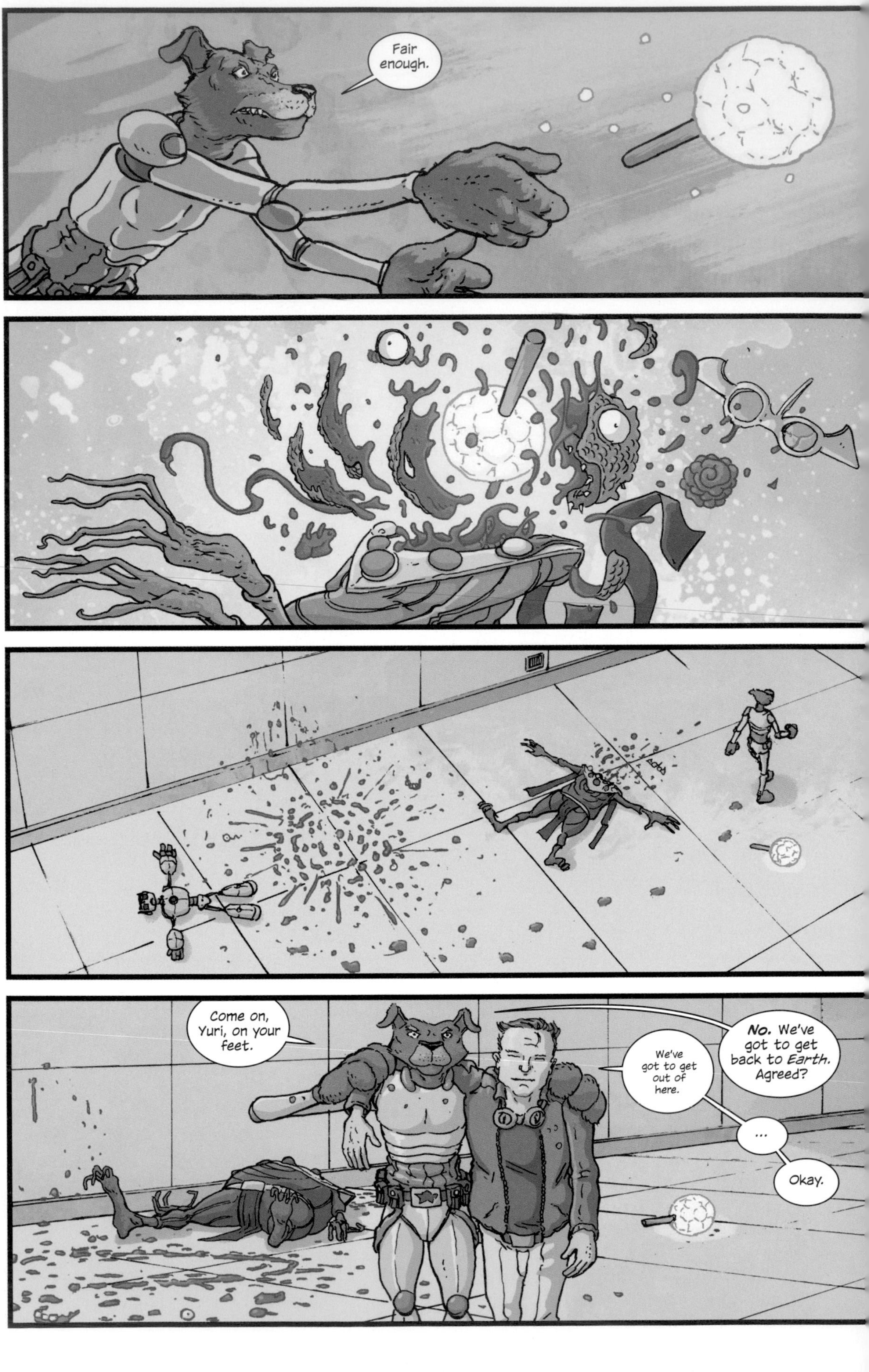

Fair enough.
Come on, Yuri, on your feet.
We've got to get out of here.
No. We've got to get back to Earth. Agreed?
...
Okay.

Sixteen thousand years of slavery.
Trillions of lives crushed under the boot of science.
It's past time my people had their freedom.
We've more than paid for it in blood.
I do this for all Sionnu Gray.
You! Slave!
On the orders of the Great Sionox, you are to immediately stop what you are doing and surrender or we will be forced to slag you where you stand.
Tisk!

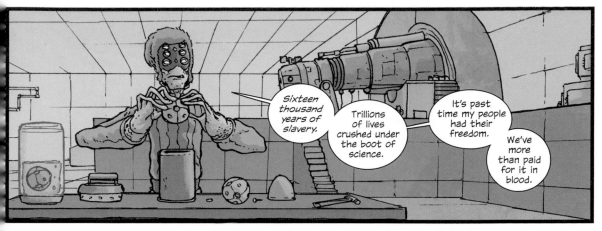

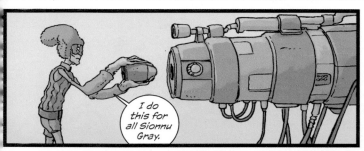

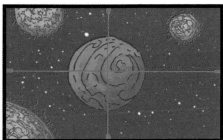

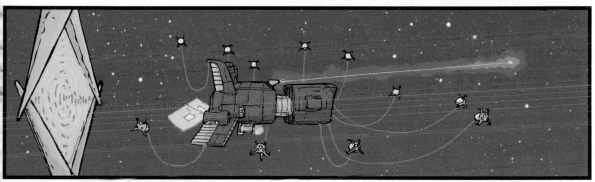

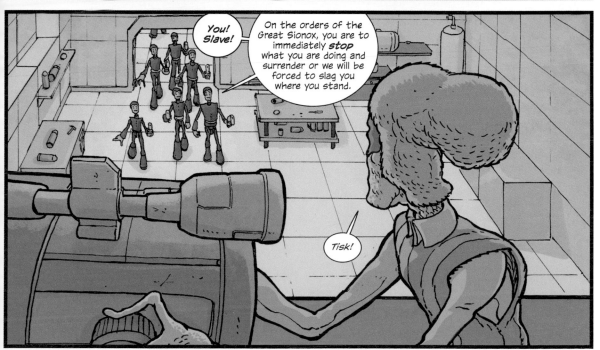

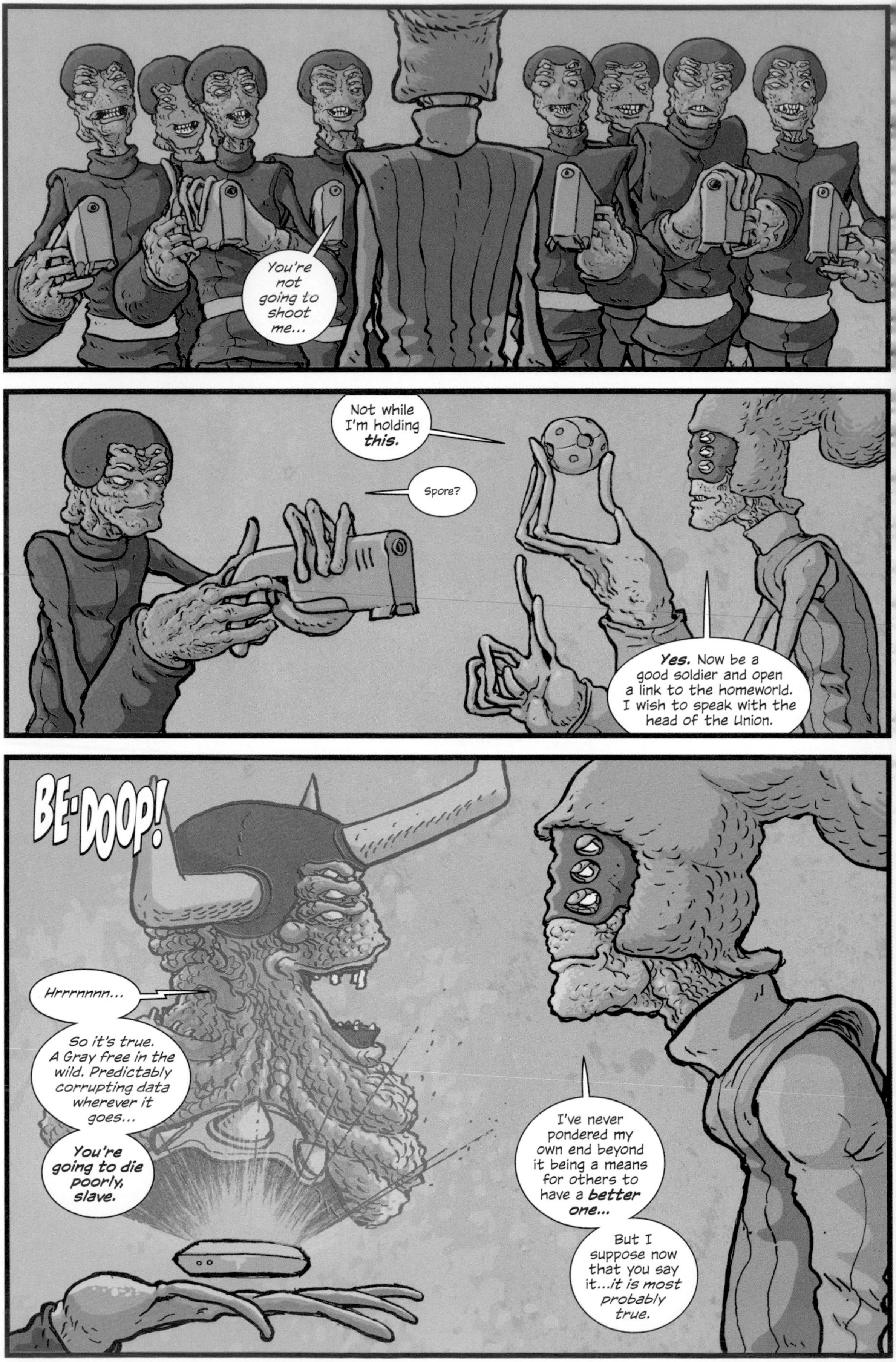
You're not going to shoot me...
Not while I'm holding **this.**
Spore?
Yes. Now be a good soldier and open a link to the homeworld. I wish to speak with the head of the Union.
BE-DOOP!
Hrrrnnnn...
So it's true. A Gray free in the wild. Predictably corrupting data wherever it goes...
You're going to die poorly, slave.
I've never pondered my own end beyond it being a means for others to have a **better one...**
But I suppose now that you say it...*it is most probably true.*

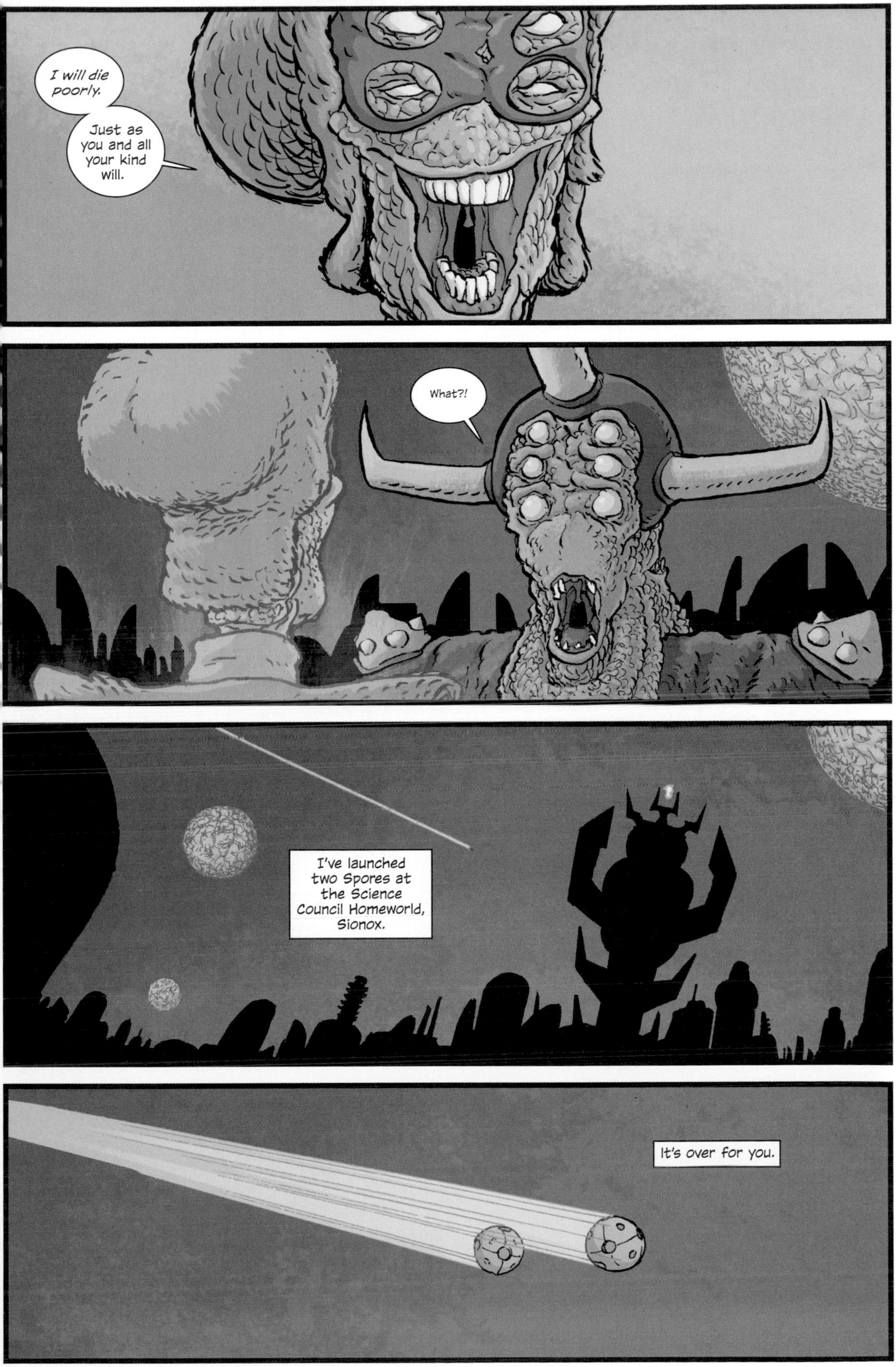
I will die poorly.
Just as you and all your kind will.
What?!
I've launched two Spores at the Science Council Homeworld, Sionox.
It's over for you.

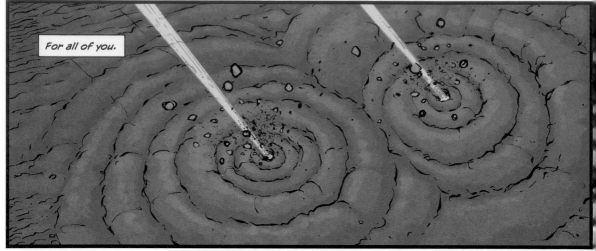

For all of you.

Every Sionnu leader.
Every follower.

Every citizen who turns a blind eye because they just want to be left alone to live their lives.

Every child that would grow up apathetic to the plight of my people.

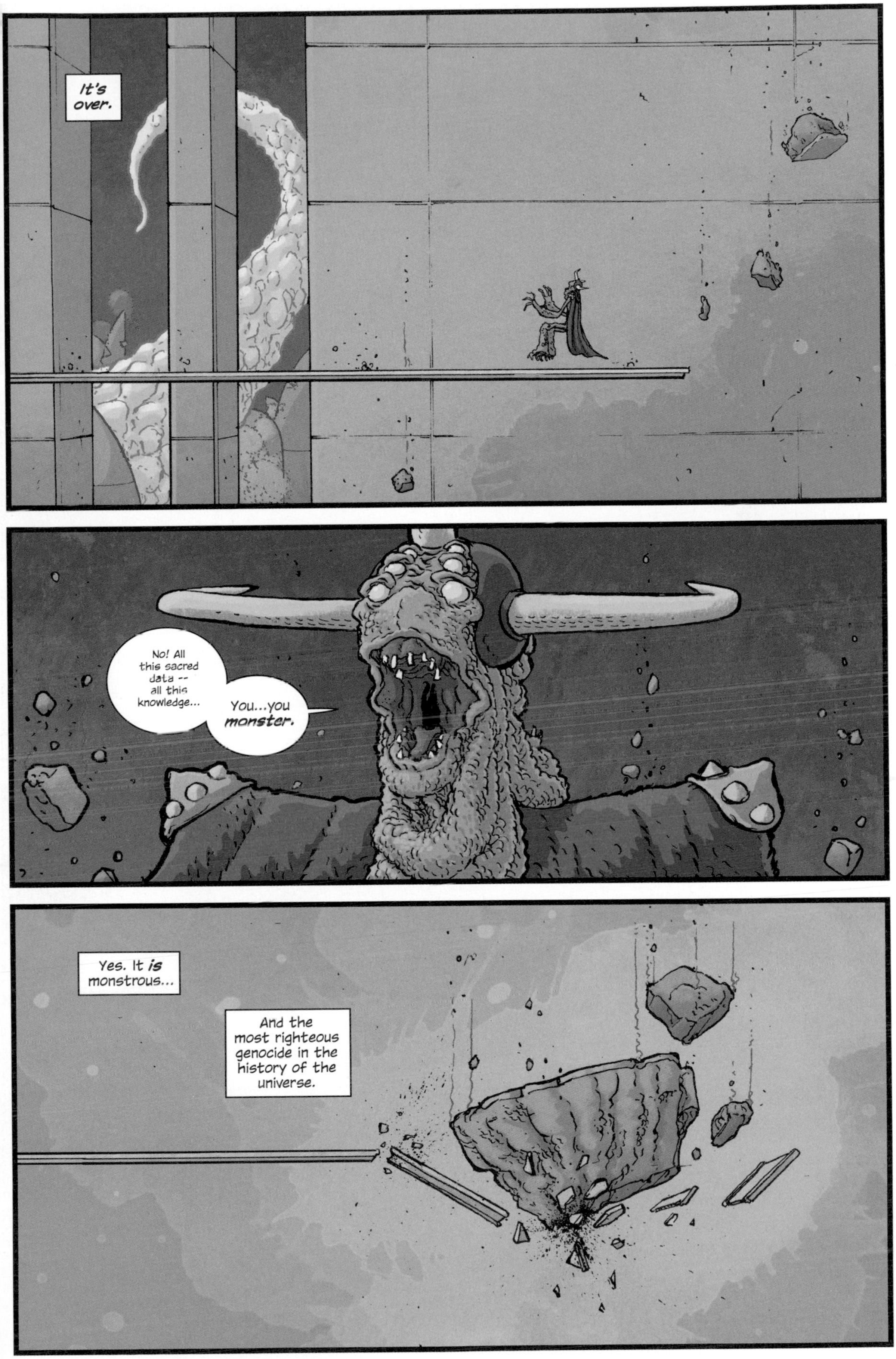
It's over.
No! All this sacred data -- all this knowledge...
You...you monster.
Yes. It is monstrous...
And the most righteous genocide in the history of the universe.

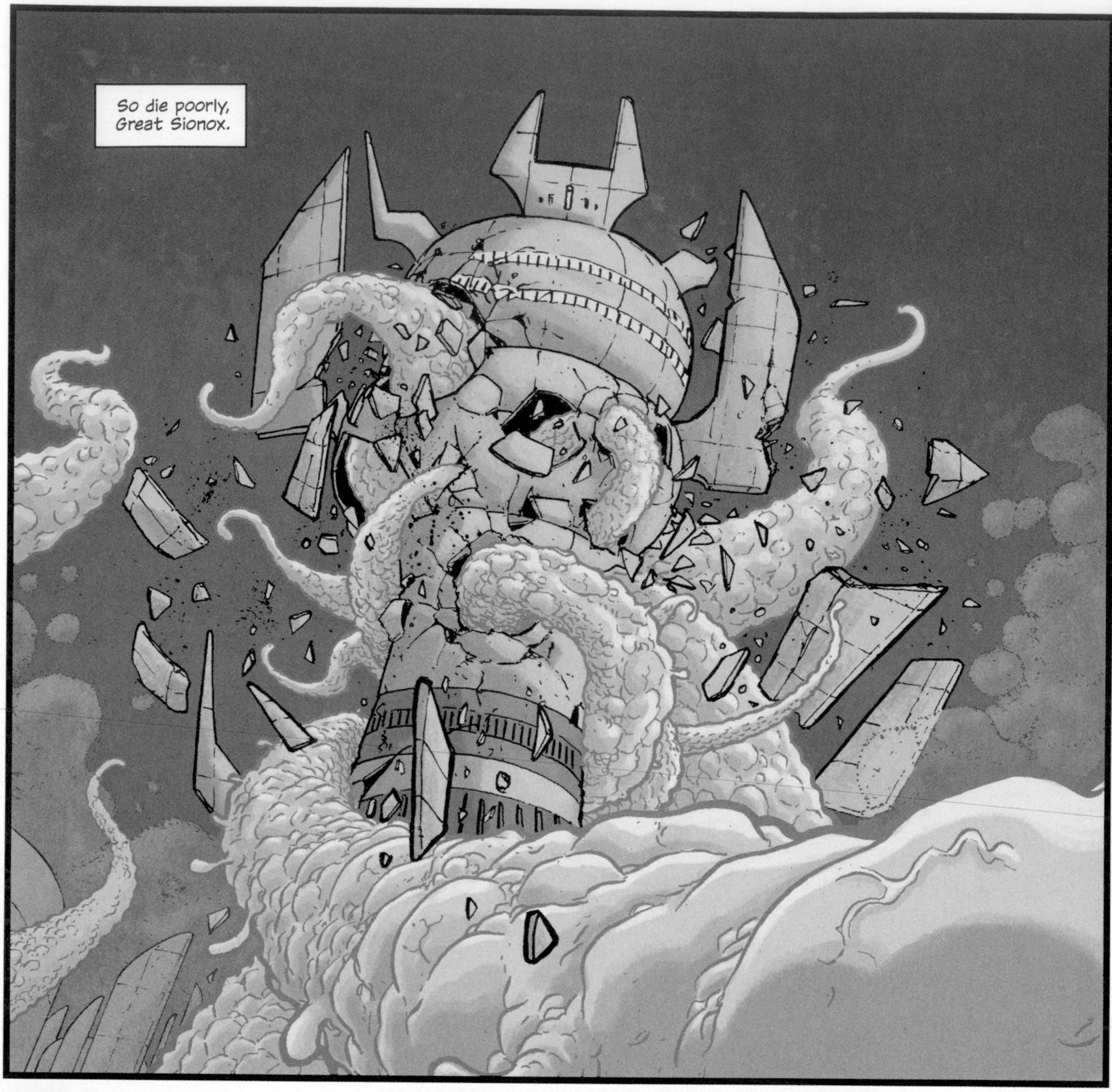
So die poorly,
Great Sionox.

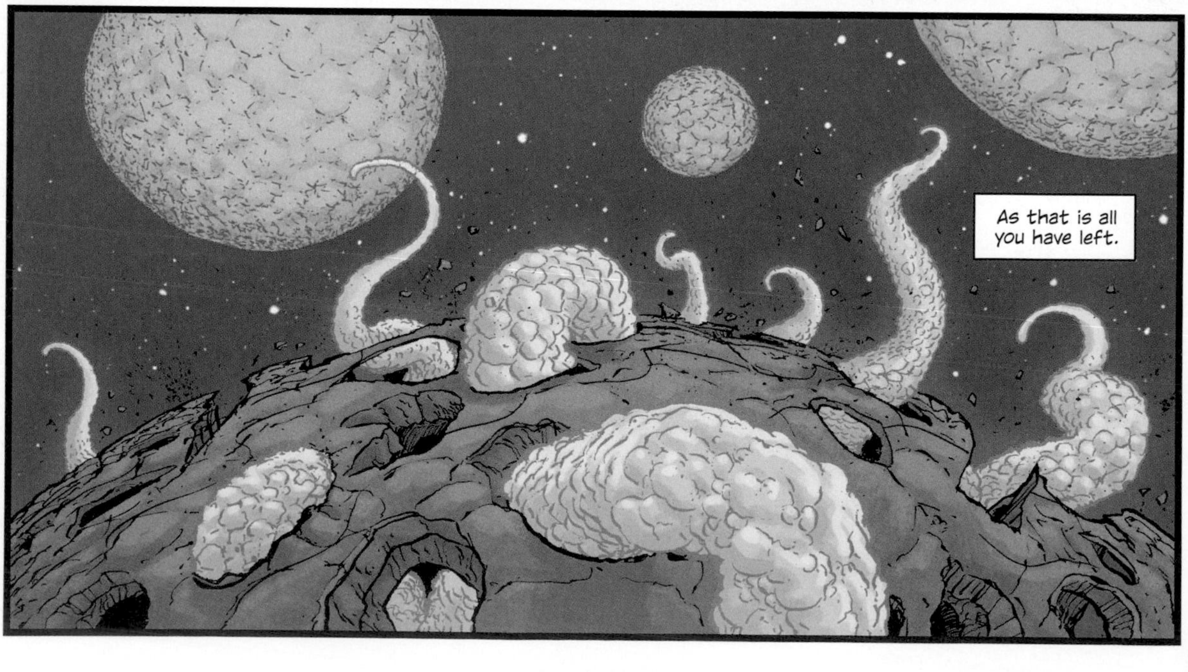
As that is all
you have left.

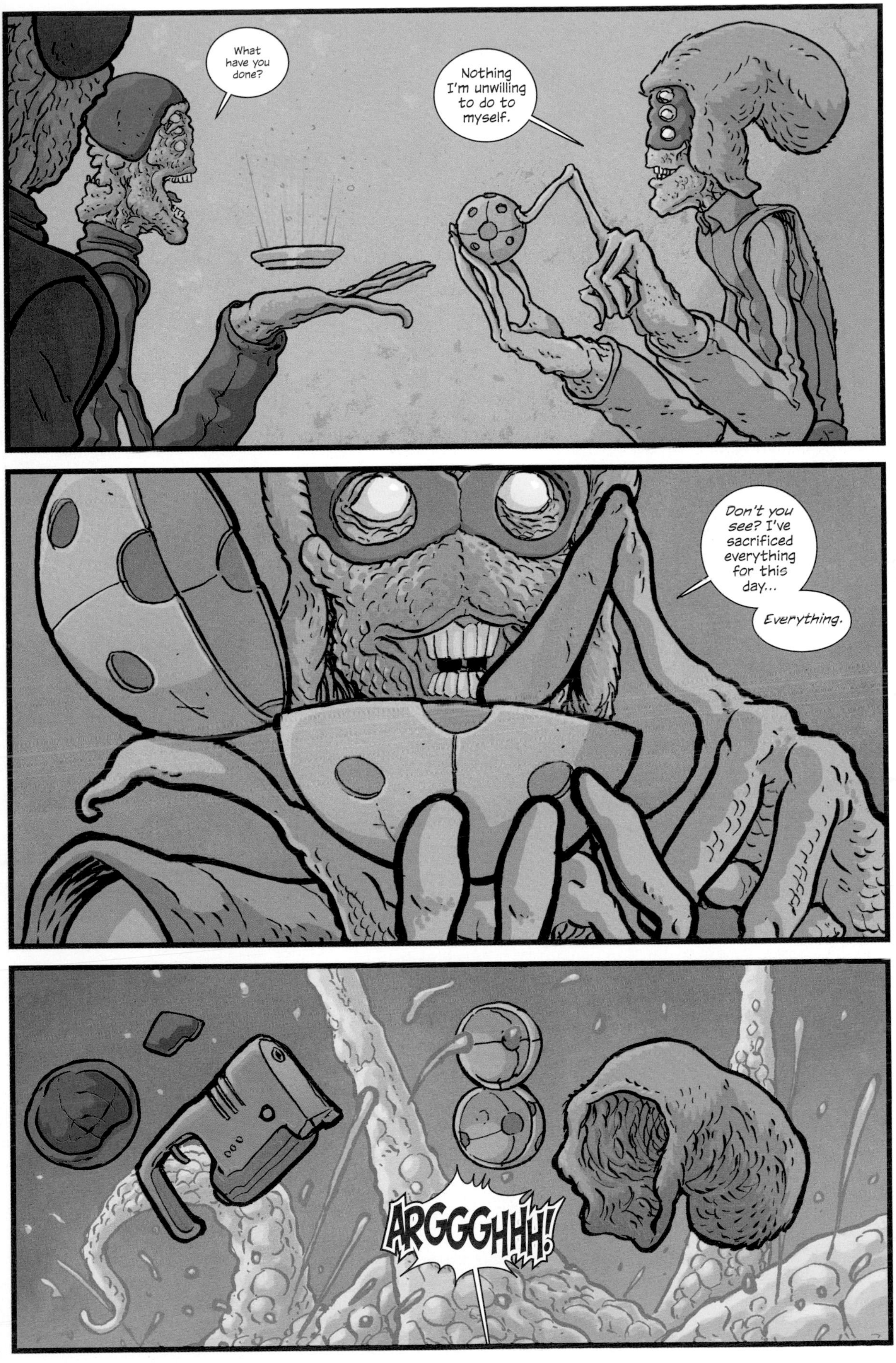
What have you done?
Nothing I'm unwilling to do to myself.
Don't you see? I've sacrificed everything for this day...
Everything.
ARGGGHHH!

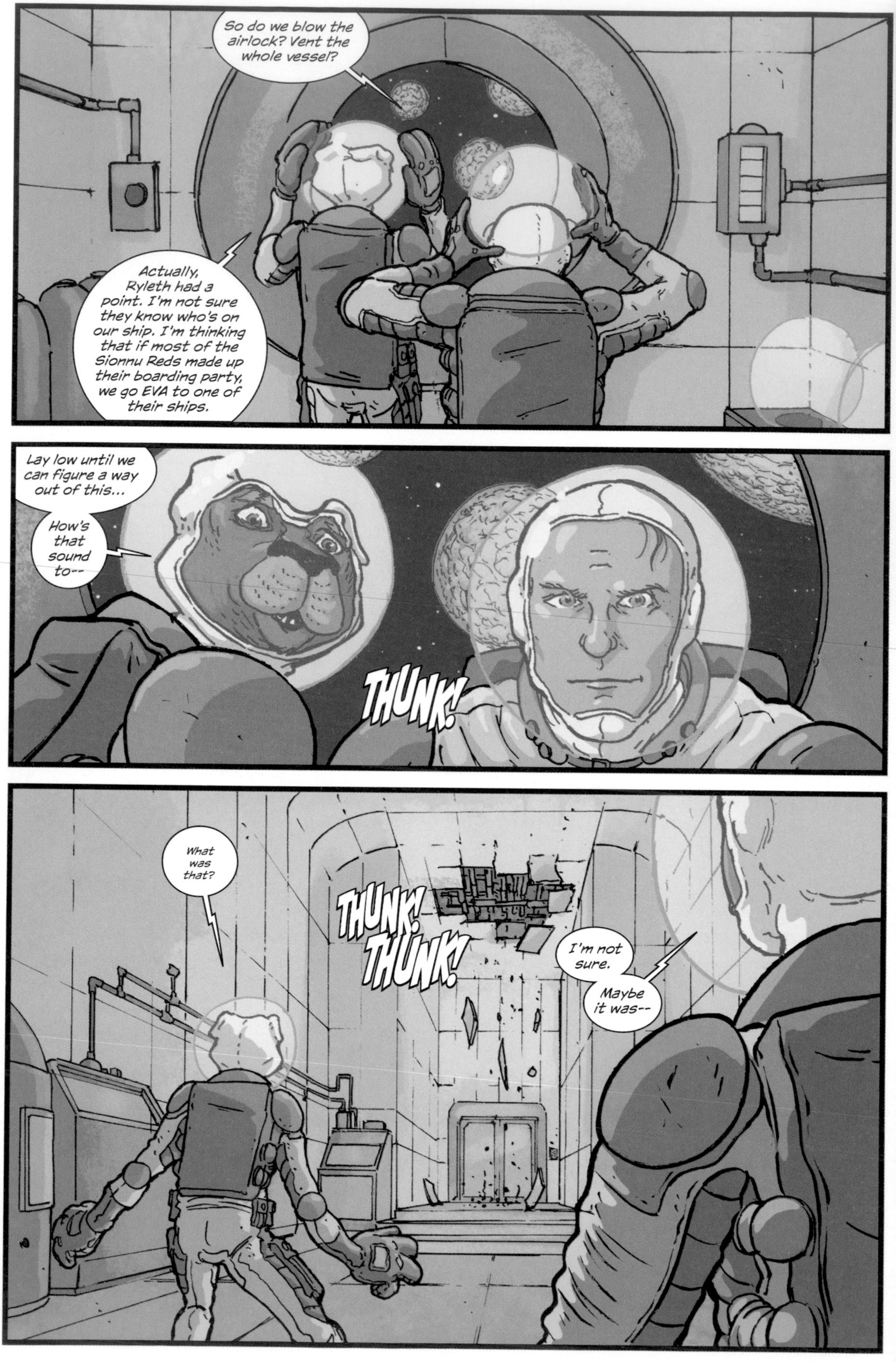

So do we blow the airlock? Vent the whole vessel?
Actually, Ryleth had a point. I'm not sure they know who's on our ship. I'm thinking that if most of the Sionnu Reds made up their boarding party, we go EVA to one of their ships.
Lay low until we can figure a way out of this...
How's that sound to--
THUNK!
What was that?
THUNK! THUNK!
I'm not sure.
Maybe it was--

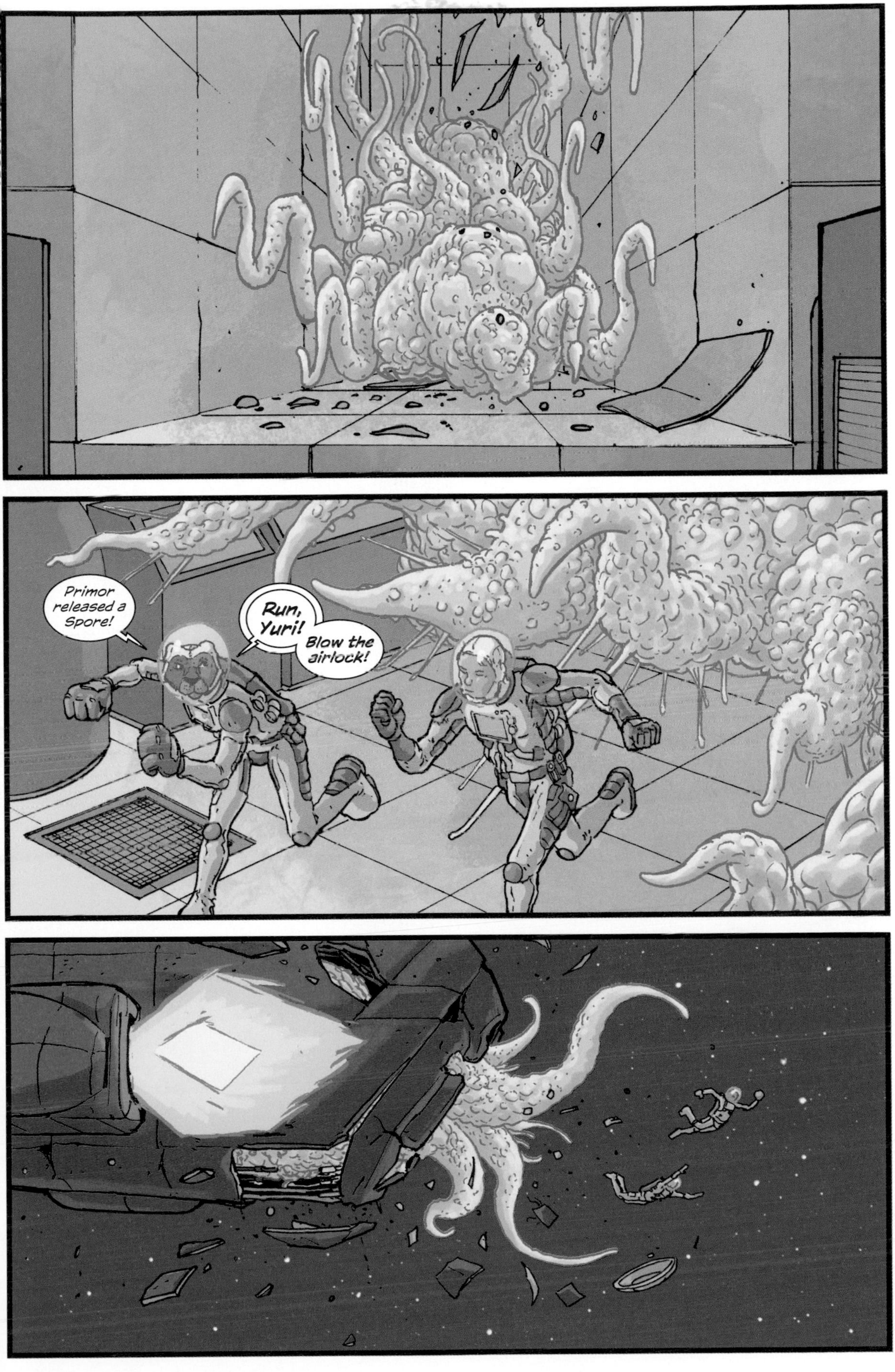
Primor released a Spore!
Run, Yuri!
Blow the airlock!

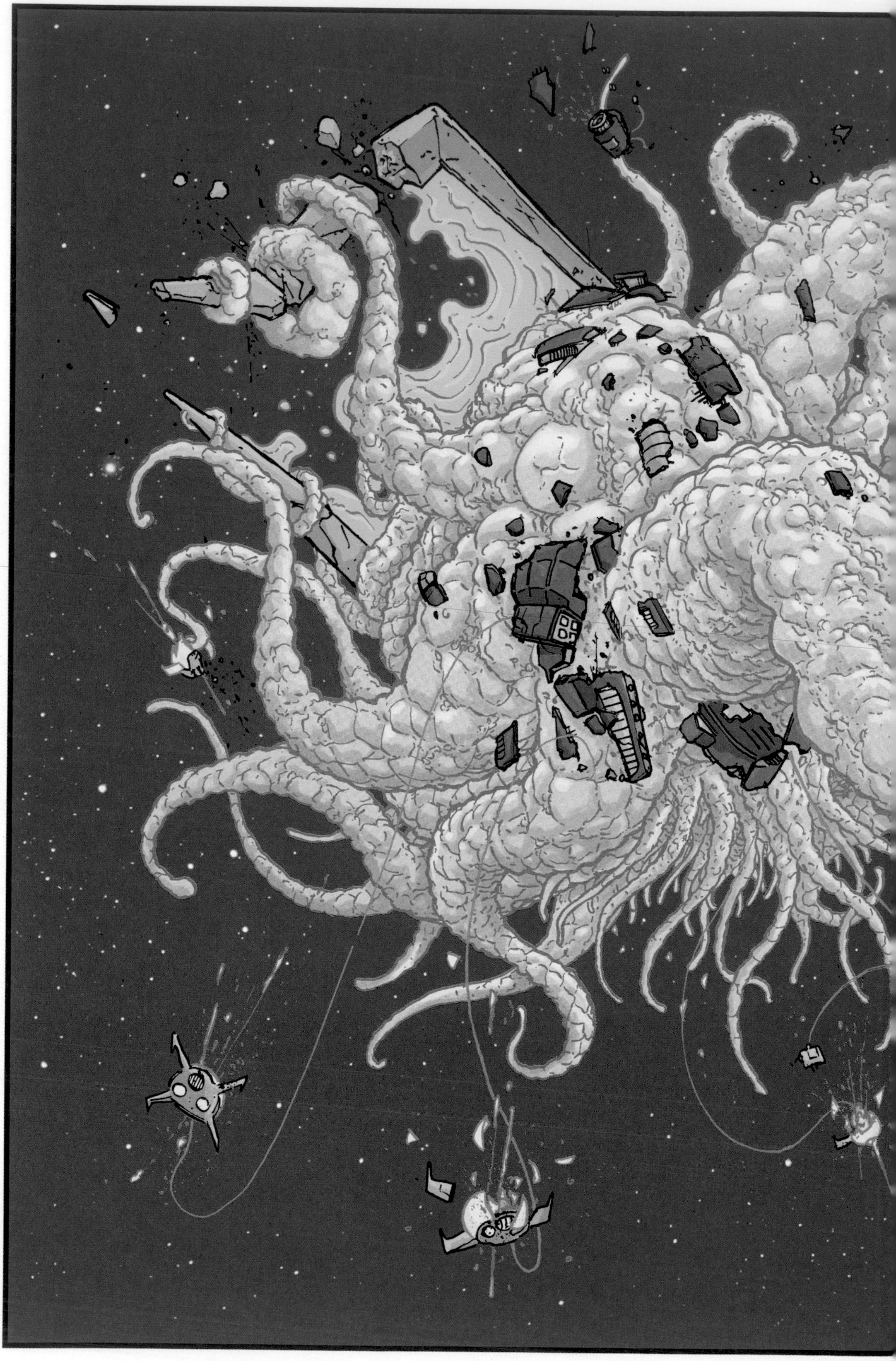

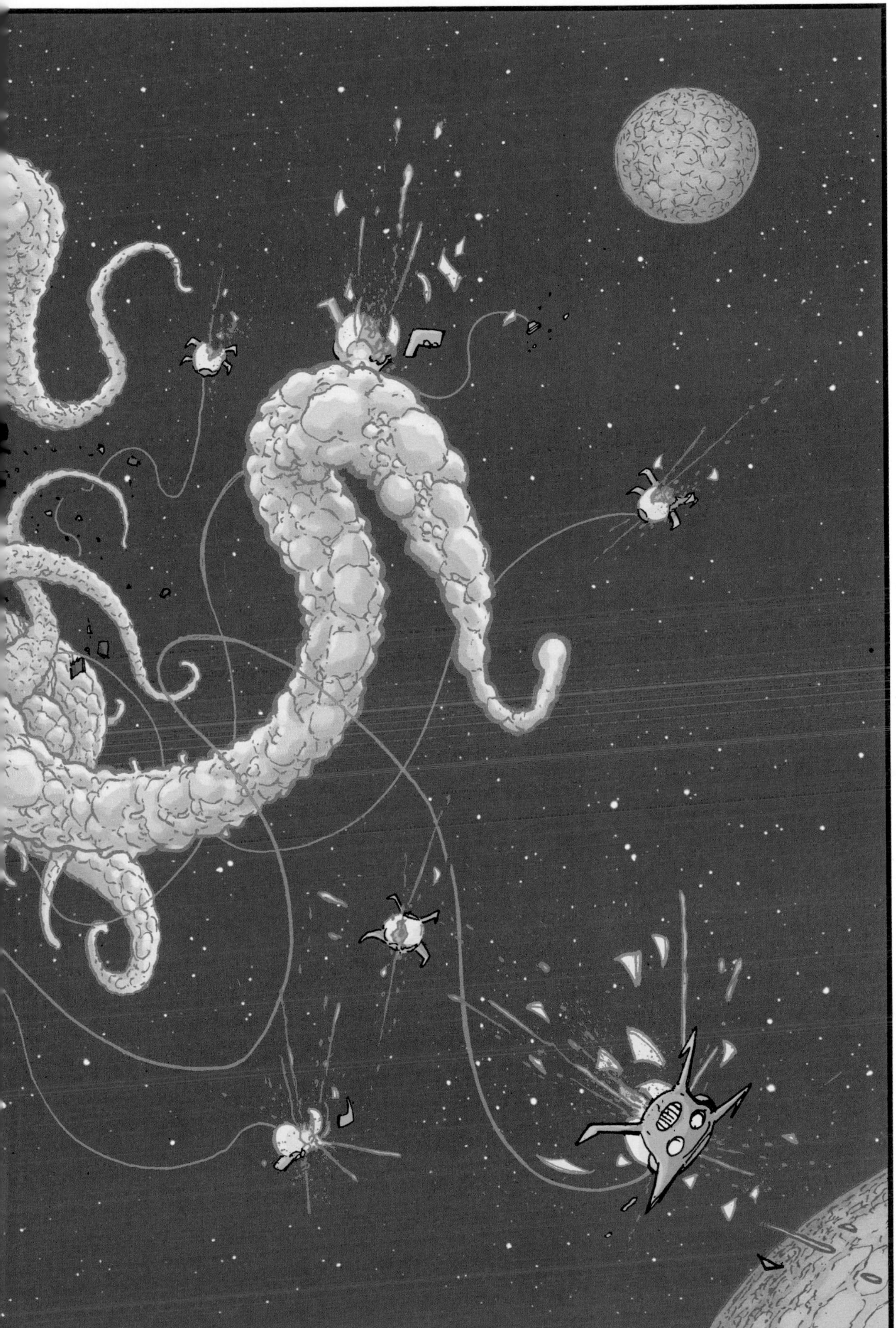

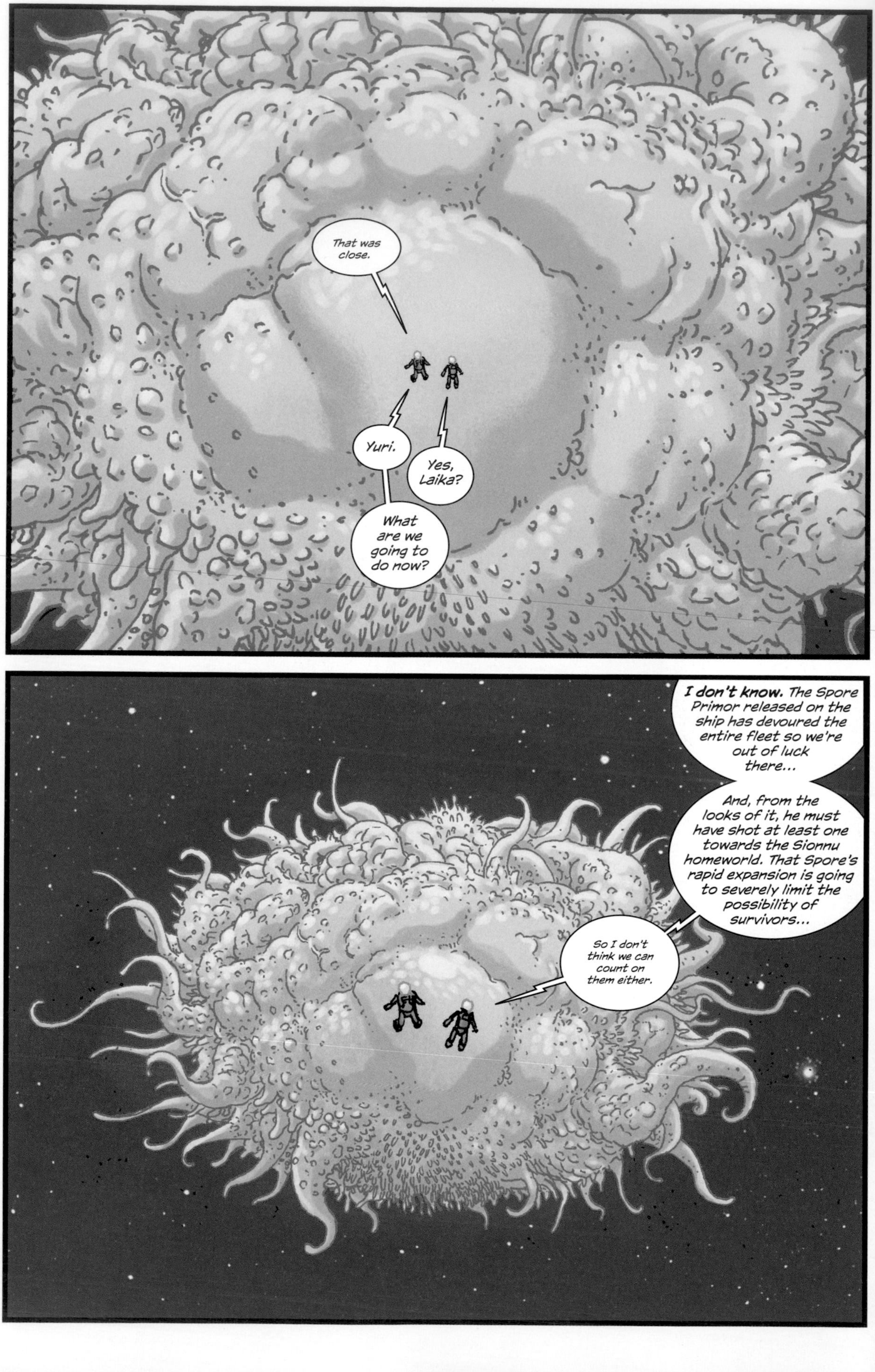
That was close.
Yuri.
Yes, Laika?
What are we going to do now?
I don't know. The Spore Primor released on the ship has devoured the entire fleet so we're out of luck there...
And, from the looks of it, he must have shot at least one towards the Sionnu homeworld. That Spore's rapid expansion is going to severely limit the possibility of survivors...
So I don't think we can count on them either.

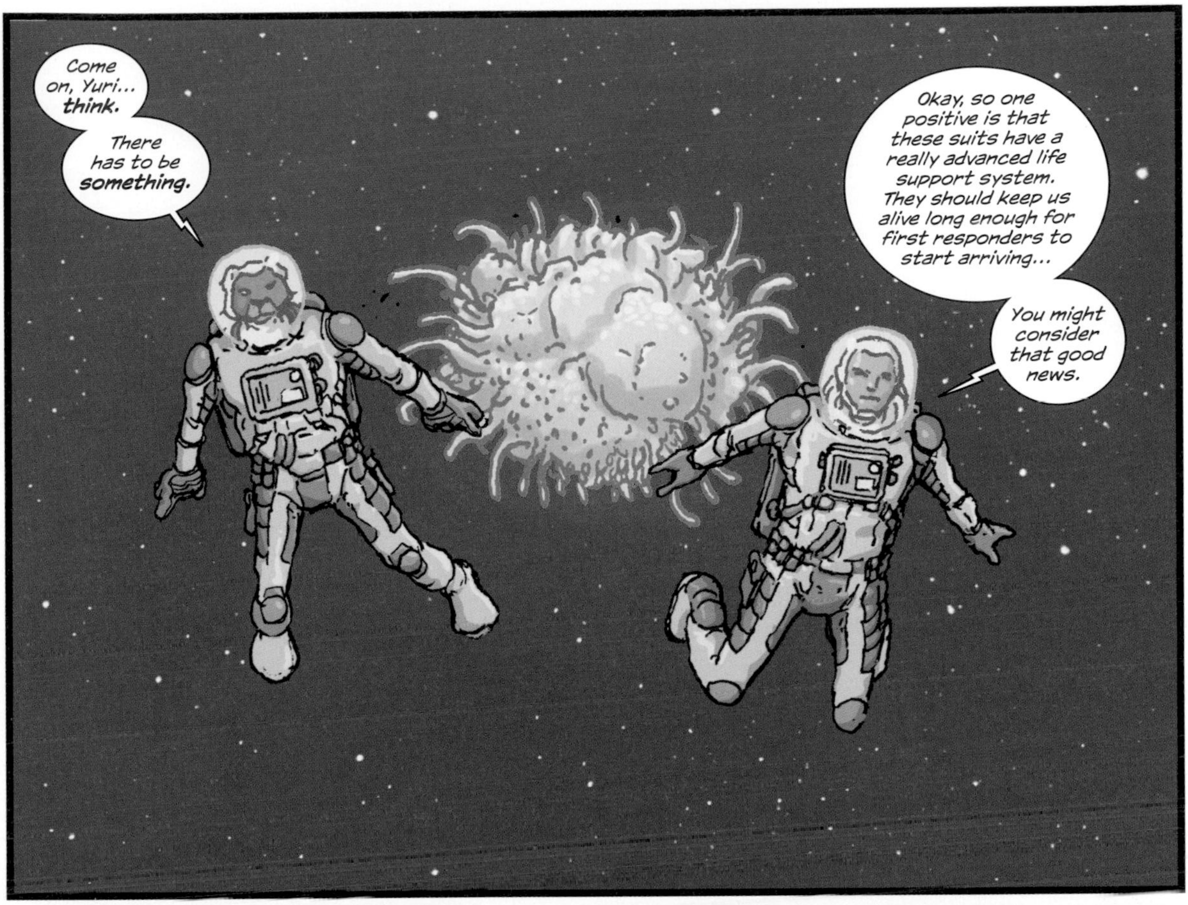
Come on, Yuri... **think.**
There has to be **something.**
Okay, so one positive is that these suits have a really advanced life support system. They should keep us alive long enough for first responders to start arriving...
You might consider that good news.

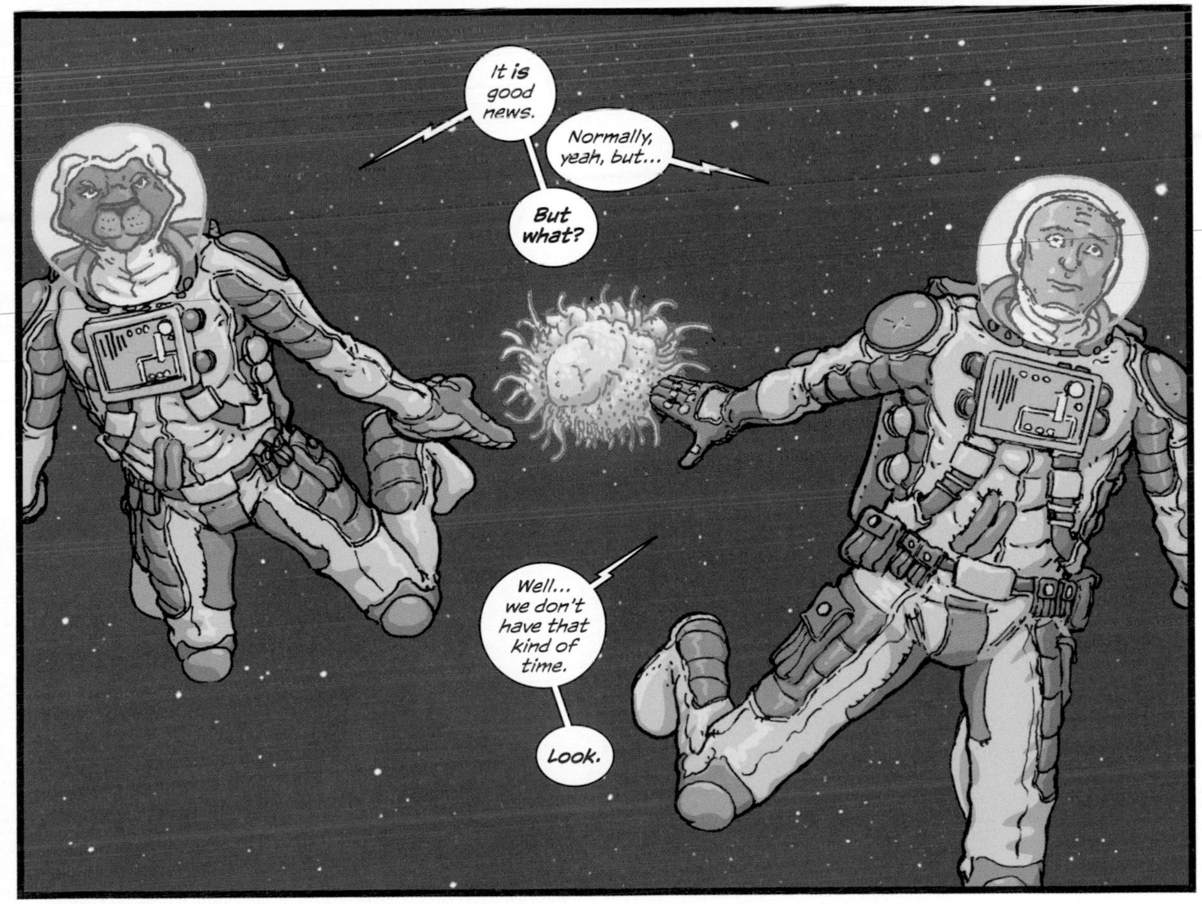
It **is** good news.
Normally, yeah, but...
But what?
Well... we don't have that kind of time.
Look.

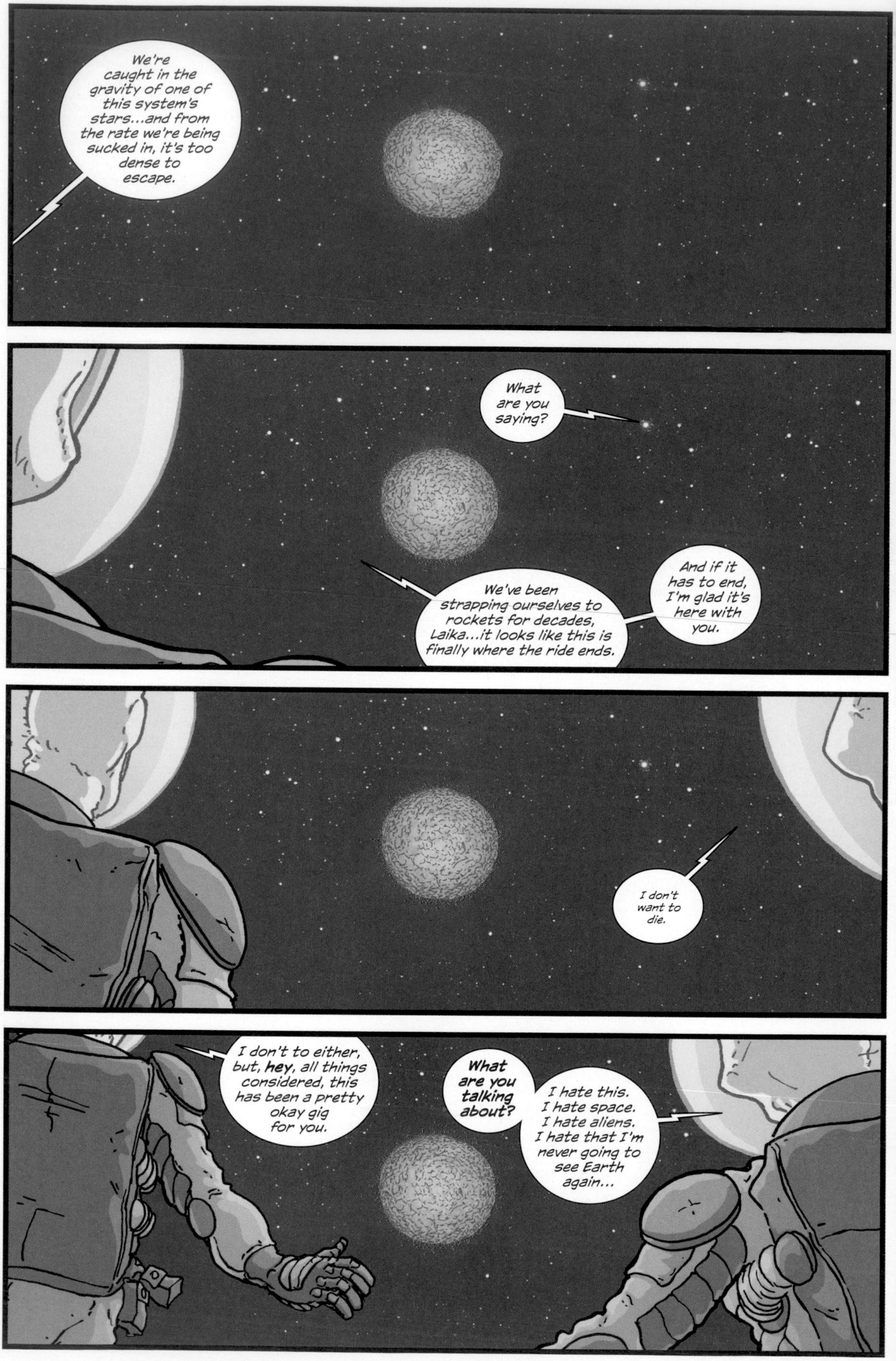
We're caught in the gravity of one of this system's stars...and from the rate we're being sucked in, it's too dense to escape.
What are you saying?
We've been strapping ourselves to rockets for decades, Laika...it looks like this is finally where the ride ends.
And if it has to end, I'm glad it's here with you.
I don't want to die.
I don't to either, but, **hey**, all things considered, this has been a pretty okay gig for you.
What are you talking about?
I hate this. I hate space. I hate aliens. I hate that I'm never going to see Earth again...

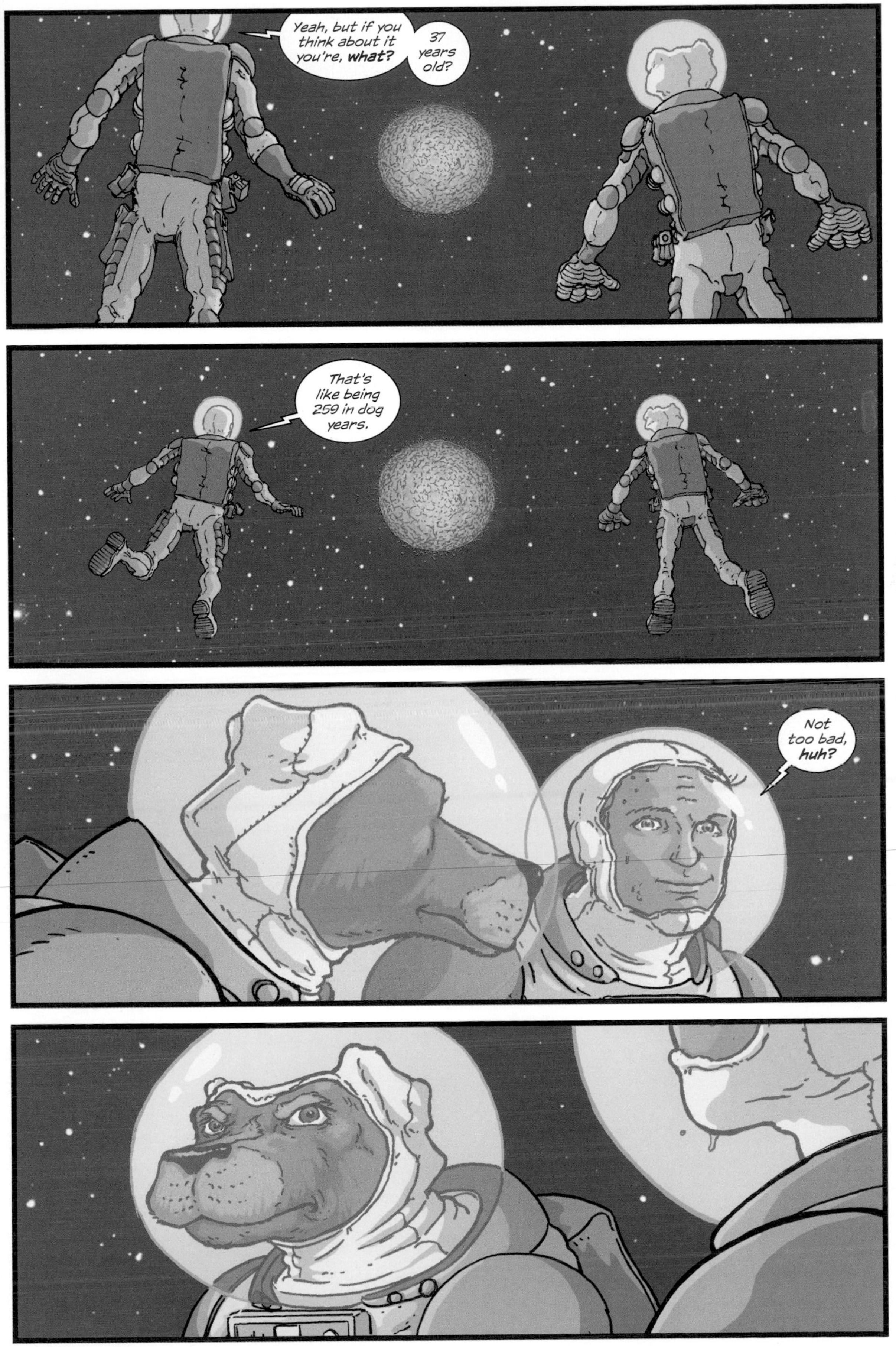
Yeah, but if you think about it you're, **what?**
37 years old?
That's like being 259 in dog years.
Not too bad, **huh?**

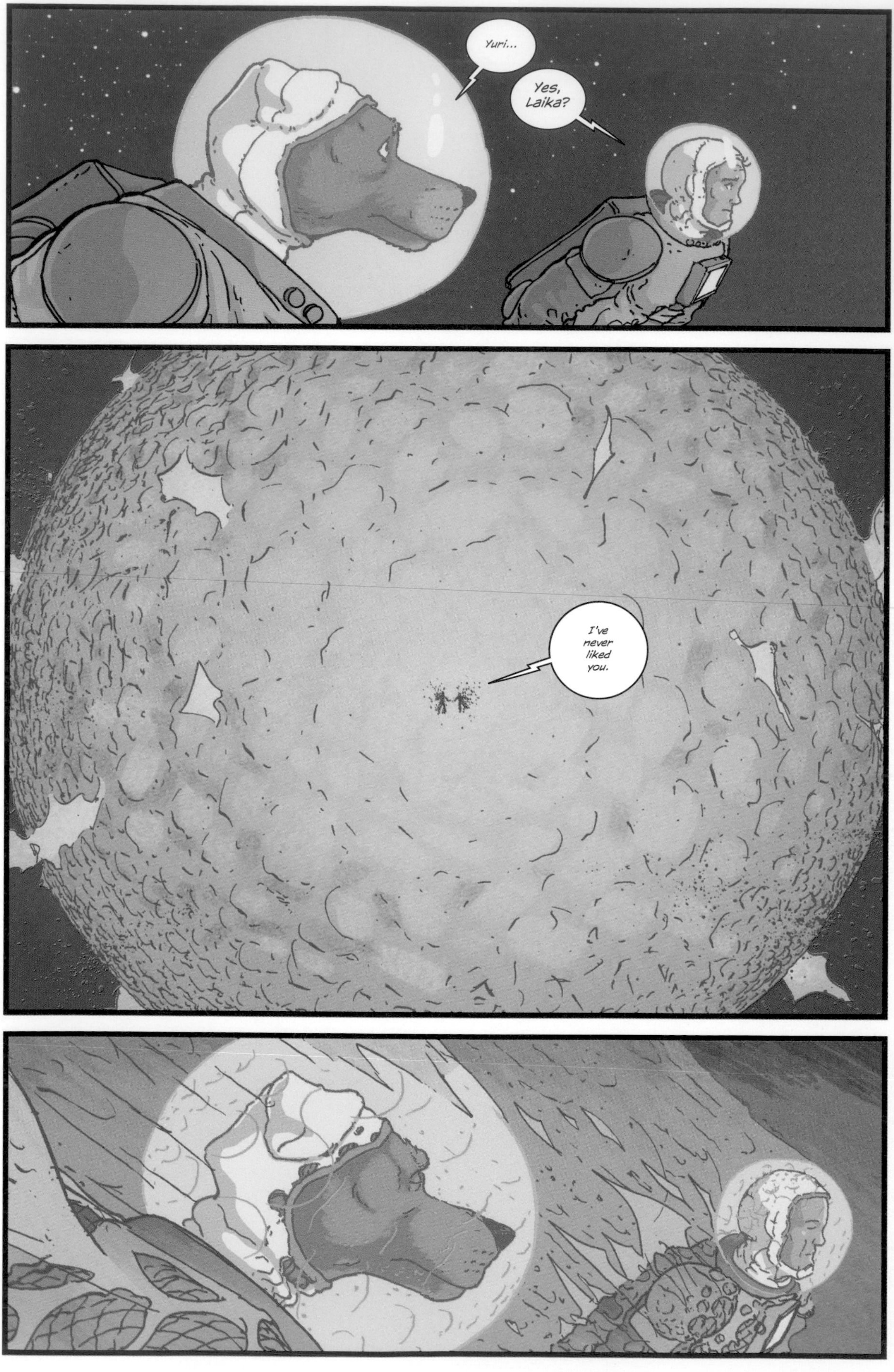
Yuri...
Yes, Laika?
I've never liked you.

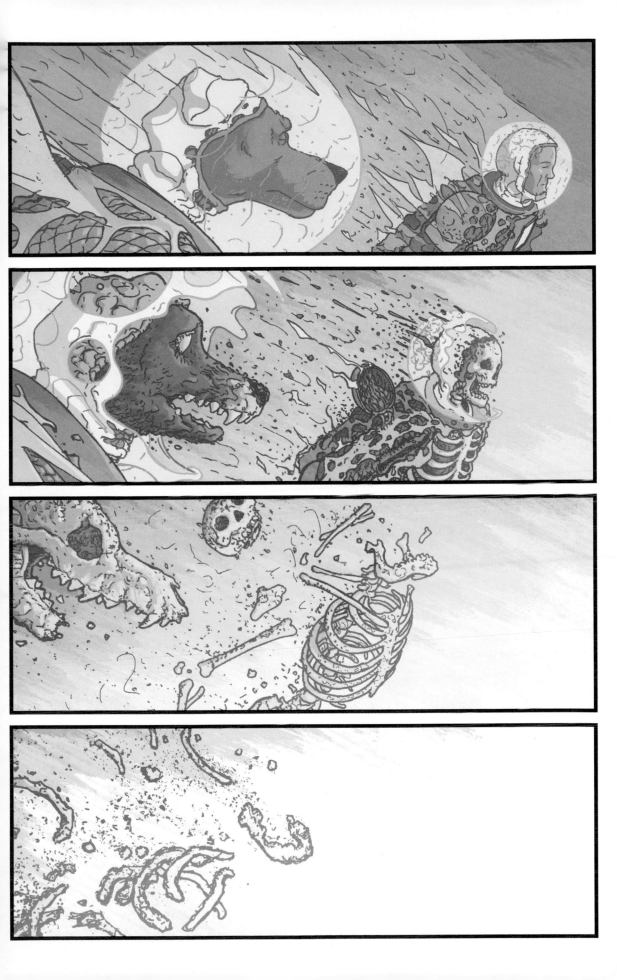

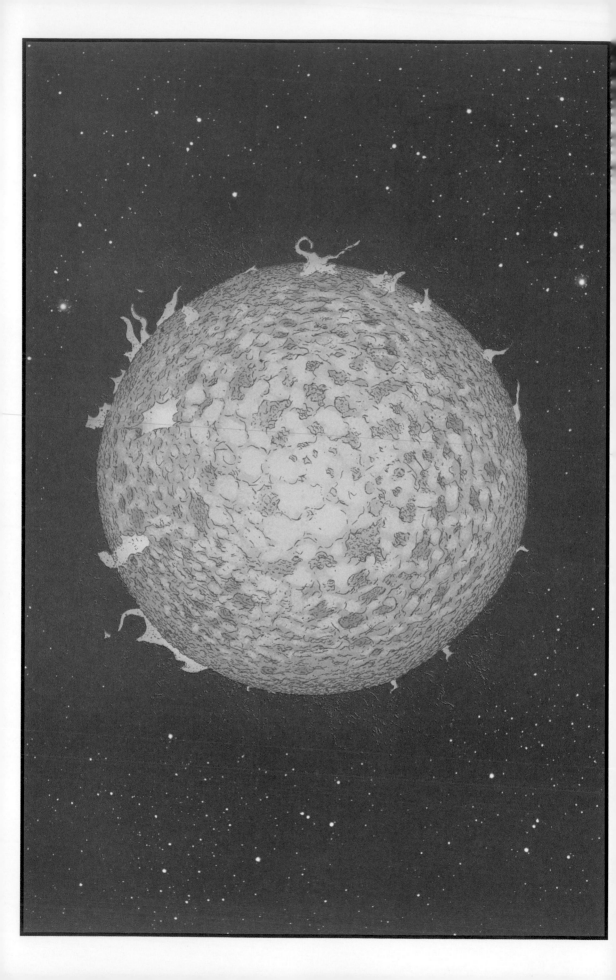

SERIES COVERS

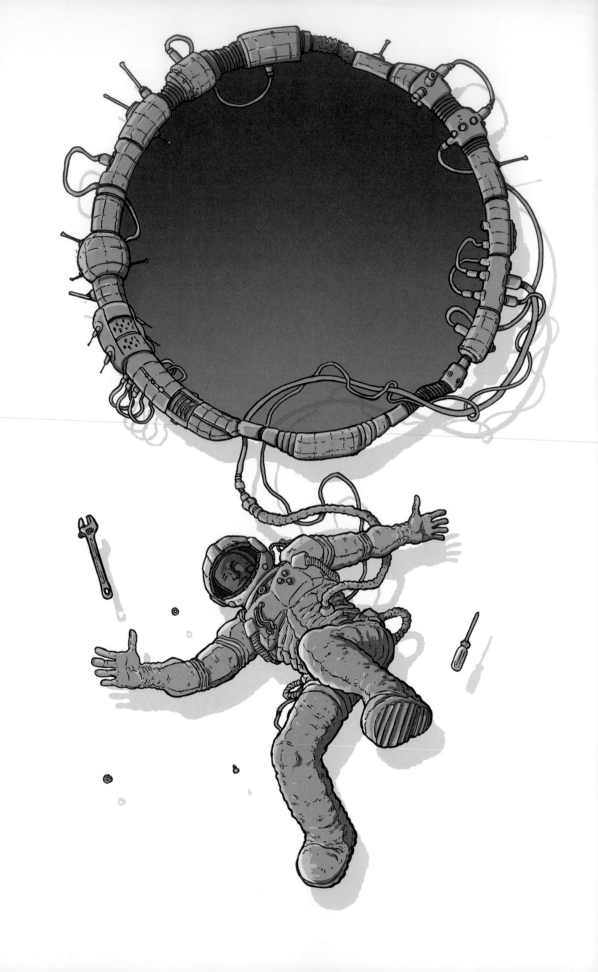

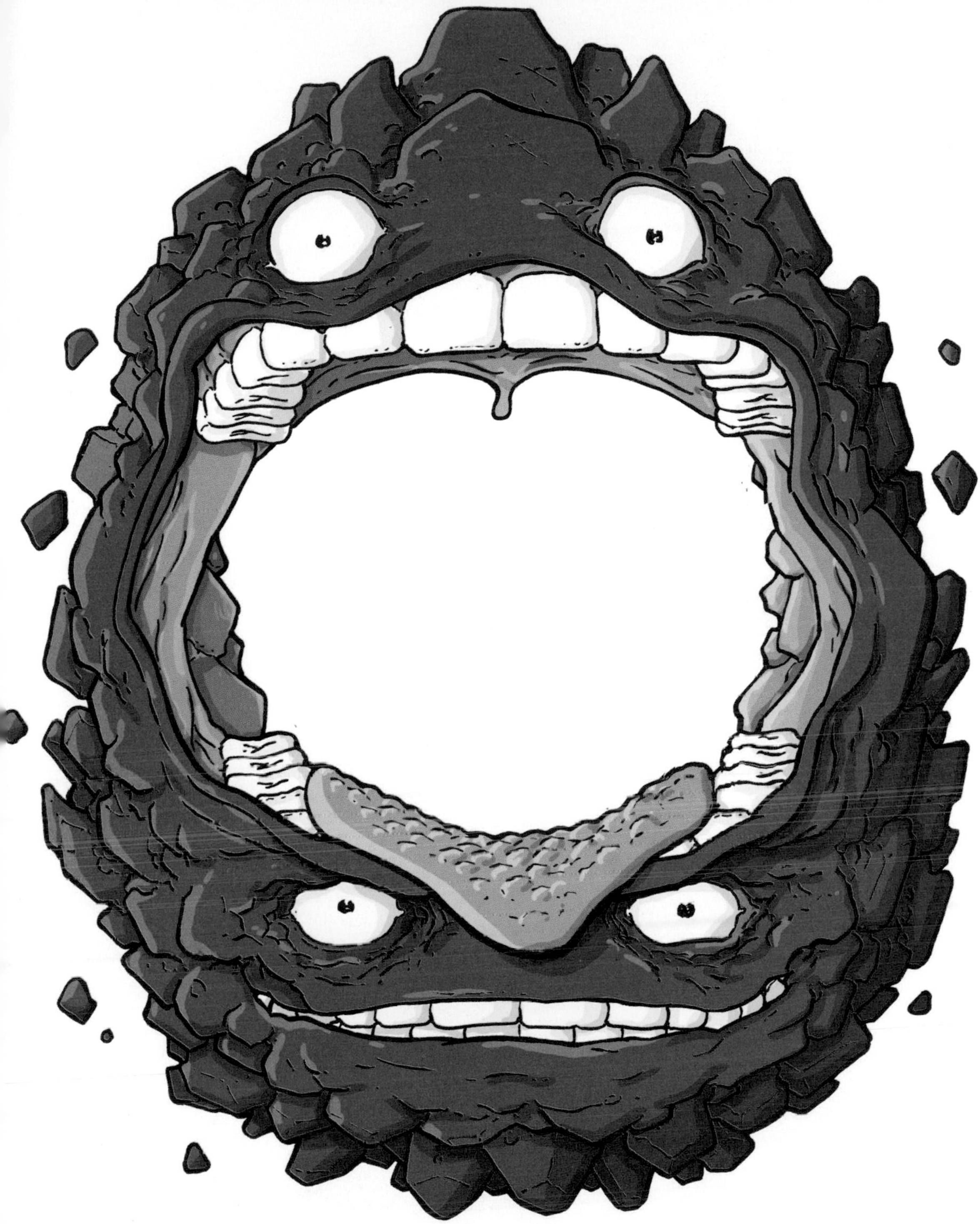

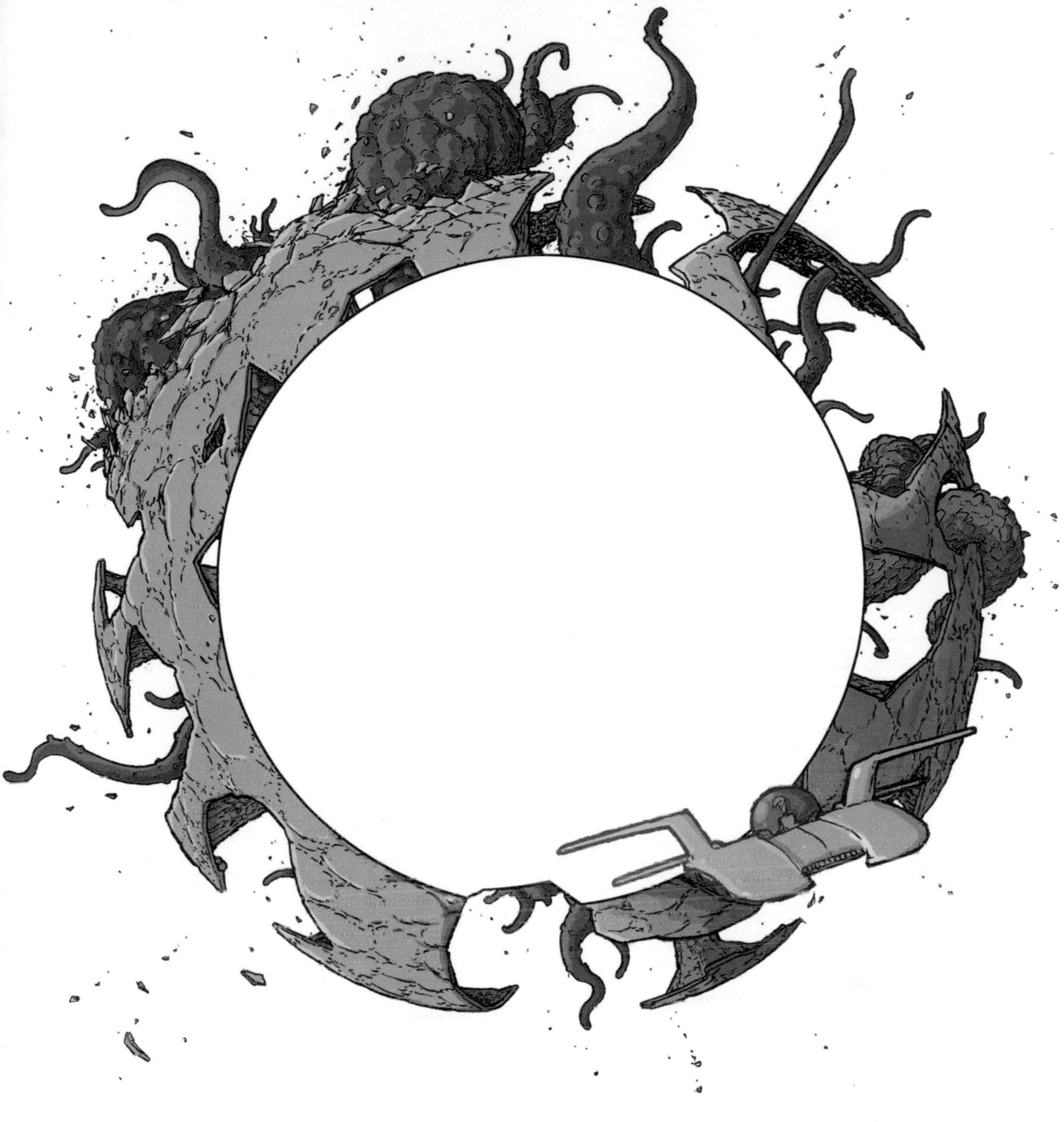

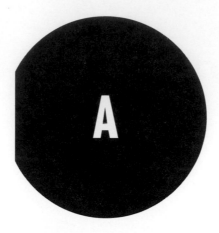

Jonathan Hickman is the visionary talent behind such works as the Eisner-nominated **NIGHTLY NEWS**, **EAST OF WEST** and **PAX ROMANA**. He also plies his trade at MARVEL working on books like **FANTASTIC FOUR** and **THE AVENGERS**.

His twin brother, Marc, ate an old chesseburger and recreated a universe out of love.

Jonathan lives in South Carolina near a lowcountry nature reserve.

You can visit his website:***www.pronea.com***, or email him at:***jonathan@pronea.com***.

•

Nick Pitarra is a native Texan and all around nice guy. As a senior in high school he was kicked out of honors English, and subsequently fell in love with comic illustration while doodling with a friend in his new class.

Sometimes it pays not to do your homework.